———— Who You Claim ————

ALTERNATIVE CRIMINOLOGY SERIES
General Editor: Jeff Ferrell

Pissing on Demand:
Workplace Drug Testing and the Rise of the Detox Industry
Ken Tunnell

Empire of Scrounge: Inside the Urban Underground of
Dumpster Diving, Trash Picking, and Street Scavenging
Jeff Ferrell

Prison, Inc.: A Convict Exposes Life inside a Private Prison
by K. C. Carceral, edited by Thomas J. Bernard

The Terrorist Identity: Explaining the Terrorist Threat
Michael P. Arena and Bruce A. Arrigo

Terrorism as Crime: From Oklahoma City to Al-Qaeda and Beyond
Mark S. Hamm

Our Bodies, Our Crimes: The Policing of Women's Reproduction in America
Jeanne Flavin

Graffiti Lives: Beyond the Tag in New York's Urban Underground
Gregory J. Snyder

Crimes of Dissent:
Civil Disobedience, Criminal Justice, and the Politics of Conscience
Jarret S. Lovell

The Culture of Punishment: Prison, Society, and Spectacle
Michelle Brown

Who You Claim: Performing Gang Identity in School and on the Streets
Robert Garot

Who You Claim

*Performing Gang Identity in
School and on the Streets*

Robert Garot

NEW YORK UNIVERSITY PRESS
New York and London

NEW YORK UNIVERSITY PRESS
New York and London
www.nyupress.org

© 2010 by New York University

Library of Congress Cataloging-in-Publication Data

Garot, Robert, 1967–
Who you claim : performing gang identity in school and
on the streets / Robert Garot.
p. cm. — (Alternative criminology series)
Includes bibliographical references and index.
ISBN-13: 978-0-8147-3212-0 (cl : alk. paper)
ISBN-10: 0-8147-3212-7 (cl : alk. paper)
ISBN-13: 978-0-8147-3213-7 (pb : alk. paper)
ISBN-10: 0-8147-3213-5 (pb : alk. paper)
1. Gang members—United States. 2. Gangs—United States.
3. Youth—United States—Attitudes. I. Title.
HV6439.U5G384   2010
364.10660973—dc22   2009035184

New York University Press books are printed on acid-free paper,
and their binding materials are chosen for strength and durability.
We strive to use environmentally responsible suppliers and materials
to the greatest extent possible in publishing our books.

Manufactured in the United States of America
c 10 9 8 7 6 5 4 3 2 1
p 10 9 8 7 6 5 4 3 2 1

Contents

For Mr. Mills, Mel
and Michelle

Acknowledgments

While whatever fault lies in this manuscript is my own, the possibility to write it, in all its stages, occurred only out of a confluence of others' goodwill. First and foremost, I thank the young people at Choices Alternative Academy (CAA [pseudonym]), who shared with me both their lives at the school and their life histories, teaching me more about my society and myself than I could put into words. Second, I thank the administrators, teachers, and staff at CAA and the attached nonprofit for graciously providing me access and responding to my naive questions.

For guiding my development as an ethnographer, I am grateful to Bob Emerson, Linda Shaw, Rachel Fretz, Jack Katz, Mel Pollner, and Harold Garfinkel, and I benefited from contact with others such as Jeffrey Alexander, Rogers Brubaker, Saul Friedlander, David Halle, John Heritage, Bill Roy, Emanuel Schegloff, Ivan Szelenyi, Diego Vigil, and Roger Waldinger. Many fellow students shared the journey, such as Terri Anderson, Rosie Ashamalla, Byron Burkholt, the late Evan Childs, Lori Cronyn, Cynthia Cruz, Derrick Gilbert, Pepper Glass, Yvette Guerra, Alexes Harris, Curtis Jackson-Jacobs, Maggi Kusenbach, Eric Magnusen, Saa Meroe, Fred Pritchard, Jennifer Reynolds, Erik Rivera, Dana Rosenfeld, Lakshmi Shrivnas, Tamara Sniezek, Cynthia Strathman, Linda Van Leuven, Darin Weinberg, and Sal Zerilli. I have been fortunate to find a supportive and nurturing environment at John Jay College that includes Rosemary Barberet, Mucahit Bilici, David Brotherton, Ric Curtis, Gayle Garfield, David Green, Andrew Karmen, David Kennedy, Danny Kessler, Lou Kontos, Kyoo Lee, Anthony Lemelle, Ariel Lubin, Susan Opotow, Valli Raja, Teresa Rockett, Barry Spunt, Douglas Thompkins, Lucia Trimbur, Susan Will, and Jock Young. Also, thanks to supportive colleagues such as Leon Anderson, Peter Becker, Tim Berard, Stacy Burns, Rob Collins, Paul Colomy, Sarah Beth Estes, Brigittine French, Joby Gardner, Doug Harper, Tony Jefferson, Donna Kaufman, Stephen Lyng, Martha Mazzarella, Norma Mendoza-Denton, Valentina Pagliai, Luca Palmas, Rafael Reyes-Ruiz, Annegret Staiger, Deana Wilkinson, and Rhys Williams. At NYU Press, Ilene

Kalish, her anonymous reviewers, and Elisabeth Magnus, my assiduous copy editor, have been most helpful. The UCLA Leroi Neimann Center and various funds at John Jay provided support for writing.

My wife's family has been wonderfully helpful, sustaining us during certain periods of writing, and my parents, Jim and Diana, have been there every step of the way. Thanks to Valentina, Elena, and Tristan for the insights and distractions. This project is dedicated to three remarkable people who passed away during the course of this project: my sister, Michelle; my advisor, Mel; and my good friend Mr. Mills.

Grateful acknowledgment is made to the following publishers for permission to reprint sections of previously published materials: "Reconsidering Retaliation: Structural Inhibitions, Emotive Dissonance, and the Acceptance of Ambivalence among Inner-City Young Men," *Ethnography* 10 (1): 63–90; "Non-violence in the Inner-City: 'Decent' and 'Street' as Strategic Resources," *Journal of African American Studies* 10 (4): 94–111; "'Where You From!': Gang Identity as Performance," *Journal of Contemporary Ethnography* 36 (1): 50–84; (with Jack Katz), "Provocative Looks: The Enforcement of Dress Codes and the Embodiment of Dress in an Inner-City Alternative School," *Ethnography* 4 (3): 415–48; and "Inner-City Teens and Face-Work: Avoiding Violence and Maintaining Honor," in *A Cultural Approach to Interpersonal Communication: Essential Readings,* edited by Leila Monaghan and Jane Goodman, 294–317 (Cambridge: Blackwell, 2007).

Preface: Emily's Tale

I am often asked how I was able to study gang members. Mostly, I have Emily to thank. When I entered her classroom and the rest of the students ignored me, Emily came and asked for help, easing the painful awkwardness of not belonging. Her long black hair flowed over a lacy, off-white long-sleeved blouse with a little tie around the collarbone. Her voice was sweet, even dainty, and I was flattered that perhaps she was flirting with me as we worked out the questions on her grammar worksheet. As I returned to her alternative school over the next four years, I was relieved that she continued to seek me out for help and send friends to talk with me.

When I asked students if they would like to be interviewed, Emily wanted to be the first. At a quiet spot in the front office, on two badly stained, overstuffed and comfortable old beige chairs, I placed my tape recorder on the table between us and she told me a tale that continues to haunt me over ten years later. She began by showing me how those lacy sleeves hid huge and ornate tattoos in medieval script, spelling out BLVD up her right arm and the name of the boulevard on her left. In the forty-five minutes of our interview she told me a classic tale of redemption through love. After seeing her brother and mother shot at fifteen, she spent three years staying away from home, smoking weed, getting drunk, smoking PCP, sniffing glue, writing on walls, getting tattoos, and beating into a bloody pulp any females intruding into the neighborhood from rival gangs. Then an older man at the local liquor store asked why she was gangbanging and began to gently court her, encouraging her to change her style of clothes and her way of talking and presenting herself. According to Emily, "He's an ex-gangbanger. He knows what's going on. He said, 'I ain't gonna die for something that ain't even mine.' See, he knows. And I still went into the fight, I wanted to be in the gangbanger life. But then, little by little, when I started going out with him, he told me, 'Oh, I don't want you to dress like that, please?' Because I liked him, I wouldn't dress like that. So then I would follow him all the time. I forgot about my homeboys. I stopped going over there. I would just, I would always be with him. And then he would tell me, 'I don't want you to smoke weed no more.' I was like, 'Whaa? You met me when I was smoking weed.' He was like, 'I don't want a girlfriend that be smokin' weed.' I was like, 'All right.' So I stopped smoking drugs."

"You just stopped altogether?"

"No, it takes little by little. Sometimes I'll tell him that I don't smoke, but when he wasn't around I would smoke. But see, sometimes he would sneak up and come to my house and I'd be hiding and he'll notice. And he told me, he said, 'Next time I catch you like that, when I surprise you when I see you at your house, don't ever talk to me again in your life.' And I took it serious. So now, I've already been with him for two years. But for a year it was pretty hard. Now it's easy."

"Yeah."

"Now he sees how I've changed."

"Uh huh."

"He'll be like, 'Damn, you've changed a lot since when I met you.'"

As the year progressed, Emily became pregnant, and this pulled her further from the gang lifestyle. According to Emily, this is a common way out of gangbanging.[1] "As time passes, my homegirl Lil' One, she got pregnant, so she didn't go around no more. My homegirl Dimples, well, she found her boyfriend and they moved to Delano, and my sister, she got pregnant, so she stopped messing around. Like all my friends got pregnant. . . . You know when I was gangbanging, I would say, 'If I ever get pregnant I will stop gangbanging,' like my homegirls and my sister did."

We commonly think of gangbangers as vicious thugs, and why shouldn't we? Gangbangers work hard to cultivate that image. Yet no human being can be so easily summarized. In many settings, being a vicious thug is simply not an option. Vicious thugs often change their ways.[2] Yet both gangbanging and distancing oneself from gangbanging require a detailed attention to the skills of presenting oneself to create or avoid potentially life-threatening situations.

Emily could never be *entirely* a gang member or a non–gang member. Even before she joined her gang her brother was involved, and she and her sister were so afraid to leave the house for fear of her brother's enemies hanging out at the foot of the steps to their apartment that they dropped out of school and convinced their father to move. Even as a gang member, Emily might want to see a movie with a friend in a part of town where her enemies lived and not be bothered with, as some put it, "the whole gang thing." Or she might be at the dinner table with her grandparents or on a field trip to a major university, like the one she took with me, where she looked around with a sense of emptiness, not finding anyone, whatever their ethnicity, who looked like her.[3] And even after all her talk of conversion, sometimes I saw her standing on the sidewalk after school, looming large with a squared, arms-folded stance and eyes squinted in a way that made my blood run cold.

As is the case with all of us, Emily's identity was composed of her social relationships: who she claimed. Competing claims, misunderstood claims, and demands to make a claim or to be claimed may pose problems anytime, anywhere: one might argue that world history has been shaped by nothing less. In Emily's neighborhood, powerful interaction rituals not only determine where one stands in relation to others but force one to be accountable for this situated social placement. Such dynamics unfold in a moment's glance and are significant enough to end a life or create one anew.

Over four years of participating with students at Emily's school, Choices Alternative Academy (CAA, a pseudonym), and interviewing forty-six of them in sessions lasting from one to twelve hours, I found repeated tales of such balancing acts, belying threatening metaphors of gang members as monsters, a plague, or a virus. What one finds in spending time with *them* is, in the famous words of the old comic strip, "We have met the enemy and he is us." Emily, for example, was almost painfully polite and hardworking.[4] But like all of us, she also had a desire for something more. Her neighborhood provided all the access one would wish to dangerous endeavors if only one cultivated the right friends, wore the right clothes, and learned to speak the right jargon to pull it off. She carefully cultivated skills, and even when she decided to distance herself from such practices she still took pride in them, and was at times seduced back into that world she knew so well.[5] This book is an effort to recognize the achievement of performing a gang identity, the dynamics out of which it grows, and the ambivalence involved in the moment-to-moment thrill and responsibility of being able to choose to wear the lacy blouse or the baggy pants, the carefree smile or the menacing glare. It is a choice that is fundamentally American.[6]

Gang Identity as Performance

Rather than containing youth in adult narratives, how might
we avoid repeating identities? How can we encourage practices
that do not depend on the intelligibility that dominant (adult)
narratives presume to be necessary? How might adults come to
see the identities we and youth adopt as creative rather than as
evolving copies?

—Susan Talburt

Over the past fifty years, social scientists have increasingly turned
from essentializing identity as a fixed characteristic to understanding identity
as fluid, contextual, and shifting. Through dress, mannerisms, and language,
individuals make and dispute claims to identity based in socially recognized
categories, and such claims and contestations become the bases for sustaining interaction. Prominent, one might even say the dominant, literatures in
grappling with the complexity of such topics as gender, race, ethnicity, and
nationalism all recognize the importance of understanding that these categories are not fixed, but strategically molded in the ways we present ourselves, and that they are always subject to the variable interpretations of our
audience.

Adolescence is especially recognized as a time when one needs to experiment with identity, as the choices one makes in terms of career and family
may have long-lasting ramifications. Being sorted or sorting oneself into a
category too soon may lead to future regrets. Even our legal structure recognizes this, providing a separate system for the young so that they need not
pay too great a price for early mistakes.[1]

Yet such insights tend to be overlooked when we speak of inner-city youth,
and especially when we talk about gang members: fear clouds our thinking.[2]
When we feel threatened by those commonly referred to as "monsters" or
"superpredators," it seems irresponsible or even dangerous to appreciate the
artful nuances of their ways of performing identity.[3]

This is unfortunate, for such fear may well play a role in maintaining the
conditions that lead to the behavior we seek to redress.[4] Out of fear arises seg-

regation, the isolation of the poor into depressing, neglected neighborhoods, far from decent jobs, goods, and services.[5] Schools, depending primarily on local taxes for survival, become run-down and dilapidated.[6] The media often contribute to such stereotypes, referring to those who must reside in such areas as the "underclass" and wildly publicizing freak events such as the "wrong way murder."[7] Out of such multiply marginalizing geographies of fear, gangs flourish, but not necessarily for the reasons we think they do.[8] Typically, gangs arise to meet the many challenges resulting from the neglect of officials;[9] they assist their families and neighbors to survive.[10] As Michael Ungar, an expert on childhood resilience, insightfully notes, the characteristics that researchers define as providing the capabilities for young people to survive in difficult circumstances "are potentially available to some children through deviant pathways to health. . . . One need only think of how gangs offer youth a street family, a sense of belonging, even hope and opportunities for 'decisive risk-taking' that impoverished families struggling with addictions and under-funded schools may not."[11] This book aims to appreciate such capacities of young people to create a lively social world, despite the limitations imposed by a social structure that all too often tends to marginalize and criminalize them.[12]

Perhaps, then, if we look closer, not to ignore the obvious role of structural forces but to appreciate how people survive despite them, we may begin to see beyond our culture of fear, to appreciate young people in the inner city just as we appreciate young people anywhere else, for their potential, their creativity, their resourcefulness, and yes, even their dangerousness.[13] Inner-city youth are humans after all, with all the wonderful, mysterious, and frightening characteristics that we have long come to associate with our troubled species.[14]

Grappling with Identity

Understanding identity is one of the primary agendas of the social sciences, yet the meaning of the term *identity* is by no means straightforward or consensually understood.[15] Many scholars distinguish between hard, strong, obdurate, fixed versions of identity on one hand and soft, weak, fluid, constructionist versions of the concept on the other.[16] According to the former, common in early anthropological accounts and much contemporary journalism, identity serves as an explanatory concept. For instance, some have posited that achieving a coherent, stable political organization in African nations or the Balkans is difficult because of *tribalism*,[17] or women are said to follow a set of moral standards that differs from that of men.[18] Such depictions are problematic on a number of grounds. On one hand, such thinking is known as a reductionist fallacy, wiping out innumerable individual variations in order to explain individuals in terms of a category that supposed "members" may not even adopt for themselves.[19] On the other hand, such thinking has been seen as justifying social exclusion and arguments in favor of genocide, slavery, war and identity politics in general. As most social scientists know well, "'Essentialism' has indeed been vigorously criticized, and constructivist gestures now accompany most discussions of 'identity.'"[20]

With regard to gangs, the idea "that membership in gangs confers identity . . . could be the single most common proposition encountered in the literature on gangs."[21] Such a version of identity echoes hard, essentializing arguments, as much of the literature on gangs evinces a determination to correlate this fixed "identity" with crime and other deleterious outcomes. Such an approach overlooks the widespread critique in the social sciences of hard versions of identity. Inasmuch as problematizing, constructionist approaches to seemingly obdurate characteristics such as gender, race, or nationalism are commonplace, practically old hat, the gang literature is by and large behind the times. This book makes a case for a soft version of gang identity.[22]

Below, I first examine some of the problems involved in efforts to essentialize gang identity and then turn to the contradictions of controlling gangs. I then briefly explore some of the most influential approaches to soft identity in terms of gender, race, ethnicity, and nationalism. Last, I note possibilities for conceptualizing gang identity as performance.

Problems with Essentializing Gang Identity

No consensus exists among gang researchers on the proper definition of a gang.[23] This lack of consensus is primarily due to contrasting research agendas, derived from contrasting epistemological stances. On one hand, researchers who have conceptualized gangs as a social problem in need of social or criminal justice remedies find the determination of gang membership unproblematic. Some note that asking youths, "Are you now or have you been a gang member?" is the most powerful and direct measure of gang membership.[24] Others have noted that "the self-nomination technique is a particularly robust measure of gang membership capable of distinguishing gang from nongang youth."[25] Such approaches overlook that a respondent's conception of a "gang" may not necessarily match what the researcher has in mind.[26] Also, *gang* and *group* are often used interchangeably, even in contexts where the consequences of using one term or the other are dramatic.[27]

The question is further complicated in light of the wide variety of gangs. Consider the following: "Classification of gangs is a daunting task, and with inclusion of other youth collectivities, it is even more so. In addition to diversity and change, youth collectivities come in many forms, which sometimes merge and change in other ways: There are drug gangs, or 'crews'; 'wilding' groups; milling crowds; smaller networks involved in delinquency; 'tagger crews'; mods, rockers, and soccer hooligans; skinheads and bikers; prison gangs; seemingly ad infinitum."[28] Nonetheless, many researchers express an urgency regarding the need to define gangs, warning that "it may be extremely difficult to develop useful policies and effective programs if two different types of groups or their behaviors are identified as the same, or the same types of groups and behaviors are regarded as different."[29] Other researchers would like a good definition of the term to counter media manipulation and sensationalization.[30] A third reason for a clear definition concerns the gathering of gang statistics. How can we determine an accurate count of gang members if we are not sure what we are counting?[31]

No definitions have yet found success, although Frederic Thrasher made a notable contribution with his classic study of Chicago gangs of the 1920s. For Thrasher, a gang is "an interstitial group originally formed spontaneously and then integrated through conflict."[32] This is a quite economic definition, elegantly integrating the social processes that Thrasher analyzed. The group is interstitial ecologically, arising in zones of transition where a deteriorating housing stock meets struggling industries. Individuals in the group are also typically at an interstitial stage in life, struggling out of childhood and into adulthood. Thrasher posited that since gangs form spontaneously from play groups, all such childhood groups are potential forms of gangs. The key factor determining the integration of the play group into a gang is contact with other groups who express disapproval or opposition, including authority figures. Thrasher's conceptualization is enduring, but some find problems with this definition in that it seems innocuous, presenting gangs as arising from play groups and downplaying their supposed criminal aspects.

Walter Miller attempted to arrive at a definition of gangs through a consensus of troubleshooters, finding six items agreed upon by 85 percent of 309 teachers, police officers, and community workers who had experience with gangs. According to their common opinion, gangs are (1) a self-formed association of peers, (2) bound together by mutual interests, (3) with identifiable leadership and (4) well-developed lines of authority, (5) acting in concert, and (6) controlling a specific territory.[33] Yet the same definition could apply to the U.S. Senate, and it overlooks what gangs mean to young people.

Other researchers argue that defining gangs is actually not important. According to Ruth Horowitz, the groups concerned with defining gangs all have their own interests and taken-for-granted assumptions and will never agree on a definition. Further, definitions tend to focus research in particular ways, narrowing the topics studied and the questions asked. New conceptions may encourage researchers to refocus the questions and develop revised understandings.[34]

Many of the most useful terms for conceptualizing gangs have been somewhat amorphous. David Matza's notion of delinquency not as a fixed characteristic but as activity one may "drift" in and out of, and through which young people may negotiate their way into adults' conventional worlds, is a useful starting point.[35] Lewis Yablonsky's concept of "near-group" also captures ambiguity in gangs, emphasizing their "informal, short-lived" qualities.[36] Much of the gang literature reifies gangs even while claiming that they "lack the structure and corporate capability to coordinate activities effectively," a finding first proposed nearly fifty years ago.[37]

Many recent studies have probed how policy and funding objectives of social control agents shape definitions of gangs more than anything about gangs per se.[38] Such policy and funding objectives also shape sociological research, resulting in a criminologists' gang rather than a "gang" as constituted and understood by members.[39]

Whether the term is clearly defined or not, the consequences for invoking it are painfully evident. Over the past ten years, most states have passed laws explicitly defining "gangs" and "gang members."[40] Persons convicted of violating the federal Criminal Street Gangs Statute (1999) can receive a sentence enhancement of up to ten years, and the California Penal Code 1999, section 186.22[b][1], states that "actively participating in any criminal street gang" can result in jail or a prison sentence. Even researchers who assume that a meaningful operationalization of gang membership might be found are uneasy with antigang laws and codes. As some gang experts have wondered, "Given the lack of consensus about what constitutes gang membership, is it viable to implement policies that subject individuals to criminal justice processing due to their alleged gang status?"[41]

The Contradictions of Control

The rhetorical and legal fiction of gangs is nothing new.[42] In 1927, Thrasher noted that "the key determinant of the transition into a gang is contact with other groups who express disapproval or opposition."[43] Such groups are not necessarily other gangs but may well be individuals in positions of authority. The continued repression of gangs through the profiling of gang members in schools and in the criminal justice system only makes them stronger.

The criminal justice system helps to constitute gangs in an arduous process whose many aspects–police profiling, police record keeping, legal processing, imprisonment, release–can be addressed here only briefly. There is a need for more grounded studies of the consequences of the bureaucratic reification of gang membership for young people.

While considerable scholarly and governmental attention has been directed to the widely accepted problem of racial profiling,[44] police departments tend to evince great pride in their efforts toward gang profiling, although one would be quite hard-pressed to differentiate the two. Easily available are assiduously maintained statistics of the Los Angeles Police Department, which keeps track of gang-related crime and, until recently, maintained precise figures on the number of gangs and gang members, *broken down by ethnicity*. For instance, in January 2006 there were apparently 463 gangs and 38,811 gang members in Los Angeles.[45] Always critical to keep in mind with such statistics is Becker's observation of the contradictory "double problem" of rule enforcers: to "demonstrate to others that the problem still exists" while showing that "attempts at enforcement are effective and worthwhile."[46]

The organizational use of such statistics is the subject of the fascinating work of Albert J. Meehan, who shows how police "record keeping practices can effectively create and manage" the fiction of gangs, typically to serve political ends. As an officer whom Meehan interviewed stated, "This is an issue for the mayor, not a real problem for the police." The "problem" thus constituted begins with callers blithely referring to a "gang of teenagers" on the corner; if they should instead simply refer to them as a "group," the dispatcher is certain to correct them, asking, "What's this, a gang?" in order to add another hashmark to the tally. Meehan finds that "activities by groups the police considered to be 'real gangs' did not constitute a significant portion of the incidents handled by the gang car that resulted, nonetheless, in 'official' gang statistics."[47]

In one of the few studies of how gang members are legally processed, Zatz shows that although gang members were not directly discriminated against in the 1,916 court referrals she studied involving 257 boys, gang identity did affect other personal, offense, and case characteristics, such as school performance, prior record, and complaint type, in court processing. She notes that "in particular, complaints calling for immediate detention following arrest significantly increased the rate of movement to more severe outcomes for gang boys, but not for their nongang counterparts," and that gang boys with prior referrals also received harsher sanctions.[48] While more ethnographic work is needed to specify the interactional details of such decisions, the work of Alexes Harris on judges' decisions to waive juveniles to adult criminal court reveals that determinations of a juvenile's "sophistication" are often based on his or her purported gang ties.[49]

While gangs on the street may be situated and contingent, perhaps the most lasting and obdurate means by which the state creates gangs is through incarceration. Unfortunately, as the U.S. prison system has grown to become by far the largest in the world, much of it privatized, ethnographic studies of prisons have decreased because of limitations imposed by institutional review boards on one hand and enhanced restrictions in prisons on the other.[50] Especially remarkable is the lack of discussion of the role of prisons in shaping gangs in much of the gang literature, when one of the strongest findings of prison studies is that incarceration has effects that contradict its supposed purposes, ensuring that convicts will mature in criminal knowledge, contacts, and sophistication.[51] Prisons are especially efficacious in ensuring the growth of gangs; depended upon as a source of social control, gangs have become firmly institutionalized there. Many gangs owe their fruition to the prison context, including the Almighty Latin King and Queen Nation and the Norteños, or Mexican Mafia.[52] At least in California prisons, it is commonly acknowledged that gangs perform the role of the police.

Such contradictions of control became glaringly evident in 2004, when attorneys representing the inmate Garrison Johnson successfully argued before the Supreme Court that California's practice of segregating prisoners by race must pass a rigorous judicial test of strict scrutiny, thereby forcing the prison administrators to provide a "compelling reason" for the violation of equal protection under the Constitution's Fourteenth Amendment.[53] In response, a number of law review articles and even the Maoist Internationalist Movement, associated with the Black Panther Party, have argued against this decision in favor of segregation for the sake of prisoners' survival.[54] Gangs in prison have apparently become so integral for social control that legitimizing turning back the clock in favor of institutional segregation becomes the new standard for political correctness.

Gangs not only maintain order inside prisons but are also integral for meeting prisoners' needs once they leave. A great deal of recent scholarship has focused on how social institutions are both disinclined and ill prepared to accommodate returning convicts, who typically become concentrated in neighborhoods that already face myriad economic and social disadvantages.[55] Historically, in states such as California convicts faced a "civil death," lacking any civil or property rights upon release, a legal status that some argue is returning despite reform movements of the 1940s and 1960s to facilitate reintegration.[56] As is often the case, gangs provide a response to such social hopelessness, becoming for many a necessary resource for survival. For instance, as Greg Scott notes, they help the returnee overcome the "gate fever" he or she faces in managing the logistical minutiae of daily life.[57] The organization of drug markets, "constant across locations, presents a familiar money-making venture to the newly released, increasingly desperate and anxious ex-convict." One's gang involvement "often *follows* one's participation in crime," acting as a cushion "to soften the blow of repeated incarceration and release." Such a cushion includes modest material gain and the social and psychological benefits of status, yet ex-convicts risk being exploited by the gang, and ties to the gang increase the probability of arrest, negative attention, and violent victimization, as well as increasing the challenges of getting a straight job. In sum, Scott's analysis shows how "the contemporary urban street gang forms in response to oppression but ultimately reproduces within its ranks the oppression it originally sought to ameliorate."[58] Such a statement could just as well apply to the state's efforts to control gang members by returning them to prisons where they must reforge their gang ties.[59]

A banal, commonsense, historically based, and culturally universal finding of the social sciences that eludes much of the gang literature is that human beings live in groups. The gang literature tends to problematize this, asking questions that anyone might address by simply reflecting on personal experience: Why does one join a gang? What does one do in a gang? How does one leave a gang? Only when gangs are demonized do such questions make sense. If not for the incorrigible suppositions regarding gangs' antisocial tendencies, the basic research questions regarding gangs would soon cease to be of interest.

There is indeed a strong argument to be made that gangs need not be a topic of criminological interest.[60] Like human beings or nation-states, gangs may forge discord or *communitas,* commit murder or provide needed assistance, and the gang literature contains the full gamut of such examples. If anything might be gleaned from over eighty years of gang research, we should learn that the more gangs are repressed, the stronger they become. Throughout the mainstream gang literature and the criminal justice system, from schools to reentry, the fear and loathing expressed in efforts to repress gangs make them all the more attractive for the young person in search of stylistic dissent.[61] Tellingly, Foucault's insights with regard to the hysteria and prohibition of children's onanism can be well applied to contemporary discourses and practices regarding gangs: "The child's 'vice' was not so much its enemy as its support; it may have been designated as the evil to be eliminated, but the extraordinary effort that went into the task that was bound to fail leads one to suspect that what was demanded of it was to persevere, to proliferate to the limits of the visible and the invisible, rather than to disappear for good. Always relying on this support, power advanced, multiplied, and branched out, penetrating further into reality at the same pace."[62]

The simultaneous repression and expansion of gangs provides yet another perverse loop in an ongoing collective spiral of pleasure and power that characterizes the violent history of the United States.[63] Yet even as our institutions of social control work to harden gang identity, for many young people growing up poor, gang identity is a resource, invoked strategically and subject to audience. In other words, gang identity is best conceptualized as performance.

Soft Versions of Identity

There are as many soft versions of identities as there are identities, but all of them have in common the use of such qualifying adjectives as *fluid, contextual,* and *contingent.* Ironically, a term initially intended to denote sameness has been increasingly turned in on itself.[64] In other words, identity is "a concept—operating 'under erasure' in the interval between reversal and emergence; an idea that cannot be thought in the old way, but without which certain key questions cannot be thought at all."[65] Hence thinking about an identity as a cause for certain behavior, or interpreting a behavior as indicative of a certain identity, is highly problematic. As Douglas Maynard notes, "For one thing, even if people can be abstractly categorized in various ways, that does not make their identities automatically relevant for direct interaction. Only periodically during conversation do parties enact their 'master' identities. For another, it is erroneous to assume that *because* of their social identities, parties become involved in patterns of domination and subordination."[66]

The idea of identity as performance may seem novel, as it is perhaps not commonplace, but the concept is not new. In 1959, Erving Goffman showed, to the delight of a popular as well as an academic readership, how we self-consciously manage (or *give*) the impressions we hope others will have of us, even as we *give off* impressions of which we are not aware. Further, how we perform ourselves has much more to do with where we find ourselves than how we define ourselves. As Goffman famously stated, "Not, then, men *[sic]* and their moments. Rather moments and their men."[67] Ethnomethodologists furthered our understanding of identity by showing, often in painstaking detail, how identity is an *accomplishment*.[68] In the 1960s Harvey Sacks, coined the term *doing being* to allude to such dynamics and provided a method to explore such insights through membership categorization analysis.[69] Such a method analyzes in technical detail how an invoked category for interpreting another person is used to sustain a range of inferences, which become the basis for observations and generalizations.[70] One of the clearest examples of an ethnomethodological approach to identity is found in D. Lawrence Wieder's analysis of "telling the convict code." Rather than using ex-convicts' supposed identity as such to explain their behavior, as is common in sociological studies of "the convict code," Wieder explored how members of a halfway house drew upon the convict code as a resource to remind each other of what sort of information should be told to the researcher, and how staff drew upon the code to account for their unsuccessful efforts to rehabilitate ex-cons.[71]

Exploring identity as performance also highlights that aspect of interaction most vital in everyday life but until recently practically absent in academic texts: the body. Elusive to capture with words, which may reify and rigidify that which is felt and taken for granted, the visceral presence of the body is marked through clothing, hairstyles, muscles, tattoos, and *ways* of walking and talking, displaying the nuances of identity work. Such practices are especially important to consider with regard to gangs, since social control agencies such as the police and schools, but especially young people themselves, pay special attention to the various ways the body may perform gang identity.[72] As Dwight Conquergood noted, "Street youth transform themselves into the 'the body of the signifier.'"[73]

The pioneers of unpacking the practices that constitute identity have been scholars of gender. In 1967, Harold Garfinkel published a long chapter in his landmark publication *Studies in Ethnomethodology*, based on extensive interviews with a woman named Agnes. Agnes was born with the genitalia of a man but managed to pass, throughout the course of her daily affairs, as a woman. Twenty years later, Candace West and Donald Zimmerman centered their analysis of "doing gender" on Garfinkel's study of how Agnes made the invisible work of producing gender visible. Hence, that someone is born with a certain set of genitalia is not sufficient for producing maleness and femaleness. As they note, "Rather than as a property of individuals, we conceive of gender as an emergent feature of social situations: both as an outcome of and a rationale for various social arrangements and as a means of legitimating one of the most fundamental divisions of society."[74] Another soft study of identity par excellence is Judith Butler's book *Gender Trouble*, which posits that "there is no primary or original that drag imitates; but gender is a kind of imitation for which there is no original."[75] In other words, "There is no gender identity behind the expressions of gender; . . . identity is performatively constituted by the very 'expressions' that are said to be its results."[76] For students to understand such insights, a common assignment in many gender studies courses is to have the men in the course pull off a believable performance as a woman for a day and ask the women in the course to "become men" for a day. As students come to terms with the work necessary to practically achieve a gendered performance, they come to marvel at how such an accomplishment is so deeply naturalized as to be unaccountable. Butler helps lift the veil from this social illusion.

In terms of race, Michael Omi and Howard Winant developed the concept of "racial formation," a "sociohistorical process by which racial categories are created, inhabited, transformed, and destroyed."[77] In their view, what counts as "race" is organized continuously and fluidly through a reciprocity between micro and macro social relations. Through political contestation at both levels, the practical, lived meaning of the concept is constantly subject to redefinition. For instance, in her book *How Jews Became White Folks,* Karen Brodkin explores how members of a group that had suffered marked discrimination and segregation in the United States came to be accepted, "like us," after World War II, in a way not unlike the Irish or Polish of previous generations.[78] John L. Jackson probes the situated intersection of race, class, and place, showing the ways African American identity is performed, sometimes inadvertently but often intentionally, in battles over gentrifying Harlem.[79] Scholars continue to debate whether "Asian" or "Latino" has become "white" and whether black students hold back academically out of a fear of appearing "white."[80]

Similarly, in studying ethnicity, Joane Nagel notes that it "is best understood as a dynamic, constantly evolving property of both individual identity and group organization."[81] Such insights echo Michael Moerman, who realized that he must stop asking the Lue of Thailand, "Who are the Lue?" since such a list was potentially endless. Instead, he focused on "when ethnic identification labels are invoked and the consequences of invoking them."

Hence, rather than using ethnicity to explain behavior, Moerman focused on how a group of people invoke and share common understandings.[82] A defining statement is provided by Ronald Cohen, who noticed that every attempt to define an ethnic group by creating a boundary is artificial and cannot account for the many *situationed* transformations of ethnic identity and/or ethnic groups.[83] A person will strategically enact and communicate the particular ethnic identity of the ethnic group that is taken for granted in a given moment or context. These enactments are based on the circumstances and the audience at the time.[84]

States play a significant part in maintaining the illusion of difference, and hence many scholars have focused on how national identity, often coincident with the construction of race and/or ethnicity, is made to seem natural and real. Benedict Anderson's book *Imagined Communities* is especially prominent in promoting this soft view of identity. It shows how the sense of fraternity provided by the idea of "nation" "makes it possible over the past two centuries, for so many millions of people, not so much to kill, as willingly to die for such limited imaginings."[85] In particular, recent studies of colonialization have focused on systems of classification and categorization, showing how rulers' practices of classifying, naming, and counting affect the politics and self-understandings of indigenous populations.[86] Another branch of research focuses on how censuses foster the idea of a bounded national society, composed of mutually exclusive cultural groups.[87] Ironies are often painfully evident in such official processes, as when the United States barred the Chinese from entry under the Chinese Exclusion Act of 1882 but allowed an exception for "merchants."[88] Despite such insights, "an understanding of *nations* as real entities continues to inform the study of nationhood and nationalism," even though "the very terms in which it is framed presuppose the existence of the entity that is to be defined."[89]

Gang Identity as Performance

Gangs might also be seen as small-scale efforts to construct nations, albeit extremely tenuous ones whose existence must be stridently affirmed lest they wither away, as they inevitably do.[90] Yet gang research adamantly attests to the existence of an entity that is problematized by its very members. To help move this research in a direction that avoids "chasing its explanatory tail,"[91] I will briefly discuss identity and adolescence and then review current work and rationales for studying gang identity as performance.

Identity and Adolescence

Much of the contemporary boom in research on identity might be traced to Erik Erikson's work, which is also a crucial starting point for understanding adolescence. As this life stage is a central time for gang involvement, Erikson's insights are also important for understanding gangs.[92] In the late 1960s, Erikson wrote *Identity: Youth and Crisis* and characterized identity as "a process 'located' in the core of the individual and yet also in the core of his communal culture, a process which establishes . . . the identity of those two identities."[93] Such a focus on identity was one of the pronounced issues of the day, since "at the same time, there was a palpable increase in anxiety among social scientists about the rise of mass society, with its decline in community, the ascendance of anonymous bureaucratic control along with the technological transformation of human activities, and a consequent rise in problems of personal definition."[94] Erikson proposed a developmental model of human life composed of eight stages. Adolescence was crucial in this model, since it was described as typically involving an identity crisis in which an individual struggles to find a place for him- or herself in community.[95] Such a period of ambivalence and unpredictability characterizes the status crisis in the transition to adulthood and, if not resolved, may lead to future crises.

Though Erikson helped sensitize the public to difficulties faced by adolescents, many feel that his insights into stages of development have hampered thinking about this life stage. Numerous surveys of young people have been implemented on the basis of what is termed a "developmental approach," sorting young people into categories deemed "developmentally appropriate" or "inappropriate." Rebecca Raby notes that in such a model "it is difficult to take children seriously," since they are seen, not as active agents, but as "first and foremost, an object of analysis that serves as an example of a previously established category, and evidence to confirm models."[96] Instead, "Adolescence is marked by a striking fluidity, as a passage in-between, a state of flux that defies clear-cut labels."[97] This book will explore how gang identity is also strikingly fluid, in that the same young person may explicitly draw upon or deny such an identity depending on the circumstance.

Gang Identity as Performance

In ecologies where gangs are active, young people may modulate ways of talking, walking, dressing, writing graffiti, wearing makeup, and hiding or revealing tattoos, playing with markers of embodied identity to obscure, reveal, or provide contradictory signals on a continuum from gang related to non–gang related. Yet few studies of gangs appear hip to these nuances. When it comes to understanding gang membership, most of the gang literature is mired in notions from the 1950s that identity simply *is*, rather than is artfully created and contingent on circumstances and audience. For an alternative, we are well advised by scholars of identity who inform us, "We should seek to explain the processes and mechanisms through which what has been called the 'political fiction' of the 'nation'—or of the 'ethnic group,' 'race,' or other putative 'identity'—can crystallize, at certain moments, as a powerful, compelling reality."[98]

Dwight Conquergood pioneered the study of gang identity as performance. For four years he lived in "Big Red," a housing complex dominated by gang members, and analyzed gang graffiti, communication, and nationalism.[99] Through such long-term immersion, he found that "gangs produce their identity through complex communication practices that are conflictually constituted and proliferated along fabricated borders, cleavages between Self and Other. Turf tensions and boundary vigilance both emplot and energize the signifying practices of gang culture. The trespass of borders and the desecration of symbols, in short, transgressions of the space of the Other—both physically and figuratively—are the performative moments of gang identity."[100]

Norma Mendoza-Denton has also made profound contributions to the gang literature, revealing how young women work a gang identity and confound notions of femininity through their strategic use of makeup and bodily comportment. Building explicitly on Judith Butler's approach to gender, she shows how the *cholas* she studied "throw into question the very gendered category that girls are expected to inhabit."[101] Simultaneously, their embodied performances of gang identity "were inscribed with the traces of conflict: assimilation, ethnic pride, covert prestige, and the pride of survival were all etched on the surface of their skins, rewritten every morning in the mirror with the help of Maybelline, Wet n' Wild, and Cover Girl." She traces the ways in which such nuances of hair, eyeliner, and lipstick "were crucial to members' identification of each others' allegiance," as powerful markers of liberation, not social injury.[102]

One of the most problematic and powerful venues for performing gang identity is school; few institutions have been more concerned about gangs, and few students attract more concern, since symbolically schools and gangs occupy opposite ends of a moral continuum.[103] Some analysts, such as Kenneth Trump, propose that school staff should be aware of "gang" identifiers, such as "graffiti, colors, tattoos, handsigns and handshakes, initiations, language, and behavior." Once such behaviors have been identified, school officials "should design a program of combined strategies based on strict enforcement of disciplinary regulations (such as dress codes) and criminal codes; provision of services to intervene with children displaying current involvement or interest in gangs; and the use of education and training for preventing gang growth in the schools and overall school community."[104] Such efforts merely multiply the ways in which gang identity can be performed and the occasions for performing it.[105] Back in 1964, Carl Werthman showed how gang members strategically invoke their street identities as a form of resistance in classrooms, especially when they interpret teachers' grading practices as arbitrary. The analysis that follows picks up from Werthman's insights, exploring how the combination of a lack of purposeful teaching and the enforcement of arbitrary rules alienates students, heightening the possibilities and rewards of performing gang identity.[106]

To understand the nuanced, strategic, contingent ways in which gang identity is performed is not simply a descriptive exercise. Rather, to grapple with the ways young people perform gang membership has important consequences, both for recognizing the positive aspects of gangs and for working to counter their negative aspects. For one, we might appreciate the strategic ways in which marginalized young people are able to create something out of nothing, enlivening their space with vibrant social and political possibilities, which may lead to political action and legitimate social and economic uplift.[107] Alternatively, we might better understand the local interaction rituals that may limit collective efficacy, promote violence, and limit individuals' ability to move freely through neighborhoods in order to see friends, get to work, or visit family.[108]

Setting and Methods

Choices Alternative Academy (CAA) was designed for the baddest of the bad: the roughest kids in the toughest neighborhood. Surrounded by two twelve-foot-high chain-link fences and two separate security gates through which one must be buzzed in, CAA is a small inner-city alternative school for young people aged fourteen to twenty-one who have dropped out of school for sixty days or more, in a six–census tract area with some of the highest crime and poverty in the western United States. As I stood on CAA's street with a community organizer, he told me, "At least six of the houses on this block are crack houses."

Initially, I was introduced to the school to survey students' school-to-work transition, and later I chose it as a setting where I could spend a sustained period of time with young people and be of service to them.[109] Built from a combination of federal and local funding, CAA was located in a large, highly populous, diverse county. The school served approximately two hundred students, roughly half of whom attended on any day. About one-third of the students were on probation, and about thirty were parents, whose children were cared for at the child care facility attached to the school. Mirroring the demographics of the neighborhood, roughly half the students were Latino, half were African American, and some were from Asian Pacific islands such as Samoa or Central American countries such as Belize. Students who were sent there often had histories involving violence, drug use, truancy, dropping out of school, and teen pregnancy.

Over a four-year period I spent my time in the school hanging out in the classroom and on the yard, tutoring, playing basketball, playing games like chess and dominoes, and talking. I waited in line for food and ate with students, often blending into their classrooms passively.[110] On only one or two occasions I took jottings in the field, as when I sat in the front office and a notepad seemed to show the office staff that I was keeping busy. I wrote extensive field notes on the evening of each day's observations, following practices handed down by Robert Emerson, Rachel Fretz, and Linda Shaw.[111] The appendix further explores the tensions of managing relations with both students and teachers, African Americans and Latinos, young men and young women.

Table 1 compares mean values of some characteristics of the six primary census tracts served by CAA to the same data for the city, county, and state in which these tracts were located. Note that CAA also received many students from outside its target area who had been transferred or expelled or were simply looking for a place to complete their high school education. As we see from the table, the median household income in the census tracts served by CAA was roughly half the median household income for the city, state, and county. The census tract with the highest median income for households with children was located furthest from CAA, while CAA was situated in the census tract with the lowest median income for households with children. This census tract, from which CAA took many of its students, also was the only one with a lower median income for households with children than for all households. Also, fewer than 50 percent of residents had graduated from high school and fewer than 5 percent had graduated from college in these census tracts, far below the city, county, and state percentages. Of graduates, most went on to work as white-collar professionals in government or

TABLE 1. *Demographic Characteristics of CAA Target Area, 2002*

	Census Tracts Served by CAA	City	County	State
Median income	$20,490	$39,012	$44,109	$49,955
State rank	3rd %	31st %	57th %	
National rank	8th %	52nd %	81st %	
Median income, households with children	$26,821	$56,257	$59,520	$66,476
State rank	5th %	45th %	61st %	
National rank	9th %	62nd %	81st %	
High school grads	42.2%	67%	70%	76.2%
College grads	3%	22.9%	22.3%	23.4%

social programs.[112] According to the local police department, the area around CAA ongoingly experienced the highest percent of "gang-related crime" in the city, measured at 14.3 percent of all gang crime in the city in the year before the school was built. One of the CAA census tracts charted the largest increase in violent crime in the city between 1980 and 1988, at 92.2 percent.[113] All the students there had experience with gangs, and many were still heavily involved with them.

Alternative schools differ markedly from typical U.S. high schools. There are no athletic teams, band, cheerleaders, or lockers, and students have no real opportunity to develop status or prestige from school involvements.[114] Many students at CAA had been transferred there for frequent episodes of fighting and violence, although others had been transferred for dealing drugs, and others were simply dropouts from traditional high schools who sought out CAA as a means to achieve a high school diploma. Hence, many students were troubled and attended the school only temporarily. Alternative schools such as CAA are an increasingly common response to school safety concerns. Many policy makers advocate such settings as an alternative to expelling students, thereby balancing the rights of violent students to receive a free education with the rights of all students to a safe environment.[115]

After a number of weeks in the setting, I began to conduct interviews with students away from their classrooms. Eventually, I came to interview forty-six students, six repeatedly, plus eleven of twelve teachers, two administrators, one security guard, and a community activist. Those who were under eighteen needed to secure parental permission prior to being interviewed. I chose the young people I interviewed on the basis of a number of criteria, seeking a racial/ethnic balance that would mirror the neighborhood and represent variation along the continuum from gangbanger to nongangbanger, nonviolent to violent. I also sought to interview students with a variety of interests, including those who excelled academically, musically, in sports, or mechanically. The range of talents and abilities of young people who have been marginalized in educational settings of last resort, such as alternative schools and special education programs, is not only remarkable but stunning, as is evident in many of the interviews. I refer to those I interview as "consultants," since I use their accounts as resources to report events I was unable to observe firsthand.[116] All names of staff, students, schools, and the local gang ("Central") and its gang color are pseudonyms.

Interviews were semistructured, open-ended conversations, lasting from one to twelve hours, and were taped and transcribed. Following Susan Driver, the aim was to "open up spaces in which to listen for culturally mediated . . . communications," to show how "youth themselves are continually theorizing identity and power as they struggle to recognize and speak themselves through personal and collective discourses."[117] Sessions with young people spanned their life history, covering such topics as places the consultant had lived, reasons for moving, descriptions of fights, drug use, experiences in school, intimate and familial relationships, hobbies, and experiences with gangs.[118] Interviews were often highly emotional and could be therapeutic for both myself and my consultant.[119] As Driver notes, "Being given the opportunity to name and share difficult experiences within a research context enables [young people] to reflect and to construct their own identities while getting feedback and support."[120] Transcripts were provided for consultants when possible, checked for accuracy, and used as the basis for further questions.

My initial stated interest was in how young people deal with violence, but my deeper aim was to "[pay] attention to creative initiatives of youth as a starting point . . . [as a] useful way to decenter adult authoritative knowledge away from institutionally bound methods, following the lead of youth to affirm the mediums, communicative styles, and social arenas connected to their everyday worlds of experience."[121] I coded and analyzed data according to the traditions of grounded theory and analytic induction, developing over four hundred inductive categories that I managed through the program Ethnograph.[122]

The tales in this book are cumulative, with the analysis building from chapter to chapter. Still, one may wish to read the Appendix first in order to gain a fuller sense of the setting, the research process, and some of the individuals involved. The book is divided into two parts. The first part explores the ecological backdrop that provides a venue and motivation for the performance of gang identity, and the second part presents my consultants' variable ways of presenting the self with regard to gangs and violence. In the first part, I explore how young people struggle to resist powerfully alienating routines of school and the often arbitrary imposition of rules at school. The second part begins with two chapters on invoking and affiliating with gangs, followed by two that probe how young people resist fights and violence. The final substantive chapter examines the variable, contingent identity performances of one young man who worked as a bureaucrat on a federal jobs program while maintaining his gang ties. The conclusion calls for community researchers to reclaim the term *gangs*, recognizing them as a vital part of many communities, and for gang researchers to recognize and probe the many manifestations of soft versions of gang identity.

Table 2 lists the young people who were interviewed for this study, their age at the time of the interview and the year of the interview.

TABLE 2. *Consultants*

Pseudonym	Ethnicity	Age
Angel	Latino	Nineteen in 2001
Antoine	African American	Eighteen in 2001
Ben	Belizean	Eighteen in 1997
Bill	African American	Eighteen in 1997
Billy	African American	Eighteen in 2001
Bix	Latino	Sixteen in 2001
Brad	African American	Eighteen in 2000
Brian	African American	Eighteen in 2001
Buck	African American	Sixteen in 2001
Carlos	Latino	Eighteen in 1997
Charlie	African American	Nineteen in 2001
Chris	Cherokee/African American	Eighteen in 1997
David	African American	Eighteen in 1997
Dion	Latino	Eighteen in 2001
Donald	African American	Fourteen in 1997

(continued)

TABLE 2. *Consultants* (continued)

Pseudonym	Ethnicity	Age
Doogan	African American	Eighteen in 2001
Earl	African American	Eighteen in 1997
Ernesto	Latino	Sixteen in 1997
Emily	Latina	Eighteen in 1997
Eric	Latino	Nineteen in 1997
Everett	African American	Eighteen in 2001
Esmeralda	Latina	Eighteen in 2000
Frank	Latino	Eighteen in 1997
Jerome	African American	Eighteen in 2001
Jaime	Latino	Eighteen in 1997
Joe	Latino	Sixteen in 1997
Johnnie	Samoan	Eighteen in 2000
Juan	Latino	Sixteen in 2001
Ken	African American	Sixteen in 2001
Lamont	African American	Eighteen in 2000
Larry	African American	Eighteen in 1997
Leroi	African American	Eighteen in 1997
Marco	Latino	Eighteen in 1997
Maria	Latina	Eighteen in 2000
Mel	Latino	Seventeen in 2001
Mikie	African American	Sixteen in 2001
Oliver	Latino	Fourteen in 1997
Oscar	Latino	Nineteen in 2001
Pete	Latino	Eighteen in 1997
Richard	African American	Sixteen in 1997
Shawn	Belizean	Twenty in 1997
Steve	Latino	Twenty in 1997
Tammy	African American	Eighteen in 2000
Terry	African American	Eighteen in 1997
Tim	African American	Eighteen in 1997
Tom	Belizean	Eighteen in 2001

Alienation in School

2

Moral Dramas at School

No sub wants to come down here, they think this is a war zone.
—Mr. Dolan, CAA teacher

It's just so ghetto. Look at this school, it's like the worst in the district. I can't stand it.
—Tammy, CAA student

A chicken and egg question haunts studies of school achievement and, by extension, criminology: Is it the behavior of students or that of schools that seals certain students' subordination? Paul Willis classically demonstrated how the students themselves, acting out of an awareness of their limited class position and their threatened masculinity, contributed most to their continued oppression; the actions of teachers and administrators were but a shadowy backdrop to the lads' antics.[1] John Ogbu did not overlook discrimination in the school to the same extent as Willis, yet his work, like Willis's, emphasized how those from historically oppressed communities, especially involuntary immigrants, were less likely to adopt school codes of behavior.[2]

Two recent articles, one by Pedro Mateu-Gelabert and Howard Lune, and the other by Rosalie Rolón Dow, offer a refreshing alternative to such approaches.[3] Both show, in contrast to Willis and Ogbu, how students ardently desire to learn but are let down by a dire lack of school management that leads to unpredictability and violence (Gelabert and Lune) or by fundamentally unengaging classroom lessons (Dow). This chapter contributes to these insights by showing how both the lack of school management referred to by Mateu-Gelabert and Lune and the lack of engaging lessons emphasized by Dow create alienating classroom conditions that *provide no opportunity for success*. Simply by living in a certain neighborhood and attending this school, students are *deprived of educational options*. Hugh Mehan notes that the designations of students' capabilities arise out of institutional arrangements or "felicity conditions," rather than out of students' attributes.[4] Students who resist such arrangements open up space for other possibilities that one might perceive as either furthering their oppression or, as this chapter argues, providing opportunities for liberation.

As Willis does, I celebrate the efforts of students to resist a pedagogy of oppression.[5] But I diverge from him in finding a spark of hope in such efforts: in a postindustrial world quite different from that of Willis's lads, a world that commodifies rebellion and offers opportunities to make money from it, they carry the potential to rise above rather than merely recapitulate one's class position.[6] Such resistance, often confused with "gangs" and "criminality" in the popular imagination, may be one of the few ways that students can have an impact on schools that do not address their needs and concerns, and one of the few ways that they can realize their voice and potential in this context.[7] When schools offer students literally nothing of value, one person's instigator of chaos can be another's community organizer, offering manifold opportunities for the development of street literacy.[8]

For the teachers and students who must inhabit and make sense of the small, semi-isolated social worlds of classrooms on a daily basis, these classrooms provide useful spaces in which they can explore the dynamics of order and resistance. Studies have focused on how resistance may be related to class, race, gender, and the structural dynamics of the classroom, typically portraying resistance as deviance or disruption, a problem to be managed so that teaching goals may be realized.[9] Yet in educational settings that do not even attempt to maintain the appearance of a "real school," resistance may be students' best hope for creating meaning in the classroom, "enchanting a disenchanted world."[10]

Alienation in the Classroom

Ostensibly, a school is a place where teachers teach students, yet at CAA this is frequently impossible. The bare minimum requirements of a school, to have teachers and students present, are often not met; absenteeism and tardiness are chronic problems among both. Once students are on campus, staff face great difficulty in having them attend class, even though the campus is quite small and easily monitored. Finally, once students are in class, students complete busywork, and if the teacher does provide a lesson its pedagogical value is often questionable.

By and large, students at CAA must do one of two things: either complete questions on a worksheet or answer questions at the end of a chapter in a book. Directed lessons are rare because of problems with absenteeism, but when teachers do provide substantive lectures these are often quite misinformative. More commonly, teachers give "life experience" lectures in hopes of edifying students by sharing practical wisdom.[11]

For the most part, teachers are planted behind their desks throughout the class period; students receive little one-on-one attention, except from occasional college volunteers. Most students are grateful for individualized attention when it is provided. Amazingly, despite the tedium, many students work hard in their classes, sitting and diligently completing worksheet after worksheet, chapter after chapter.[12]

At CAA, no course ever begins or ends. Students work at their own pace to complete a course, joining a class when they need it and leaving once they are finished. Motivated students can take weeks to complete a course; others take years. In the school's early days, students knew they had completed a course once they reached seventy-five points. Since each semester had seventy-five days, a student would receive one point for each hour of "work." There was no standardization for the way points were given, and students were not working to meet clear objectives. Thus points were awarded arbitrarily for tasks such as sweeping the class, completing a worksheet, or simply sitting quietly.

A number of years after the school was founded, the principal began to ask teachers to write down for students the goals to be completed in order to finish a class. Many teachers rebelled fiercely against this innovation, calling it an administrative trespass on their autonomy. Nonetheless, the principal was adamant, and the Goal Sheet (GS) became the norm. While the GS was designed to have students work toward and present a final project, such as a poster, a paper, or a speech to demonstrate mastery of a topic, usually it consisted simply of a set number of worksheets to be completed or chapter questions to be answered.

Basic teacher expectations are well reflected in the following tape-recorded interaction between two teachers while I interviewed one of them.

TEACHER A: I look at this, I'm like, "When is the day gonna be over!" *[laughs] [Louder, pleading tone]* When is it gonna be *over!*"

TEACHER B: Well, I try to make it to a half-day and then, you know, break it up into little pieces. A part and B part.

TEACHER A: That's what I used to do when I worked an eight-hour shift. Two hours, take a break. Two hours, take a lunch. Two hours, take another break. Then I got two hours left.

TEACHER B: After twenty-five years of this, man, I don't know if I can go back to an eight-hour shift anymore. Eight, ten hours. Twelve?

TEACHER A: *[low, whispering]* I'm not gonna do this for no twenty-five years. [hearty laughter]

For such teachers, teaching was akin to unsavory labor: a job that had to be endured, minute to minute, hour to hour. As one confided, "I'm beginning to buy into 'Plan ahead, have a program for them, and insist on the attendance' and so forth." Yet he had not yet begun to lesson-plan during the ten months I observed him at the school.

Many students simply had no teacher show up. For weeks during my fieldwork, one teacher, whom I'll refer to as Ms. A, was inexplicably absent. She left no lesson plans, her manuals were locked in a cabinet, and substitute teachers had no idea what to do. Below, I noticed Ms. A's students as I interviewed Ms. Mates, who shared a room with Ms. A that was divided by a flimsy partition.

Sean, Tom, Antoine, and a few others dragged themselves into class lethargically, with frustration and disappointment. "She's gone again?!" they complained as they entered. Mr. Merritt, the vice principal, made an announcement on the PA that Ms. A wanted her students to continue to complete their assignments and that she would return soon. I heard noise over the partition between the classrooms, and soon Mr. Merritt himself entered the room. Somewhat frantically, he asked Ms. Mates if she had any worksheets or assignments for that class. Rolling her eyes, she pulled out a large three-ring binder and took out a page, and he thanked her. "That's the benefit of having experienced teachers on staff," he said, winking at me. "Any sort of extra assignment or filler needed, there it is." Ms. Mates grunted in response.

After our interview, I visited the class. A substitute teacher sat at the teacher's desk. The students looked to be in pain, frustrated, and miserable, but still with their somewhat rebellious senses of humor. Sean was talking to himself at the front table when I entered. I sat down next to Tom and looked into his bloodshot eyes. He had a ragtag dictionary in front of him and aimlessly flipped through pages. "Man, this sucks," he told me. He said all they had to do was look up sixteen words and write sentences with them. Antoine had actually done it, and the sub graded it, noticing that one sentence was missing a period and emphasizing to Antoine how important that was. Antoine took the paper with a limp hand that fell with the paper. I pointed out to Tom that all the words started with "p." "That don't mean nothin'," he said. "She just picks out any words. Today, they just happen to begin with 'p.'" "Oh," I said.

Such is the routine of a pedagogy of oppression, in which words, crafted over centuries, are transformed into encumbering weights, frustrating students who must tediously look up their meanings in dictionaries. The substitute tried to be enthusiastic and even chastised students for not working harder. I was amazed at the students' compliance.[13]

Teachers who did attend often arrived well after 8:00, when school was scheduled to begin, leaving students who showed up on time with nothing to do but hang around with friends on the yard until their teacher arrived at 8:15, 8:30, or later. As Angel told me one morning when I found him on the yard, "Since my teacher usually doesn't show up on time, why should I?"

Such students were a concern for security guards, who were charged with "clearing the yard." Security guards were often unaware of whether the teacher had arrived yet, and this lack of knowledge was a ready resource for students, who could easily push the guards to exasperation.

> A group of three Latinos stood outside the second gate. One, Jorge, was reading the newspaper that the security guard, Louis, had brought for himself. "Why aren't you in class?" Louis demanded. "My teacher ain't here yet," Jorge said, shrugging with a grin. "Yeah, our teacher ain't here yet," the others chimed in. "That's not true," Louis said. "At least go stand back there and check." The students laughed a little, not budging. "I'm gonna give you two minutes," Louis said, but after five minutes they were still standing around, and Louis said nothing.

Hence teachers' poor attendance practices, which resulted in student loitering, were also a resource for students to justify their loitering. If teachers were not yet in class, students had nowhere to go except the yard, which was ostensibly prohibited. Louis had to watch the front of the school and scan students with a hand-held metal detector, and without a walkie-talkie he had no way of finding if the teacher was in class or not. In this case he resorted to a weak, vague threat, which the students ignored with a chuckle. Teachers' tardiness thus undermined security guards, leaving them few alternatives to being manipulated and humiliated by students' wiles.

In addition to these times when teachers who were supposed to be teaching were absent, one day per week at CAA was formally designated a nonteaching day. Every Friday was "social rec." (social recreation) day at CAA, during which students simply practiced "hanging out" by playing basketball, dominoes, and board games, as well as rapping and dancing. While such activities may have more learning content than worksheets and chapter reviews (discussed below) and can be a boon for ethnographers, they were entirely unstructured and optional. As can be imagined, after three or four hours of this students tended to become frustrated, and especially in hot weather fights were not unusual.

Grading

It was an open secret that grading at CAA was a farce, and it was hard to find grades that were justified. Students rarely received papers back from teachers, and teachers often had no way to explain a grade. Typically fewer than a half-dozen parents attended parent conferences, but when an effort was made to contact all parents to inform them of Open House, many more showed up than usual. This was especially stressful for teachers who had not determined grades. Below, one teacher counseled a young woman's mother.

> He said that [the student] had good behavior in class and that if she applied herself she could really do something with herself. With a shrug, he added, "If she does apply herself. I know she can do it if she wants to, she just has to want to bad enough." Holding his palms up, he quickly mumbled that he had not given any of his students anything better than a "C," since he had not graded the papers and so wasn't exactly sure of the grade they should receive.

The parent in this conference did not ask why the teacher had not completed the grading yet or inquire into the basis of his grades. Rather, she stood for a while nodding, then shook hands and left. Nonetheless, teachers did feel rather put upon, as in the following incident involving a second teacher:

> The teacher came over to me, wiping sweat from his forehead and shaking his head. "I don't know, this is kinda stressful," he said.
> "Is this the first time you've had conferences?" I asked.
> "No, my second time, but last time we only had four parents come in the whole school," he said.

One attraction for potential employees at CAA was that they were not held strictly accountable for grading practices, as a third teacher revealed in our interview.

"What was your first impression coming here to this school?" I asked.

"I thought, this is really easy work. The academic demands here are relatively low. Hey, as long as I stay, I can stay. I was really happy about that."

"What are the academic demands?"

"If a kid can get close, you pass him. If you've got an excuse to pass him, you pass him."

When I asked him to elaborate, he told me of a specific incident from which he inferred that administrators were telling him that passing students was the key, not quibbling over whether they deserved it. "There was one record that got screwed up. That was the record of this girl who didn't really have a snowball's chance. Kind of marginal. She thought she'd pass, and I said, 'Well, is she gonna come back tomorrow?' Here she is trying to graduate. I'm in the office where these things are handled, and the question came up, 'Did she pass or not?' She's all upset because the record didn't get through. I didn't know the grade book from my asshole. The person asking for the decision did not ask me in any detail whatsoever what she did to qualify. 'Did she pass or not?' And the light went on in my head and I said, 'Yes! She completed assignments for me, and she explained it to me, therefore she passed.'"

Such practices were well known at CAA. In the field note excerpt below, a teacher spoke of more covert ways in which grades were changed without applying pressure to the teacher as in the excerpt above.

"Sometimes I feel that as a student here, I wouldn't be awfully motivated," I said.

"Oh no. How could you be? I try to do my best to motivate them, but school as a whole, no. I don't see how they can be motivated. They can sit here and be in a classroom two, three years without finishing up. They can sit in a class and not do anything, semester after semester, and nothing's done about it. I was in a meeting, and an administrator was saying, 'People are giving them A's, and they're not doing A work.' I looked at this person and thought, 'This person has given people grades for classes that they didn't take, so they could graduate. This person has tried to change the grades that people have given them. Another teacher said he found out—someone showed him—'Is this your signature?' He said, 'No.' Someone signed his name and said this student passed a class with a grade. That happened to me too. They do all kinds of stuff here. I guess it won't hurt anybody because these kids are not college level."

In this excerpt, I had not asked specifically about grading practices, yet this teacher linked such practices to my statement that I would be unmotivated as a student at CAA. First, she told how students could be in a class year after year without finishing the class, yet nothing would be done about it. She then spoke of administrators who, though criticizing teachers for providing easy grades, provided grades for classes students had not taken, changed teachers' grades, and even forged teachers' signatures to allow students to pass. Although she had qualms about such practices, she rationalized them with a statement that spoke volumes about social priorities toward inner-city students.[14]

Worksheets

My field notes were full of efforts to help students complete worksheets. In some classes, the entire curriculum consisted of a packet of worksheets, usually copied out of workbooks. Sometimes they were kept in file folders, so that once a student completed one sheet he or she returned to the files to find the next. In other classes, students received a stapled packet to work through. Oliver, a second-generation, fourteen-year-old Latino, was working through one such packet. He fluently mixed English and Spanish but had limited reading ability in each language. He could have benefited from any sort of ESL lesson; instead, he was stuck with a complicated worksheet in which he had to apply eight rules for plural nouns to a list of one hundred nouns that had already been made plural—a confusing task even for one with proficiency in making plurals. As with any worksheet at CAA, the justification for using it was unclear. It was used, as books were used, simply because it was available. No one had explained his worksheet to him and he had not asked for help. Teachers often passed out such work with minimal directions and provided credit without checking answers. Students practically never asked to see their graded work. Oliver worked on this same packet on plural nouns the entire time I worked with him, from January to June of 1997.[15]

In such a class, in which a worksheet was all a student had, inability to complete a worksheet could lead to inability to complete a class and could potentially present an obstacle to graduation. Emily, also a second-generation Latino, was to underline the subject of a sentence once and the predicate twice, but she continued to underline objects as subjects, then confused verbs with subjects, drawing out an assignment meant to take minutes into days. Meanwhile, many students sitting behind her had already given up and were using the class time to socialize.

Chapter Questions

Answering the questions at the end of a chapter in a book may seem a more useful task than completing worksheets. Rather than simply trying to finish a meaningless exercise, students looked for information to provide in response to various questions. Nevertheless, as with worksheets, the relevance of the textbooks was rarely demonstrated. The large and bulky textbooks were an oppressive presence in the classroom: a student had to simply plow through them, chapter by chapter, until a requirement had been met. Students never read the textbook. Instead, they became expert scanners, able to find headings and information in italics or bold print with lightning speed and then write a response to the prompt. Below, Billy expressed frustration about completing a GS for a health class.

He had a health book, and he showed me his GS, stating that he must complete ten chapters for class credit. "What chapter are you on?" I asked him. "Eight," he said. "No, nine." He opened the book and started talking about how meaningless and frustrating this is. He said they don't learn anything, the books are useless and totally meaningless for his interests. "What would you be interested in learning?" I asked him. "Something about business," he said, "how to make money."

Billy was complaining about a textbook that was relatively new and user-friendly, with large color photographs, charts and graphs, and easily readable sections. In most classes students weren't so fortunate. Dion, a bilingual second-generation Latino with learning difficulties, struggled with a large, cumbersome, old edition on government, full of confusing terminology, lacking in photographs, and with much out-of-date information. One can well imagine the extensive tagging and missing pages on such a volume, evidence of the frustrations of prior students.

I worked with Dion for the period on a chapter concerning due process of law. He had a hard time reading—pronouncing most of the words incorrectly—as many were quite difficult. Dion was supposed to write about the difference between procedural and substantive due process, and it frustrated him, although he only needed to copy a sentence. The words seemed too large and abstract even when I read the examples. Eventually, he became frustrated and resisted, and I felt I was being unfair in prodding him to continue. This probably explained why he usually simply sat in class staring into space. I never saw the teacher in this classroom get up from his desk and work with students one on one.

Not only was the task of completing an assignment arduous and frustrating, but students knew that once they finished they were likely to never see the work again, and that if it was graded it might well be graded incorrectly.

At times, teachers found sources outside worksheets and textbooks. Yet even when they had done the work to find such a source, they seldom motivated students by introducing it, connecting it to projects, helping students complete those projects, or discussing the relevance of the reading to other themes in students' lives.

The teacher passed out two stapled pages with two versions of a story featuring the meeting of conquistadors and natives. He simply said, "Read it," so I did, along with the others. And that was it. A girl asked him what to do, and he sounded offended, responding in an almost defensive, high-pitched, somewhat mocking voice, "Write what it's about. You know what it's about, right?"

Directed Lessons

Occasionally, teachers offered lessons that were not dependent on worksheets or answering questions out of books. Such lessons often consisted of watching a film or answering questions on a field trip. At times, teachers would try to apply lessons out of manuals, but not always with the greatest success. Below, a teacher followed one such lesson in a conflict resolution manual, asking students to tape papers to their backs and then write messages on them about what they thought of each other.

Billy was especially happy about the exercise, writing on Robert's back, "Stupid Ass Mexican," and on another, "Dumb." Meanwhile, someone had written "Lazy" on his back. Another kid, Brad, got "Tall new guy," and another, "Needs to focus." When the teacher asked them to look at what people had written, everyone seemed a bit disappointed, much less excited than they had been when they were writing. Billy was smiling, saying, "Lemme see this." When he pulled his paper off his back, he looked crestfallen, and snickered with disdain. The teacher smiled at their responses, and told them that this shows how others see us differently than we see ourselves.

Directed lessons could be painful to watch, not only because some teachers seemed not to have mastered the subject matter they were presenting, but also because, perhaps on account of such insecurity, their presentation of the lesson was often suffused with bravado and arrogance, as if to constantly remind students that the teacher was more intelligent than them. Below, a teacher improvised a grammar lesson as a follow-up to a journal prompt.

I spent the morning tutoring Michael, helping him write a response to the prompt, "I had a great Thanksgiving dinner. We." The teacher walked to the front of the class and told me he didn't put ". . ." after the "We" because then he'd have people writing the ". . ." on their papers. "What'd you do?" he bellowed. "We ate," they responded. After "We," the teacher wrote "eat," and looked out with a deadpan expression. "Ate," students said, but he didn't correct it, so I wasn't not sure if the "eat" was pedagogical or not. He went on to teach a lesson, apparently on conjugating verbs. "You have to know your pretenses," he said. "'We' is what? That's second person. 'I' is what? That's first person. 'You' is what? That's third person," he continued. "'I went' is what? Past pretense, right. What about if it happens right now?" "I went," someone called out. The teacher was stuck. "Lemme think about this." After a pause, he announced, "I guess you're right, if it's today, it's also 'went,' so that's present pretense. What about the future?" "I am going," Melvin called out. "Right. 'I am going,'" the teacher said. "You've got to learn your participles," he said. "And always use the right pretense."

Below is another kind of directed lesson that, while not directly relevant to standardized academic curricula, was a standard part of instruction at CAA. Whether the purpose was to inspire students or simply kill time, students were subjected to such lectures on an ongoing basis, which explains how Mitch was able to anticipate the points so presciently.

The instructor put three boxes up on the board, numbering them 1–3. "Look, he's gonna talk about jail," Mitch said. The lecture began with: "You basically got three options in your life. This first box is your number one plan. This is the main thing everyone wants to do. For most people of color, it's either one of two things, sports or entertainment. I was just like the rest of you. I played football, and I was *very* serious. You can see how buff I am now, and just imagine how buff I was then." He was wearing a sports jersey with the sleeves cut off, revealing buff arms with veins popping out. "I'd say 90 percent of people don't get this." He wrote "90 percent" above the box with an arrow pointing up. "You know why people don't get to do the thing they really want to do in life? Because they're too *lazy*." The students laughed and hissed. "You'd rather be out smoking pot, gettin' high, and fooling around rather than doin' what you need to do.

"So what do the people do who don't get to do their plan A? If they're smart, they go on to the second box, to their Plan B. So about 90 percent of the people who don't get to Plan A have to move on, they need a backup plan. This is my backup plan. I did what I could do in sports and entertainment, and then I moved on to this. I make almost fifty cents *a minute* teaching you. I get paid the same whether you listen or not." This quieted the students down a bit. "So what's the third box?"

"Jail," Mitch said. The teacher drew bars over the third box.

"See, what'd I tell you," Mitch said with a snicker, dismissing the talk with a wave of his hand.

"You deal drugs, you work the streets, this is where you'll end up, people."

Here the instructor commented on his sense of students' chances, based on his sense of his own chances. Whether his depiction represented realistic structural conditions or not, the repetitiveness of the discourse, the lack of consideration of other options, the lack of guidance, and the repetition of threat reinforced the notion of school as a fearful, alienating place rather than a nurturing one. As Jean Anyon stated, such lectures are also "instantiations of the lived professional culture that degrades students."[16] Since staff were doing little to prepare students for the first two options, once could only assume they were preparing them for the third.[17]

Student Resistance

In a series of recent studies based on extensive classroom observations, Daniel McFarland argues that structural conditions of classrooms, rather than the class or race of students, lead to student resistance.[18] Classrooms with teachers who use fewer directed lessons and fail to connect classroom material to students' experiences tend to have more disruptive episodes, especially if individual students' disruptions are reinforced by cliques. McFarland states, "Serious forms of resistance . . . are change-oriented efforts that galvanize the social order and commence a dramatic series of events."[19]

Such resistance is often infrapolitical.[20] Maryann Dickar, drawing on the work of James C. Scott, notes that "infrapolitical resistance, like infrared rays, is barely visible resistance that quietly seeks to limit the demands of the powerful." Such tactics include "a thousand little tricks," such as lateness, chatting, overstating obstacles, and gold-bricking. Teachers spend endless hours commiserating in faculty lounges about these tactics and trying to address them through rules, but mostly through procedures in the classroom.[21] According to such authors, the lack of a clearly articulated political message in such behavior is what makes it subject to less policing, although, in a point this analysis echoes, it is quite political and coherent.

This section will look at two types of student resistance. The first is skipping class. Such a tactic may not seem to require great skill, but the excerpts below belie that assumption. The second type of student resistance comprises ways of undermining some of the above teaching practices. The key question for school staff faced with such behavior is: How far will they collude? In many cases, staff, apparently as alienated by institutional routines as their students, seemed to facilitate such behaviors and in so doing delegitimized themselves as teachers and the school as an educational institution. As we will see, the creative possibilities of street culture quickly appeared to fill the void.

"Room Steppin'"

In light of the pedagogy of oppression at CAA, absenteeism became a logical alternative to school.[22] On one occasion, nearly *every student* at the school chose to attend a house party at one student's home instead of school. On days when a house party was not scheduled, roughly half of the students attended, but it was a rotating half, rarely consisting of the same students. In interviews with eleven of twelve teachers, most justified their shoddy practices with reference to student absenteeism, failing to recognize that students' perspectives did the reverse.

Although CAA was quite a small campus, staff had considerable difficulty enforcing student attendance.[23] Instead, students often wandered aimlessly from room to room or hung out with the PE class playing basketball outside. When I asked an administrator about practices to keep the school safe, I learned that there was a term for this: "When something's gonna go down, then somebody's gonna get antsy. They're gonna be *room-steppin'*, trying to find out what's going on, who's got what. It's just a matter of being totally aware of your students."

While this administrator used "room stepping" as an indicator of potential ensuing violence, *he did not indicate that it was forbidden,* thus hinting at a powerful source of administrative collusion. Rather, it was up to the security guards to decide that perhaps students shouldn't just hang out on the yard while class was in session, as one explained:

> I met with some of the other security people, told 'em, "Hey, you know what? We gotta do something about these kids being out of class. Our job is to make sure they in class. If they in class, if they sitting in their seat, even if they learn one thing, they learn one thing, but they can't learn that out here." I implemented a rule where, after nutrition, no one's allowed to use the bathroom, first fifteen minutes, because we just had nutrition. That kept a lot of people in class. Passing period, if you wanna use the restroom, that's your time to use the restroom. After that, if the bell rings you in class, nobody uses the bathroom for the first fifteen, twenty minutes. So that kept a lot of people in class. My thing was, keep 'em in class. If we keep the campus clean, there's no time for nobody to get in no fights, no time for people to argue. They have the opportunity to learn, and even though they may not wanna learn, by them being in the class and listening, they're gonna pick up something. So my object was to have this campus clear.

As the guards went about this task, they asked students repeatedly throughout the day, "Are you supposed to be out here?" followed by "What class you supposed to be in?" or better yet, ordering (often yelling), "Get to class!" There was no assurance, however, that the class the student "got to" was the class to which he or she was assigned, as in the following incident, which was not at all uncommon:

> Harold was at the desk where Malik usually sat.
> "Harold, are you in this class?" Mr. Dolan asked.
> "I don't have a class now," Harold said.
> "Yes you do. Get to class," Mr. Dolan said, and went back to helping a student. Mr. Ogburn came in and said, "Come on, Harold, let's go," and escorted Harold out. Harold started screaming a Kurt Cobain song as he left. I followed them outside, where Mr. Ogburn had a brief talk with him, and then Harold went next door to another classroom.

Sometimes, by a parent's request, the school would have a student carry a pass to each teacher, to be signed each day to ensure that they had attended all their classes. Students would get around this by asking teachers to sign multiple slips at once, as one of the office workers explained:

Ms. Smith told me that the student had a history of ditching, so she had to bring this pass around to all her teachers and get it signed. "The other day, she wanted me to fill out two of them," she said laughing.

"Well, that would defeat the whole purpose," I said.

"That's what I told her," she said. "In the past she somehow managed to get one signed without being here."

One young woman exercised considerable skill in order to attend school bodily without attending officially.

A young woman came in wearing a tight, multicolored tube top and a pink CD player with headphones, and Bill, the security guard, let her in the outside gate, then the inside gate. She started walking toward a class, and Bill said, "Wait a minute, did you sign in this morning?" "I don't have to sign in, I'm not really here," she said. "Oh yes you do," Bill said. She kept walking as Bill went up the ramp to the office, and I followed. He called for the vice principal and told him, "I have a young lady out here who says she doesn't wanna sign in." "Oh no," Merritt said, and came out with a head of steam, pounding his feet as he arrived and calling out, "Young lady! You'd better get it together! What are you doin' here? Either you sign in or you leave!" "Pffff," she said, throwing down her arms in angry exasperation. "You better get yo' act together," he called out, going back into the office. She went outside the gates, and when she was back on the sidewalk, she made faces and cursed under her breath as she brought out her CD player again.

This incident, unfathomable to me at the time, was logical in light of the strange attendance practices at the school.

"Why didn't she wanna sign in?" I asked Bill.

"She just wanted to be able to go from class to class and see her friends. Then if a teacher'd ask her if she was in their class, she'd say she wasn't in school today. She thought she could be in school"—Bill put out one hand—"and not be in school"—he put out the other hand. Then he crossed both hands and waved them together to show this was not allowed. "It's just a way for her to cause trouble. She didn't wanna be accountable like any other student."

Further, the student knew that accountability was unlikely to be demanded of her at CAA; she knew she could exploit the school as a setting to merely socialize, something she had been able to accomplish in the past when an ethnographer hadn't been standing by observing the daily rush of events.

On one occasion I decided to quietly follow one student, Joey, to find out how he managed to stay on the yard when it was time to be in class.

I meandered with a group of students making their way to Ms. Camp's room. Some were hanging around outside, sort of dragging their feet, so I did the same. Joey went into the office for something, and I followed him at a distance and then went in there too. At least a half-dozen kids were crowded around the counter. After a few minutes, an office worker shouted at the students, "Get to class!" which cleared them out of the office. Joey stepped outside again, and on his slow way up to his class saw a security guard, Bill, on the other side of the high fence. "Mr. Thomas, can I have some of that cold water?" he asked. Bill nodded, so Joey came over and passed a dollar through the fence. Then Joey had an excuse to wait around. Louis, another security guard, asked what he was doing. "Waiting for Bill," he said. "He's goin' to get me some of that cold water."

As we waited, Joey talked with some young women, and Louis came along behind to shepherd them to class. One of them became upset and started swinging her arms. Louis backed up and puffed up a bit, and she stopped. She treated it as if it were teasing, but Louis looked tense. "Get to class," he ordered.

Bill returned with the water bottle and Joey complained, "Oh, I wanted the bigger one." Bill said the smaller one was the only one they had that was cold. "Why aren't you in class now?" Bill asked. "I was conversating with him," Joey said, pointing to me as his alibi.

In this excerpt, Joey demonstrated a remarkable mastery of tactics for nonattendance. First, he physically resisted by walking slowly toward his classroom. Then, since there was often a commotion in the office after nutrition (probably caused partially by students doing just what Joey was doing), he went to the office to blend in with the crowd. After he was kicked out of the office, he drew upon his personal relationship with a guard and the knowledge that the guard could get him a chilled bottle of water out of the locked refrigerator in a classroom for a dollar.[24] This provided Joey with a justifiable reason for being outside when he was questioned by another guard. Joey tried to prolong his stay by asking Bill for a larger bottle, and when Bill resisted and asked him to account for why he was not in class, I suddenly found myself part of Joey's repertoire of excuses. My interviews, apart from whatever other value they might have had for students, also provided them with reasons for avoiding class.

Student Resistance in the Classroom

As McFarland notes, student resistance can take passive or active forms.[25] Passive resistance at CAA was omnipresent; even students who appeared to be working were often engaging in another activity. With little teacher supervision, even in small classes with classroom aides, students could become lost for hours in pointless tasks:

> Emily was working on a government lesson on English rule over the colonies. She kept whiting out the questions she had copied because she didn't have enough room to write her answers. By the end of the period, her paper was full of whiteout. "You don't need to white that out," I said. "Yes I do," she said, and another five minutes were lost.

Sometimes everyone in class was involved in nonacademic activities, as I observed in the following incident.

> None of the twelve students in the room were working on anything school related. They were crammed as far back as possible away from the teacher's desk, looking through magazines, talking and writing notes, and throwing balls of paper into an ever-rising mountain of trash on the floor. One student, Jorge, noticed a man trying to climb the fence outside the window and opened the window and shouted, "Police!" The man jumped off the fence quickly, which made everyone laugh. Jorge seemed quite proud of himself, smiling, mentioning how funny it had been when that guy jumped down. The teacher in the front of the room continued looking through papers.

As I typed such notes that evening, I wrote, "It's so difficult to kill time in a class—it makes me feel angry and goofy." Students in such a counterfeit classroom, surely feeling emotions akin to my own, engaged here in such common time-killing practices as talking, reading newspapers, and passing notes.[26] They were also alert to capture any opportunity for action, which in this case was a verbal outburst. Such an adaptation to the environment was often facilitated by the school, as we saw in the section on grading above.

Sometimes students chose more active modes of resistance. CAA was often the last chance at an education for students who had dropped out or received disciplinary transfers from other schools, and they could easily jeopardize it by becoming a nuisance or disciplinary problem. Yet such a risk was worthwhile for many students because it was one of their few resources to overcome the mind-dulling environment.

Melvin, a student just barely able to read who was classified as having low intelligence, had worked with me to complete a world history assignment based on answering questions at the end of the chapter. In the following incident he played the trickster, making his teacher look stupid.

> I saw that Melvin had written an answer that contradicted the book. I told him I thought he should erase it, but he said the teacher wouldn't know the difference. "Let's see," Melvin offered. I watched while he handed in the paper.
>
> "Are you sure you know the answers?" Melvin asked the teacher.
>
> "Are you kidding? I've studied world history for years." The teacher marked every answer right, and Melvin turned to me and we grinned at each other.

Lecturing teachers also provided ripe opportunities for action, as the students Billy and Mitch demonstrated.

> "You are the future," the teacher said.
>
> Billy masturbated with his left hand in his pants and tried to contradict the teacher at any chance possible. Repeatedly he imitated someone smoking weed, bringing his pinched fingers up to his mouth and toking, or pantomimed guzzling alcohol. He did this four, five times.
>
> "Yet this is all you want to do with yourselves," the teacher continued, "is go around, gettin' high. Instead, you should be out there building up the world."
>
> "Show us how!" Mitch called out, "instead of talking to us like we're in prison."
>
> "You've got to take the responsibility," the teacher said.
>
> "Shhh," Mitch said, shaking his head.

During this typical lecture, Billy, who appeared stoned to me, colluded with his teacher, in a sense contributing to the lecture by playing its foil. Mitch, on the other hand, refused to play along and demanded a point to the discussion, only to be pounded with the ideology of individual responsibility.[27]

Sometimes students acted on sentiments such as Mitch's, engaging in small-scale civil disobedience against inane classroom environments.

"What are you working on?" I asked Richard.
　"We're on strike," he said, laughing along with two girls.
　"How come?"
　"Because he's such a jerk," he said, referring to his teacher.
　"Is that why hardly anyone's in the class right now?"
　"They all left," he said. "They're sick of him."
　"Really? They just got up and left?"
　"Yeah."

On various occasions, I saw students at CAA "take over" a class. Since all the students were doing busywork while the uninvolved teacher was just sitting at a desk in the back of the room, everyone enjoyed the respite of a student providing a presentation of his or her own. Such a lesson, however, was not likely to have followed the school district's curriculum guidelines:

Tim came up to the front, picked up the chalk, and began his presentation. He asked how much money they would make per week at their jobs, and he wrote down the number provided. One student said $150, then another called out $175. Tim wrote these down without a word. Eventually the number rose to $245. "Okay, $245," Tim said. Then, without another word, he placed a zero on the end of this and put down the chalk, saying, "That's the lesson for the day." Class was over, so he exited, leaving everyone rather stunned.

Tim displayed a number of excellent presentation strategies and a cogent example of street literacy.[28] First, rather than imposing a preconceived ideology on students, distilled through a graphic organizer such as three large boxes, he gently solicited students' input. Unlike many of his teachers' presentations, Tim's had the class's full attention, as we waited to see what he was planning. Was this a math lesson? we wondered. His technique of writing down the numbers without speaking was especially effective in heightening the suspense. Placing a zero after the highest amount was the coup de grâce, implying that drug dealing could bring in ten times more money than a "straight" job. Tim's perceived street identity was enough to make the point remarkably clear and unmistakable for the students watching, whether they were completing worksheets or not. Four years later, Tim paid a visit to the school, looking dapper in the preppy shirt he wore as an area sales representative for a local phone company. Laughing with the principal and vice principal, he had returned to the school to share some of his success.

The Hidden Curriculum at CAA

As anyone who has experience in inner-city schools can testify, the students who need the most assistance receive the least. Many of the characteristics of the Harlem elementary school Gerry Rosenfeld described in 1971 resemble those of CAA; in many respects not much has changed with regard to certain types of inner-city education for at least forty years. A question for future research, then, is not simply to explain such conditions but to understand why they are so enduring.[29] Given such dire circumstances, sensible topics for research are not "Why do inner-city teens resort to violence?" but "How do inner-city teens manage to not resort to violence?"

This chapter has criticized teachers for not doing more to assist students academically. Indeed, teachers and security guards often show complicity in students' tactics to avoid learning, by providing meaningless assignments, showing up late to school (if they attend at all), signing multiple attendance slips at once, or even retrieving "cold water" for a student. As I observed this school over four years and staff became increasingly comfortable with allowing me to see how they (dys)functioned, I began to wonder if I was imposing an exogenous category of adequacy on the school, expecting them to abide by norms that had little relevance in this setting. The chicken/egg questions also applies to teachers: Do they come in as bad teachers, or do the schools turn them into bad teachers?

At the time of the fieldwork, William J. Wilson's and Philippe Bourgois's influential monographs, as well as studies that built on these frameworks, such as Jean Anyon's, linking poor schools to deindustrialization, had recently appeared, yet many local activists were adamant that the problems of the school could not be reduced to a simple lack of jobs.[30] For instance, a major retail outlet had recently opened nearby, the government was offering numerous employment packages with solid benefits, and the local Jobs Training Partnership Act Program (JTPA, since changed to the School-to-Work Opportunities Act) was constantly recruiting hundreds of teens for their rolls. That does not leave us, however, with simply blaming the "culture of the school" or, worse yet, the neighborhood itself for the school's ills. As

Pedro Mateu-Gilbert, Howard Lune, and Rosalie Dow point out, many of the students wanted to learn, and actually many teachers wanted to teach. Even the principal wanted a functional high school. Yet one primary factor worked against such goals.

That factor was fear.[31] On the most obvious level, the notion that the school and the neighborhood were fearful places kept many good teachers away. And many of those who knew the area well enough to see through such myths were attracted because they had heard it was "an easy job." While over half the teachers at CAA lacked teaching credentials, for those competent teachers who did arrive, the run-down facilities and lack of decent supplies could be discouraging: the institutional inertia against well-run classrooms could be too much to overcome, despite the best intentions. When the principal attempted even the most piecemeal efforts at accountability, such as the introduction of goal sheets to require a modicum of lesson planning, she faced staunch resistance from faculty. Knowing well the difficulty of finding replacements, she resigned herself to the staff she had, although she sometimes confided to me, "I don't cherish having anyone on my staff with an attitude about students like that." As Gerry Rosenfeld noted, "The principal seems more concerned with maintaining a stable staff, irrespective of its quality at times, than with effective school-community ties and fashioning relevant learning programs."[32]

Such institutional inertia arose from a deep-seated neglect, in the media and at every level of government, from the White House to the humble taxpayer. As in Sudhir Venkatesh's landmark study of the Robert Taylor Homes, where the Blackstone Saints filled the void in services left by the police and the housing authority, in this alternative school the students, many of whom were gang members, provided meaningful lessons.[33] The principal liked to tell me about how a shooting that had occurred before CAA opened left some government officials wondering if a school in this area was even an appropriate idea. In such a climate of fear, the mere existence of CAA seemed something of a miracle, leaving local officials loath to "rock the boat" lest they lose one of the few resources available in the community. Hence, fear became an excuse for apathy.[34]

Students who chose not to be the dupes of such institutionalized neglect were more than happy to engage with it, achieving failure.[35] Some students were lost in the void of "doing nothing,"[36] but others who employed the teachers to skirt attendance policies, fooled them into accepting incorrect work, or simply took over classrooms on their own terms filled a vacuum, exercising their voices where there was little chance for the expression of possibility or success. Until teachers, principals, and others are willing to take the same sort of risks as students to dealienate education, such resistance may be the best hope that such students can find within the confines of classroom walls to create something meaningful.[37] If one considers CAA in terms of the hidden curriculum, perhaps what was really being taught was the worthwhile pursuit of gangs.[38]

3

The Contradictions of
Controlling Student Dress

Sitting in a discussion with me in a careers class, Billy complained, "Why can't the guys wear braids at school?" "Why is it so important to you?" I asked him. "It's my hair!" he said with indignation. "Yeah, it's your identity!" Mario said.

This book shows how students' resistance in school, as well as their experiences with gangs and fights, arises out of an environment replete with deeply alienating experiences. Others have focused on the alienation experienced in repetitive, low-wage service jobs, at home watching TV, or "doing nothing."[1] While the last chapter looked at how alienation can result from being in counterfeit classrooms where insults to students' intelligence, potential, and dignity are commonplace, this chapter examines how alienation can also spring from the enforcement of arbitrary, inconsistent, and meaningless rules, and explores some of the intricacies and nuances by which students find meaning in dress.

The way one dresses is a highly charged, important decision for human beings everywhere. Dress is literally how we wear the social. It is a tacit invitation to interact with current or potential friends, and a barrier to interact with those who might think, and thus dress, differently. Dress thus marks, stratifies, and facilitates interaction, yet it is usually unremarkable and overlooked.[2]

This was not the case at CAA, where dress and other markers of adornment such as hairstyle and jewelry were ongoing topics of interest and conversation. Part of being powerful means having one's personal stylistic choices unquestioned. Students at CAA, on the other hand, like most high school students in the United States, were reminded of their powerlessness on a daily basis, as they had to subject their clothing choices to the scrutiny of authority figures simply to enter the school.[3] Students did not necessarily mind waiting, or even being frisked with a hand-held metal detector, so much as the frustrating experience of having their clothing choices systematically *misunderstood*.

Dress codes were justified at CAA, and by the Supreme Court, as a school safety measure. *Yet there is no fixed way of dressing like a gang member.* Rather, gang members signal affiliation through seemingly minor and easily overlooked markers: a certain color worn in a certain way, a hat tilted to the left or the right, a certain brand of shoes, the advertisement of a certain product or sports team, the width and color of one's shoelaces, whether clothing is ironed or not, and how it's ironed. Further, dress alone is insufficient to signal gang membership, in at least four ways. First, a wannabe (see chapter 5) could be fully decked out as a gangster and yet not be recognized as such (at least not by actual gang members) no matter how he dresses. In contrast, a reputable OG (original gangster) doesn't need to dress in any specific way to please anybody—reputation makes an outward demonstration of allegiances superfluous. Second, the combination of items of clothing, along with accessories, is important for creating the overall gestalt of a "gang member." A young person may well look like a gang member to an outsider, but if certain key aspects of the ensemble are missing, such as the combination of items of clothing, or of clothing along with a certain haircut or item of jewelry, he or she may well be overlooked by gang members. Third, these characteristic markers are fluid and changing, much too quickly for anyone to regulate. One way of "representing" works in this neighborhood but not the next; one style was vogue last week but not this week. Such changes may even entail ways of subverting changing dress codes, in a potentially infinite, perverse loop between the panoptic gaze of authority and the wily creativity of youth.[4] Fourth, the most important aspect of appearing as a gang member has to do not with the clothes but with *how the clothes are worn.* How one embodies one's clothes, by sagging them, or walking with a certain style, or cocking the head just a little bit, is impervious to legal regulation, easily escaping supervision, and is the fundamental way of marking gang membership, no matter what color, style, or brand one is wearing. This is the primary source of frustration students have with dress codes: *they reflect a deep misunderstanding of how young people create meaning and live it.*

The imposition of "safety" as a reason to control young people's stylistic choices is also perverse, as it imposes a meaning that may be far off the mark from what the young person intended. Even in the so-called most "dangerous" neighborhoods, safety or danger is typically far from the most important signifier of dress. Rather, like most young people, kids at CAA often dressed a certain way in the hope of appearing attractive to the opposite sex. The tricky side of this for many young men is that dressing like a gangster is one powerful way to look attractive. Yet young men were not helpless in this matter, as Frank will teach us below. Even if the police, teachers, and some young women cannot tell the difference between a young man who is dressed like a gangbanger and one who *acts* like one, other gang members can. Also, for kids in the inner city, dress has all the vibrant meanings that dress has for anyone, anywhere else: it is a way to signal interests, to appear fashionable, or simply to look nice, as we will see in the second part of this chapter. Narrowing the meanings of dress to a mere safety issue is an insult to the range of young people's interests, their creativity in expressing those interests, and their sophistication in judging matters of dress for themselves. Let us begin then, with exploring how such a stance toward student dress could possibly be justified, stated in policy, and enforced.

The Dress Code at CAA
Justifications

The dress code and its enforcement were common topics of conversation for staff at CAA. Typically, staff simultaneously damned the morality of contemporary teenagers and nostalgically extolled their own virtuousness as teenagers. For instance, one day in January I was hanging around with a security guard at CAA, Mr. McClain, as he talked with Isa, a caregiver from the day care center, and Diane, a roving aide. Mr. McClain, a large, tall man with the body of a football linebacker, Diane, wearing a black blouse and slacks, and I, in a long-sleeved collared gray cotton shirt and blue jeans, were on one side of the inner fence in front of the office, and Isa, who wore the blue blouse with jeans under a full apron characteristic of day care workers, was on the other side. All the staff members were African American, and Isa and Diane were about a generation older than McClain, in their forties, while he was in his mid-twenties. I am white and was in my thirties.

As Isa was passing from the parking lot to the day care center, she commented that it was a shame that so many of "these girls have babies," an ironic statement since her job was to serve just such children. Her comment was pitched indiscriminately to Diane as she was emerging from the office, to McClain, and to me.

McClain said, "It's no wonder." In hushed tones, and with his hand shielding his mouth, he added, "Do you see the kinds of clothes they wear up here in the summer?"

"Oh, I know!" Isa rejoined, her eyes wide with disbelief.

Diane nodded in affirmation.

"I can't stand the clothes these girls wear nowadays, with their titties hanging out and all that," Isa declared. "Back in our day, a boy'd get a whippin' if his butt was hanging out like a lot of these boys have it. Yesterday—" (she looked at me, pointing her finger), "I saw a boy with his pants right here!" (motioning just above the knee). "How can he walk?!"

"It's like wearing a skirt," I responded.

"You just couldn't do that in my day!" Isa went on.

"Mm hmm!" McClain chimed in, his voice and eyebrows rising.

"You'd get a swat!" Isa said.

"With holes in the paddle!" said Diane.

"It all went downhill when they made that illegal," Isa continued. "Now, anything goes, because they can get away with it."

"Freaky deaky," added McClain. "They got them studs in they tongues and all that too!"

Isa slapped her hand in the air dismissively, as if shooing an insect. "They just don't listen anymore, but you bet they do to me!" With a stern, unflinching look in her eyes, she added, "These other teachers will be calling a student, and they don't pay any attention. If I call you, you better not *not* come! They know that!"

We nodded our heads and chuckled as Isa made her way to the child care center and Diane headed toward the classrooms.

This scene is quite telling, for the conversation's topics moved from childbearing, to dress, to punishment, to authority, all seamlessly linked. Isa began with the moral observation that it was a shame so many of "these girls" had babies, thereby bringing all of us together even as we stood on opposite sides of a chain-linked fence that rose over our heads. McClain attributed the pregnancies to the seductive clothing worn by the girls, and Isa invoked the lack of discipline "nowadays," signified by the low way boys wore their pants, which she mocked (long shirts cover their boxers). She further linked such dress to the demise of corporal punishment, a common theme expressed by many staff, including the principal. After the mention of tongue studs, she concluded her discourse with the observation that "they just don't listen anymore . . . they don't pay any attention," and she affirmed her power over students, leaving her techniques for doing so mysterious yet irreproachable.

Isa's performance demonstrated her moral authority and brought together the staff members (whose paths do not cross every day) in a common accord. For instance, although McClain had not been present "in Isa's day," he affirmed, with rising intonation and eyebrows, that students could not dress in such a manner at that time. Diane and I both found ourselves practically finishing Isa's sentences as Diane added, "With holes in the paddle," and I said, "It's like wearing a skirt." The final word in this rapid, highly participatory, animated, passing conversation was an assertion of hierarchical control: students must obey their elders. It follows that if they did (compelled by corporal punishment), they would dress more conservatively, which would lead to fewer teen mothers.

In interpreting teenagers' actions, staff members tended to conflate issues in this manner, while for teenagers, as we will see below, dress had a highly distinct significance as a matter of personal liberty, self-expression, and identity. Especially revealing in the conversation is how clearly a student's dress was linked to an adult's power. Like dependent automatons, children should come when they're called and, by implication, dress as they're told to dress. As in the legal and policy-oriented decisions cited above, pedagogical concerns were apparently beside the point.

Policies

At CAA, students were first introduced to the dress code at orientation, where an office administrator went over the rules for the school, consisting primarily of prohibitions of what could be perceived as markers of gang affiliation: no colored shoestrings, no sagging pants, no hats or earrings, no sports logos on shirts, no BK (British Knights) or CK (Calvin Klein) tennis shoes, no sunglasses, and no belts with letters or colors.[5] Later, the code was expanded to exclude beepers and CD players, and students were called to wear black and white on Tuesdays and Thursdays. During student orientation, the facilitator went down the list, adding, "And no green because, as you know, that is Central's [the main local gang's] colors." In response, some of the African American young men said, "Shhh," or "Ha," smiling with irony.

Students often treated signs and announcements concerning the dress code dismissively. Sometimes the principal made such announcements through the PA system, one of which I heard while I was sitting in Ms. River's class. "No boys are to be allowed to come to school with braids," the principal stated. I asked Maria why not, and she responded, "They think it's gang affiliated," rolling her eyes and smirking. At other times, individual teachers announced the dress code to their class, as when Ms. Rivers announced that Tuesdays and Thursdays were black and white days. "Everyone has to wear black and white, or else you won't be allowed in," she said. "And no CDs or Walkmen are allowed on campus." "Why not?" a young man in the front asked. "I'm just reading what it says here," she responded.

Enforcement

The enforcement of the dress code was never just about dress. Rather, teachers and administrators used the dress code as a resource for accomplishing something else, such as control of an unruly student, intimidation, or humor. Often, it was unclear just what an authority figure was up to, since whatever the student was wearing had been fine up to the point when it was singled out. Fundamentally, the dress code provided a means of enforcing authority. It was a resource for teachers and administrators to give students the message that they had no privacy, that their choices were not their own, and that it was up to the whims of those in power to condemn such private decisions or allow them to pass. Also, as we will see below, enforcement was accomplished in personal tones and threats: "*I'm* going to take it"; "*You're* not going to get it back." The message students heard was a bullying one: "I'm bigger than you and more powerful than you, and this means I can take things from you." In short, dress codes provided a sanction for tyranny, which at best led to student alienation.

In class, I never noticed a teacher chastise a student for a dress code violation if that student was working calmly and quietly. However, if a student was rebellious or obstinate, then issues of dress came to the fore. Suddenly, the student was made accountable, often quite dramatically, by a teacher's threat. On my first day of observations at the school, Mr. Merritt chastised one young man I was tutoring, Chris, just as I arrived. Chris was sitting at the back table of the class with friends, chatting and laughing. I suspected that this had been fine until I arrived and that Mr. Merritt used Chris's earring as a pretext for intimidating him into settling down and working with me. "Get that earring out of your ear or I'm going to take it out and you won't be getting it back!" Mr. Merritt said, referring to a small diamond stud earring in Chris's left ear. "I've told you before!" Reluctantly, wincing with annoyance, Chris removed the earring, making my entrée into the school that much more difficult.

Later, when Mr. Merritt was promoted to vice principal, such personal attacks characterized many of his interactions with students. For instance, in mid-May 1997, on my twenty-fifth day of observations, I was sitting on a bench, leaning back against a fence adjacent to the child care play yard and eating a doughnut, when Mr. Merritt walked across the yard during nutrition and called out to David, "I'm thinkin' about gettin' me some earrings!" David stopped during his basketball game without making a big fuss, removed them, and put them in his pocket. Later, Mr. Merritt chastised another player in the game, Philip, for his closely braided hair.

"I couldn't find my comb this morning," Philip said. "You gonna have a lot more time to look for that comb if you keep coming like that," Merritt told him, looking straight in his eyes. Philip's shoulders drooped; a bit put down, he took Merritt seriously.

In both of these instances, Merritt interrupted a basketball game, singling out players who might have been stopped on their way into the school, and singled out these specific young men, when many others sported earrings, braids, or both. In each case he seemed to derive a certain satisfaction out of imposing his will to arrest their collaborative activity, accenting the intervention with his personal brand of humor. As students stopped what they were doing and put the earring away, or begged to be allowed to remain in school, Merritt seemed to walk a little taller, for once the master of a yard usually full of students cutting class or wandering from room to room.

"Exceptions"

Every day at CAA, students could be easily found who violated some feature of the dress code but were allowed to pass. Traditionally, dress codes have been designed to ensure modesty, but as safety concerns trumped modesty, more and more immodest students were allowed to pass, though not without some negotiation first. Watching such interactions was akin to watching the kids' card game War, where cards are thrown randomly and the higher card wins. Through a bit of negotiation, the young women in the incidents described below were allowed to pass despite wearing skimpy outfits in the sunny springtime weather.

Two pregnant Latinas arrived in short, tight summer dresses that were tied in the back. Mr. Merritt looked at them, sighed and slapped down his hands. "Do you know what day today is?"

They looked at him and shook their heads innocently.

"How do we usually dress on Tuesday?" he demanded.

"I wasn't even going to come here today. I was going to go to college," Maria said.

"So why didn't you go?"

"I got up too late, so I decided to come here."

"You know we have a dress code here."

"I know," she said. "It's just I was already dressed, and I didn't want to change."

"All right, get to class. But don't forget next time!" They left.

Mr. Merritt pointed out the color of the dresses, not their size, as a violation of the code, highlighting safety rather than modesty as his concern. Instead of answering Merritt's loaded question, "How do we usually dress on Tuesday?" Maria countered that she had dressed for a more worldly and respectable venue than CAA, thereby temporarily derailing Merritt's questions. Rather than sending students home from a school where attendance was already abysmal, he let them through with the bold directive "Get to class" and a veiled threat, "Don't forget next time," masking his failure to enforce the code.

Another negotiated exception occurred when the office secretaries intervened on behalf of Tammy, who had been sent by a teacher for the skimpiness of her dress. She was wearing a short violet one-piece outfit that consisted of a low cut, cleavage-revealing top and extremely short shorts. Her saving grace was a white zip-up sweat jacket over the dress. But apparently this didn't mollify Merritt, for she came out of his private office asking to sign out. This attracted the attention of all the office staff.

"That's not too much," Sally said.

"Just zip up your jacket," Ms. Smith said.

"He can't just send you home for that," Jennifer said.

"Last year, we had a girl here in a *bikini*!" Ms. Smith said. "Now that was too much. But this? This isn't that bad at all."

Tammy zipped up her jacket. "How's that?"

"That's just fine, dear," Ms. Smith said, and the others nodded in agreement.

"Now you just go back to class and we'll take care of this," Sally said.

Uncertainty about Dress Codes

Since styles that supposedly reveal gang affiliations constantly change, so do the rules. One rule that did not exist in 1997 but did exist in 2001 concerned braided hair (or cornrows). Young African American women were allowed to have as many braids as they wished, but the young men were limited to two braids. At times I thought a young man was wearing braids, but he corrected me, telling me, "These are twisties"—hair twisted into rows rather than braided into them. Since rules changed so often and were frequently overlooked, many students shared my uncertainty about the rules. As Doogan asked me, "What's the thing about wearing braids here? Is there a rule against that?" "Let me see, how many braids do you have?" I asked, looking at his head. "Just two? That should be fine." "Not what they told me," he said. "They told me I couldn't have any braids." Then he sighed, shaking his head, and shrugged. "Do you know why they told me that?" "I have no idea," I said.

Yet I wasn't the only semiprofessional at the school who was confused by changing dress codes. One substitute teacher, a petite Anglo woman who played in a rock band at night, told me with pride about how she had come to know some of the kids, like Vester, an especially dark African American young man with cornrows who was playing basketball outside as we chatted. She said he had been pretty distant with her until she told his girlfriend that she had a good-looking boyfriend, and then he was nicer. She said she had complimented him on his hair that day, not knowing that school staff had threatened to throw him out because it looked too much like a gang style.

Code Enforcement and Student Resistance

When students were not docile and did not quietly abide by dress code policies—in effect, when they stood up for themselves in their effort to forge an identity—issues of power and authority between staff and students came to the fore:

As we were getting ready to board the bus for a field trip, Mr. Thurman, a teacher and occasional administrator, told a group of African American young men, some with beanies or caps, to take their hats off. They simply looked at him. "I mean it," he said.

"Why do we have to take our hats off?" one of the young men asked, his head tilted sideways and eyebrows raised. Thurman told him that that was what you had to do to stay out of trouble. One student took a hat off, then put it on again. The rest didn't take theirs off, and they left them on in the bus as well. Thurman ignored them.[6]

What are a teacher's choices in such a situation? Basically, only two. One is to escalate the situation to compel conformity. Making such a demand transforms a pedagogical experience (here, a field trip) into a minor battle in an endless war, consuming a great deal of a teacher's time and energy. The other choice is to "let it ride." Like the first alternative, this one comes with great risks: the teacher has effectively lost face and weakened his authority. If he cannot compel a student to remove a hat, how can he expect a student to respect him?

Facing such options, how did the administrators respond? As soon as the students were on the bus, Mr. Thurman and Ms. Reynolds, the principal of the school, briefly discussed this matter. Then Ms. Reynolds boarded the bus and announced, "I'm very disappointed we found a lot of cell phones and CD players." She added that she was also disappointed in their hats, their hairstyles, and their language. Then she said, "Starting Monday, we are going to start enforcing all the school rules. So make sure you comply with them on Monday." The following week, signs were posted on 8 1/2 x 11 paper, announcing that students must wear black and white on Tuesdays and Thursdays and that pagers, cell phones, CD players, and braids (for young men) would not be allowed. Hence, rather than continuing to confront the students wearing hats (who were all described to me by two teachers as being gang members from Central) and perhaps preventing them from attending the field trip, Ms. Reynolds opted for a temporary retreat to muster her forces for a full attack on Monday. This heightened focus on control accentuated teachers' power struggles and contributed to alienating students from the school. The cases below followed the principal's statement.

> On a spring day in 2001, Danny, a stocky African American young man, arrived at the office, waiting to be searched so he could enter. He wore overalls drooping to his knees and held up by blue shoulder straps, as well as a shirt with "5 Fubu" written prominently across the front that was white at the top and faded to blue lower down.
>
> Mr. Merritt saw him and demanded, "What do you think you're wearing up here?"
>
> "This is black and white."
>
> "No sir, that is not black and white."
>
> "Well just give me a blue pass then" (to go home).
>
> "I will not. You tuck in those straps."
>
> "I can't tuck in the straps. It doesn't go that way."
>
> "You're going to tuck in those straps or go home."
>
> "I'll go home then, because it just doesn't look right with the straps tucked in."
>
> "Suit yourself, there's the door."
>
> "Where's my blue slip?"
>
> "I'm not giving you no blue slip."
>
> Danny left.

Danny's first interaction at school on this day was marked, not by "Hello" or "Welcome to school," but by the vice principal's demand to account for an implied infraction.[7] Danny picked up on this implication, but his explanation was troublesome, for as Merritt pointed out, anyone who saw Danny and could recognize the color "blue" could see that he was not wearing solely black and white. Danny's response invited a dismissal for the day, leading one to think that perhaps he had intentionally worn these clothes so that he could receive an excused absence from school, which he could then show to the police. Merritt refused to grant the pass but tacitly compromised with Danny, asking him only to tuck in his blue shoulder straps. Danny refused to make this accommodation since "it doesn't look right," so Merritt invited him to leave the school, and Danny accepted. Perhaps Danny came to school intentionally wearing the wrong clothes to receive the blue slip; if so, the dress code merely provided a way for him to attempt to manipulate school authority. If not, and Danny was simply upholding his pride in his fashion sense (which seemed to me the case at the time), then the imposition of the dress code resulted in a complete loss for the day. Whatever opportunities Danny might have had to learn or socialize, and the school's opportunity to be paid for his attendance, were forfeited because he wore blue.

Such discipline could transform a hard-working, intelligent student into one who was angry and rebellious. One African American young man at CAA was remarkable for his dignity and composure as much as for his isolation. A former model for major fashion designers, Jerome had been kicked out of his house in a suburban area by abusive parents. He found an apartment with roommates and paid for rent and bills as a minor while still in high school until this became too burdensome. He then came to the inner city to live with his grandparents for a couple months to earn his diploma. On one morning, I sat in the waiting room as he entered with another student and was challenged by a school secretary, Sally:

"How come you didn't wear black and white today?"

"This is black and white," Jerome said.

Sally pointed to his conservative long-sleeved shirt with a button-down collar, with thin plaid strips of white, black, and blue.

"They told me that was okay!" he protested.

"Well, it isn't. Here, you'll have to sign this, which is what everyone who doesn't wear black and white has to sign."

"Man," he said, squinting his eyes in deep disgust, as he signed.

"And that attitude is unnecessary. There's no call to talk back to me in that way!" she said forcefully, and he glared at her hard. "You should see Ms. Reynolds [the principal]," she said.

Jerome, like Danny, was not greeted with "Good morning" or "Welcome" but instead was called to account for his violation of the dress code. Like Danny, he responded, "This is black and white," yet he was on firmer footing than Danny, since his shirt contained only thin stripes of blue and had passed muster on previous occasions, as he proclaimed in an astonished, outraged tone. Sally, however, overrode his protest and had him place his infraction on record. When Jerome responded with "Man" and Sally rebuked him for "talking back," the tension of the power struggle for the institutionally appropriate definition of Jerome's clothes was palpable, and Sally escalated the confrontation by sending him to see the principal. Thus, in the challenge to students' face that is sometimes required in enforcing dress codes, the fundamental impetus for dress codes is laid bare: *not student safety but adult authority.*[8]

I stood at the doorway to Ms. Reynolds's office as she spoke to Jerome. "Why didn't you wear black and white?" she asked him. He stood up tall, in a quite imposing manner and simply made a slight shrug. "Let me see what you're wearing. Oh, that's not too bad," she said, her eyes wide and somewhat surprised. "Just next time, try not to have any blue in it." He nodded his head ever so slightly, obviously annoyed. "Now get to class, and be sure to wear black and white on Thursday." He left, expressionless, a slight "pshaw" of air escaping his mouth.

Directly afterwards, I asked Jerome if he'd like to do an interview and he was happy to participate. After about forty minutes he complained about how CAA wasted his time:

This morning, I haven't been sleeping much at all, but she just kind of made me really mad. I never snapped at her at all, but she kind of pissed me off today. . . . What teachers don't understand is that I don't care. They can put me in trouble, they can suspend me. I don't really care. To sit there and throw a fit would be something a little kid would do. You wanna suspend me? I'll just go to work. I'll just spend some time in gathering my thoughts. I don't care what you do. You can sit me into a room, I don't care. Just give me some work to do. Don't waste my time like that. . . . I don't like when they talk to me like a little kid, like a little teenager. You don't talk to me like I'm just another ordinary teenager, 'cause I know that I'm not.

In this statement, Jerome spoke of how he perceived the enforcement of the dress code not as a matter of safety but as a matter of power. Dismissing the entire interaction as "a waste of time," he described the enforcement of the dress code as belittling: staff were addressing him "like a little kid, like a little teenager." What came across most clearly was how this needless confrontation alienated Jerome; he repeated *four times*, "I don't care." In effect, his statements indicated his awareness that for the staff what he wore was more important than who he was.[9]

Students' Dress and Identity

What meanings did dress have for students? Many commentators complain of intense jealousy among young people who use clothes to make a class-based fashion statement, occasionally shooting each other for a pair of sneakers.[10] Despite the drama of such rare occurrences, I often noticed young men, usually African American, praising each other's choice of clothes or describing where they had purchased their clothes and how much they cost. This affiliative, affirmative stance around clothes is exemplified in a gesture enacted in a number of African American films and featured in songs by MC Hammer, Usher, and Ghostface Killah: to "pop your collar." I asked Bill, one of the security officers, to explain it to me after I'd seen many young men doing it to each other and to me. "Oh, well," he smiled, trying to find the words. "It means you're sharp, you got it together." Despite such a respect for fashion, I did not notice the converse—students putting each other down for dressing down. In fact, I often noticed students at school simply wearing sweat pants and a sweater without any apparent negative consequences.

However, as for all of us, the meanings of dress for young people in the inner city do not simply revolve around fashion statements but also indicate affiliations. Below, I examine how dress is an important marker of place and serves as a resource for using skills to skirt dangers and flexibly mold identity. I then explore a number of illustrative cases in which young men spoke of "leaving gangs," not in terms of changing their clothing style, but in terms of changing how they *wore* their clothes. Schools are not "cracking down on gangs" through dress codes that inhibit "gang styles." Gang membership may or may not be superficially signaled by clothes; it is just as well signaled in ways that schools have no authority over, such as a student's tattoos and ways of walking and talking. A more significant question is, So what if a student is in a gang? Should young people be judged by their social ties or their actions?

Dress, Place, and Identity

In describing the need for a gang intervention program in Cleveland, Michael Walker and Linda Schmidt note how students would carry their clothes in bags so that they could change into the proper colors as they crossed gang boundaries.[11] Shawn faced a similar problem as he rode the bus from his half-sister's house, where the abiding color was red, to CAA, where it was green. One afternoon, after I bought him lunch, we sat in my car in front of his sister's house, where the brick wall in her backyard had been covered with red tags after Shawn moved in, a gesture that he understood as a bit of a threat. "I guess they want to see if I'll cover it up. I don't touch it," he said. He said he had to watch what he put on in the morning because he couldn't wear Crip colors by his home but couldn't wear Blood colors at CAA. As he talked, I considered that his choice of shirts was telling: a long-sleeved collared shirt with thin blue, red, and green stripes over black pants secured with a jamaica-colored knit belt. I asked him if he could wear blue jeans around his neighborhood. He told me that he had many pairs of nice blue jeans but that he couldn't wear them on his way to school, so he usually wore black pants. I asked if Bloods wore blue jeans. He said they did, but that it didn't matter too much if you were already a Blood.

Hence, a known "Blood" may well dress like something else, secure that his reputation will outweigh his stylistic choices. He would probably be overlooked by a police officer trying to identify "Bloods" by their colors. That officer might instead erroneously pick up somebody like Shawn, who is simply trying to blend in and make his way safely to school.

The Nuances of Dressing "Cool"

One of my most insightful informants on matters of dress was Frank, who described how he adopted some gang styles because they were cool but modulated them so that they would not be recognized by gangsters as gang affiliated.[12] About thirty minutes into our interview we had the following exchange:

"You said that they were gonna jump this guy or they were giving him a hard time 'cause he looked like a gangster, he was dressing that way."

"Yeah," Frank said.

"Do you, in the clothes that you wear, do you try not to look like a gangster?"

"Yeah, mm hmm. Even though I dress baggy, but I don't really like to wear baggy-ass clothes. Some baggies I'm definitely against. Me, just this baggy, but not like a gangster. I just dress like normal. Not normal, but, you know, baggy, but not looking like a gangster, just like that. There's some guys that dress baggy but looking like gangsters, you know, with the creases up and buttoned shirts and everything."

"Creases in the T-shirts," I said.

"Yeah, and then in the pants, and that's what makes them look like gangsters, and bald headed, you know? And that's what helps me a lot, that I'm not bald headed. But if they see a bald-headed guy with baggy clothes, they gonna think he's a gangster. But that's why they'll cruise the bald-headed guys with clothes baggy and white shirts . . . "

"Uh huh. So you can wear your clothes baggy but not too baggy."

"Baggy, but yeah, not too baggy, you know. And you gotta be careful about how you dress baggy. Like there's some baggy with Nikes, creases, and white shirt, they'll think that's a gangster right there. But if you wear your, some Filas or baggy with no creases, you know, just iron them without no creases and a white shirt, it would be like, no, he ain't no gangster."

For Frank, a folk sociologist of dress, no one item or color determined gang affiliation but rather a whole gestalt gleaned from all elements fitting together.[13] Working the ambiguities between "normal" and "gangster," he was grateful for his curly hair, which he was certain not to cut too short, and he was careful to iron but not crease his T-shirts.[14] Hence, as he told me elsewhere in the interview, by appearing somewhat like a gangster he could appear cool and attractive to girls but avoid being mistaken as a gangster by those who could read the ambiguities.[15] Unfortunately, the police and teachers are rarely among those who can decipher such fine distinctions.[16]

In our follow-up interview four years later, we sat in his car in front of the school at 9:00 a.m. after his all-night security shift. With his baby cooing in the back seat, Frank told me how he had subsequently increased his sense of safety by allowing his hair to grow into a long ponytail down his back. Unfortunately, he had later been forced to cut this in order to get, ironically enough, a security job. This was a difficult change for him, as he explained to me:

"I'm still missing my hair, man. To be honest, I used to love my hair. To me it's like they changed my image. That was me, with the long hair. The way I dressed kind of went with the hair, you know? Now when you cut your hair, you gotta look for a way that goes with you. It doesn't really look right when you had long hair and then you just throw it out."

"So how did you dress before?"

"I used to dress more New Yorker style."

"What is that?"

"More baggy probably. Something that will really look good with the hair. But like when you bald, you gotta look for some clothes, because if you dress too baggy and your head looks bald, they think gang. And that's what I think about it."

"So your clothes aren't as baggy anymore?"

"Not anymore. They're smaller. Once in a while, like some baggy pants, but I don't really like to wear them, because my head looks clean. You get gangsters looking at you."

"So now that you're balder, you have to wear tighter clothes."

"Yeah. Don't even try to provoke the gangsters."

"Just by being baggy and bald. That's funny that that would provoke them."

"Yeah, I know. It's crazy."

Of course, school dress codes have no inkling of such nuances. The code at CAA specified "no baggy clothes," although it did not specify creases, and it could not specify all the possible combinations of "baggies with Nikes," "baggie with Nikes and bald," or "Ben Davis baggies." In all my time at CAA I never noticed that bagginess was made an issue, although it was forbidden according to the dress code. During my first immersion, staff focused on young men's earrings; during my second, braids were prohibited for African American young men, and students were required to wear black and white on Tuesdays and Thursdays. Uniforms could be seen as one way of avoiding this problem altogether, yet as my consultants explained, even the most conservative dress can be seen as gang related, depending on how it is worn.

Further, for those who do not comport themselves like gang members, gangs have little relevance. For instance, Antoine, an eighteen-year-old African American, told how his embodiment showed those who were in gangs that gangs were not relevant for him: "They come up to me, be like, 'You know, you should be from so and so.' I be like, 'Man, you know that's not me, man.' I don't even act or talk or look like a gangbanger really, you know. So that's not me, 'cause I wasn't raised like that." Or as Ben stated when I asked him to explain why he thought no one would ever try to recruit him into a gang, "Look at me. I don't really look like a gangbanger." Ben's round shape and friendly demeanor simply precluded gangs from approaching him. Hence, dress alone is insufficient to specify gang involvement. As Norma Mendoza-Denton states, "In order to be 'mistaken' for a gang member by other members, [one] would have to follow highly stylized rules of speech, hair, makeup [for girls], style of clothing, and even have a certain gait, in which case there wouldn't be much of a 'mistake.'"[17] Moreover, young people working within the context of a staging area, like a school, will find ways to index markers of affiliation or disaffiliation, whether or not these are dress related.[18]

Yet young people are often unsure about just what the markers of gang membership are. Below is another of Tim's teachable moments in a class in which little else was happening:

Tim showed how the way you wear your hat gives away your gang affiliation. He put his hat with the bill on the left and said that was one gang (he mentioned the name), he put it with the bill on the right and said that was another gang. "What if you have it in the back?" someone asked. "Front or back means you a square," Tim said with a smile. "What was it again?" someone asked. Tim went through it quickly, putting his bill to the left, saying "Crips" (for instance), to the right, "Bloods," and then front and back, "square."

On this particular day, students had the opportunity to "school" each other on gang matters. Such "schooling" was a quick and ready substitute for a teacher's lack of lesson plans, and in response the teacher "did being elsewhere" in a virtuoso performance of civil inattention as he probed his attendance sheets.[19] At another time, Joey, an African American, warned Bix, a Latino, that his wide blue shoelaces could lead to trouble, and Bix nodded in appreciation.

Dress and Embodiment

Aside from consulting a sensitive folk sociologist like Frank, I spoke with interviewees who were especially perceptive about issues concerning dress because they were leaving gangs and thus consciously working on remolding their identity. Most books on gangs have a section on leaving the gang, describing how members "mature out" of a gang or may be "courted out" in a hazing ritual.[20] A less common focus of such studies is the work that gang members must do on themselves to become conscious of prereflective ways of presenting the self in order to change those ways and appear non–gang affiliated. A number of my consultants were quite articulate in describing such processes. Like Agnes, Harold Garfinkel's famous transgendered interviewee who discussed her work to "do female," these young men were able to discuss their conscious efforts to mold their identity, "doing non-gang."[21]

Both Earl and Johnnie were eighteen, of stocky build and medium height. Earl was an African American interviewed in 1997, and Johnnie was a Samoan interviewed in 2001. Note how both young men spoke about the difficulty of leaving gangs, not in terms of the potentially explosive consequences of severing gang ties, but in terms of changing the way they embodied their clothes. In our interview below, Earl wore a red shirt with a black collar and a short zipper cinching the top, black pants, and leather loafers.

"You can't really say you from the hood no more," Earl said. "Once you give it up, that's it."

"Was that hard?"

"Yeah, at first, but that was one o' the small minor things. It wadn't too hard for me to give up bangin'. It was hard for me to give up the way I dress! That took me almost a whole year to change the way I dress."

"'Cause you had to buy new clothes?"

"Nah. Because I had to choose the way I wore my clothes, you know. New clothes automatically come, it's just the way you wear 'em, you know. 'Cause see, I could have on a T-shirt right now, like you wearin' a T-shirt, and I could wear the T-shirt the way you wear it, but it's the *way* that I wear that T-shirt. It's the way I act when I wear that T-shirt. 'Cause I could wear a T-shirt and some jeans, like you wearin', and I could have my jeans pulled all the way down below my butt, you know. And be wearin', what kinda shoes you wearin'?"

"Just boots."

"Some boots like that. And wearin', and saggin' it, and be lookin' like a gang member. I have to wear it the way you wearin' it right now, with my pants pulled up, shirt nice, you know, pressed."

"I don't have it tucked in or anything," I said, laughing.

"Well it's not tucked in, but still, you know, pants pulled up, and it's the way you present yourself. It took me a while to learn that."

As Earl stated, it was not his dress but how he wore his dress that he had to learn to change as a non-gang member. He artfully described how the clothes I wore, or the clothes of the plant manager, with a few alterations, could appear to be gang affiliated, *depending on how one would wear them.* While "the clothes came automatically," Earl took over a year to learn how to *wear* the clothes, and even then found to his surprise that others still pointed out that at times he looked like a gang member. Earl was sensitive enough to know that while clothes may be readily changed, embodied habitus is more intractable and must be repeatedly, reflexively brought to conscious attention.[22] Can schools regulate the way students wear their clothes? Is it in schools' interest to do so?

Johnnie provided insights similar to Earl's during our three-hour interview in 2001. An Asian Pacific Islander from a family of ten, he wore a red T-shirt sporting a surfing logo, baggy jeans, tan work boots, and a centimeter-wide gold chain around his neck. Below, he shared his insights into how the way a person carries him- or herself might be read on the streets.

"Only problem I really had was the area it was in. It was around Bloods. I wasn't no Crip or anything, it's just I didn't like 'em. Not that I don't like 'em, but I was sure they wadn't gonna like me, how I carry myself. So one day—"

"Tell me about that, the way you carry yourself. What was it about the way that you carried yourself?"

"A lot is based on how a person walks, how he talks, and if he has long hair, the way he wears his long hair, the colors he wears, you know."

"Do you dress differently or walk differently than a Blood walks?"

"I walk as somebody who would be affiliated with, you know what I'm sayin', a gang or some'in."

"Oh, okay."

"Motherfuckers got walks. Walk nerdy" (he demonstrated). "Nigga walk like this." He took long, lunging strides, swaying his shoulders back and forth with the arms swinging wide, making large claims on space, in dramatic contrast to his prior "nerdy walk." "Hell no. You know what I'm sayin', them niggas, they mob like, you just bangin' or some'in, and you got that hard-core walk, 'Like, wait up, homie, where you from?'"

"Right."

"I wadn't trippin' off that. That was never no big issue to me, but it was an issue concerning my safety. I didn't wanna get smoked. I didn't wanna get shot."

Johnnie did have to change what he wore, but more significant than that for signaling his affiliations, and for ensuring his safety, was changing how he embodied his clothes.[23] The key to his discourse was not his words but his embodied demonstration of "mobbing." By its very presence, it *invites* the gang performative demand, "Like, wait up, homie, where you from" (discussed in chapter 4).[24] "Mobbing," typically done in a large group, is the signifier of gang affiliation par excellence, yet no school codes outlaw this type of behavior. Large, lunging strides, dominating public space in an age-old manner described by Jack Katz in his discussion of "parading," are the sine qua non of gang identification.[25] As John L. Jackson notes, "Ordinary people anchor their notions of identity to behavioral arguments that place the onus for that difference not just on the surface of the body but in bodies' motions."[26]

Teachers do recognize such embodied practices when they see them, and sometimes they try to correct them. Below, Ms. Reynolds corrected Johnnie's posture as he read a passage about Harriet Tubman for African American History Month.

Johnnie stood at the podium, reading about Harriet Tubman to a packed double classroom of about seventy people. After he finished, Ms. Reynolds walked up to him, explaining that this was a "teachable moment." She told him to stand up straight and not lean on his forearms. "Do you want me to read the whole thing again?" he asked. "No, just the last line," she said. He read it again, as if forcing himself to stand up straight, and a couple kids smiled and shouted, "Whoop" when he finished.

Earl and Johnnie had to learn such a demeanor to avoid the sorts of hassles that accompany appearing like a gang member.

What Dress Means to Young People

An earring, cornrows, baggy pants, T-shirts, T-shirts with creases, T-shirts with creases and Nikes, tattoos, mobbing: adults rarely have a clue about what these styles signify. They only know their own gut-level fear as they encounter a teen who appears somehow defiant with his hair in braids or a diamond stud in his ear. To overcome that fear, school staff attempt to express authority, but in so doing they encourage rather than defuse rebellion.

Some might argue that rules should be further elaborated and more consistently applied. Yet such a reaction would lead to an infinite regress.[27]

Even if each and every possible detail of student dress could be specified and enforced, it would not begin to address the ways in which students do gangs. For gang affiliations are marked not merely through dress but through the body.[28] By enforcing dress codes, school officials are trying to outlaw an embodied way of being, seizing on features of dress in a desperate effort to find something concrete to regulate. Such regulation only alienates students, leading them to strengthen their counterschool "oppositional cultures."[29] Once school staff members focus more on developing a meaningful pedagogy than on merely controlling students, concern for enforcing dress codes will become as meaningless for them as it is for those under their tutelage.[30] All that "safety-related" dress codes ultimately accomplish is to pay homage to the power and influence of the local gang.

Yet the fundamental issue is not what adults make of dress but what dress means to young people. Dress can be witty, ironic, mocking, sarcastic, bold, lackadaisical, or refined. Yet these meanings are not self-evident—rarely are they simply stamped on a T-shirt, and even then they are subject to misinterpretation. When one hears a young person such as Frank, Earl, or Johnnie talk about the deep meaning of his clothes and how he wears them, one cannot help but be stunned at how such discourses are simply not heard in discussions of dress codes. Somehow, public discourses concerning "safety" disregard the meanings of those whose safety is to be secured.

The point of this chapter has been to appreciate the work of young people to skirt the boundaries of school control and local gang appearances while embodying the identity they choose, or are searching for. Where the resources or contacts to mountain climb, skydive, or ride fast motorcycles tend to be lacking, it is hard not to admire how simply walking down the street may be recognizable as a form of action. The following chapters will focus further on how gangs provide resources for working the possibilities of identity in inner-city communities.

II

Performing Gang Identity on the Streets

4

Claims

Part I of this book showed how young people, subject to a disorganized curriculum, lackadaisical and accusatory teachers, and arbitrarily imposed dress codes that are based on a systematic misunderstanding of the meanings of their clothing choices, were not recognized for their humanity or potential. Part II now focuses on the creation of lively experiential possibilities that marginalized young people ingeniously develop to compensate for the lack of opportunities and the dehumanization and degradation they experience in their current social structures.

Seeing oneself as a victim is neither comfortable nor sustainable. The sense of being a victim gnaws at one's core, providing a compulsion to transcend degradation and actualize oneself as an agent again. If the victimizer is a specific person, the desire to actualize oneself may focus on a lust for revenge. But if one has been marginalized and excluded structurally, alienated from the very services that are supposed to assist, one has other options than rage. One might play the trickster like Melvin, delighting as his teacher boasts his knowledge while accepting incorrect answers, or Joey, asking a security guard to go fetch him "some of that cold water."

As much as the practices of gangs victimize, they are also responses to victimization. We often think of gangs as enduring social groups that impose themselves on a neighborhood. But a variety of "gangs" may coexist in one locale, and young people may be involved in such groups in a variety of ways. Gang researchers have long noted how gangs come in different forms,[1] but they have not discussed the ambivalence of each young person's choice, or how each such choice involves nuanced skills in negotiating various situated risks. Young people are not mere dupes of gangs. Rather, they situate themselves strategically in relation to local gangs and use gangs, always in a contingent way, to mark the self. This chapter will focus on how such strategic situatedness is enacted and accounted for.

On inner-city streets in the contemporary United States, demanding of another, "Where you from" is the clearest, firmest way to distinguish oneself as a gang member, as one who is willing to stand up for one's gang and take whatever risks might arise from such an affiliation.² It is a way of proving toughness, courage, heart, and hardness, equally for men and women. These three little words, pronounced in the right situation, in the right way, directly in the face of the right person, place everything on the line: not only one's reputation but perhaps one's life. They call forth and reify the binary opposition on which all forms of violence utterly depend.

Such an interaction ritual is also an integral tool for flexibly, variably presenting the self. However enduring or tangible a gang affiliation may seem, failure to claim it in response to the challenge "Where you from" can make it disappear. The respondent to this demand must read the situation and the person making the demand to decide if and how he or she chooses to claim a gang. Streets in which such demands are an ever-present possibility become thereby saturated with opportunities for action, and any young person who leaves his or her house must feel confident about having the proper skills and be willing to assume the risks of responding. No response, not even a nonresponse, is without risks. Thus asking about a young person's gang affiliation is primarily relevant not to gang researchers but to young people. "Where you from," "Who you claimin," and "What you be about" are locally recognized interrogation devices and central practices for demonstrating a gang identity and forcing the respondent to make an identity claim in terms of gangs. Thus gang ecologies provide myriad opportunities for grappling with how identity is accomplished.³

The demand "Where you from," intended to resolve any ambiguity, actually becomes merely another resource to be worked in the contingent, variable effort in which young people everywhere engage in molding the self. Such an emotional challenge to identity creates action.⁴ After briefly describing the social dynamics of "hitting up," this chapter explores the performance of gang identity through hitting up, first in terms of the skills involved and then in terms of the risks.

"Hitting Up"

In the inner-city setting of this study, to "bang on," "sweat," or "hit up" another means that one young person, whom I will call the instigator, approaches another, whom I will call the respondent, on a street, in a park, at school, at a flea market, or in some other public place, and in the local vernacular "tells" (not "asks") the other, "Where you from." Anyone who lives in this locale knows that the instigator is demanding to know the respondent's gang affiliation. A variant of "Where you from" is "What you write," used by taggers.

A number of tacit assumptions can be immediately made when someone "hits up." First, the instigator must be a member of a gang, since "everyone knows" that only gang members "hit up" (in fact, "hitting up" is the characteristic act that constitutes gang membership), and only a gang member would find it relevant to know the gang affiliation of a stranger. Second, even as many see "hitting up" as an act of violence in itself, by "hitting up" one shows one is willing to engage in violence, including but not limited to rape, mayhem, assault, robbery, and murder. If the respondent claims a rival gang affiliation, violence is supposedly assured. Yet even if the respondent does not claim a rival gang, "hitting up" is often a prelude to violence. Third, the instigator is showing, by making the demand, that he perceives the respondent to embody a habitus similar enough to his own that the prompt will have meaning for the respondent.[5] Yet the posing of the prompt also demonstrates that the instigator and the respondent are strangers, at least insofar as their potential gang affiliations are unknown to each other.

An instigator may hit up a respondent for a number of reasons. The ostensible reason for a young person to hit up is to uphold a gang's boundaries and punish intruders from rival gangs, thereby showing that he is "down for the hood," possibly leading to "props" (praise) from "big homies" (older, sponsoring gang members). But inner-city young people are much too resourceful to simply stick to the standard script. They also spoke of being hit up as a prelude to robbery, a fight, or a shooting. As Shawn, a twenty-year-old Belizean, stated, "When somebody come up and ask me where I'm from, I still gotta brace myself to whatever he wanna do. He could wanna ask me where I'm from just to see if I'm down for myself. Or maybe he wanna jack me, just askin' me where I'm from." Part of the thrill of "hitting up" and the menace of being hit up is its unpredictability: the respondent has no idea what the instigator may be planning. The two possibilities Shawn mentions–to see if he's "down for himself" (able to hold his own in a fight), clearly a test of subjective dominance and masculinity, or to jack (steal from) him–do not necessarily follow from the manifest reason for the question: to determine the respondent's gang affiliation.[6]

In choosing their targets, instigators are folk sociologists who are likely to hit up someone on the basis of both ascribed characteristics, such as age (usually fifteen to twenty-five) and gender (instigators usually hit up those of the same gender), and temporary characteristics, such as clothing style (they are more likely to hit up individuals wearing clothing whose colors diverge from the colors of the neighborhood gang), although clothing alone is neither a necessary nor sufficient reason. Instigators may also look to hit up others who appear tough or "hard" and who walk with long, lunging strides, a style of walking known as "mobbing," associated with gang members.

Within the ritualized script of "hitting up," the respondent can make two possible responses to the instigator's challenge. The first is negative, in that the respondent does not make any positive claims on his own behalf. The most typical responses of this sort are "Nowhere," and "I don't bang." Such responses leave the respondent in a rather submissive, inferior position with regard to the instigator, since the instigator has already implied that he is in a gang and is "down for his hood," whereas the respondent, as a person "from nowhere," is claiming no identity and no backup for himself. From the standpoint of the instigator, such a person is typically trying to escape a potentially violent situation regardless of whether he is really in a gang or not: he stands for nothing, is willing to defend nothing, and doesn't really belong anywhere. The subjective moral dominance established here is similar to that established in robberies.[7]

In a second type of response to the challenge, the respondent "claims" his gang. The respondent, however, does not know the instigator's gang and therefore does not know if his response may lead to violence from the instigator. Even if the instigator may appear small in stature, he may conceal a weapon such as a gun or knife, or he may have a host of friends nearby ready to assist him. Hence, even hard-core gangbangers often do not claim to be affiliated with their gang when they are "hit up," especially if they are deep in rival territory. This is known as "ranking out." Even if a respondent is not in a gang, he is often accused of being a "ranker" by the instigator if he does not claim a gang. The term *ranker* is seen as synonymous with a host of other terms that impugn one's masculinity, such as *bitch, punk, pussy,* and *lemon.* If a respondent is in a gang, he may fear that the fact that he "ranked out" will get back to his gang. According to local gang lore, the punishment for "ranking out" ranges from "getting checked" (getting punched by or having to fight with a fellow gang member), to receiving "discipline" (having to fight with a number of fellow gang members), to "getting the green light," meaning that fellow gang members may shoot the "ranker" on sight. (Such notorious legends are often associated with "La M," the Mexican Mafia.)

However, the potential violence that may result from being hit up should not be overplayed, as many nonviolent outcomes are possible even in highly volatile circumstances. In fact, in one instance "hitting up" led to a peaceful, if tense, outcome for two young rivals for one young woman's affections. In such cases, the respondent claims a gang or a set that is friendly with the instigator's gang. "Hitting up" may even bode the beginning of a friendship, as the instigator and respondent begin "calling" the names of those they know, finding common acquaintances. Alternatively, an instigator may be satisfied that the respondent is not a member of a gang and then not try to further antagonize him by calling him a ranker. Or the respondent may be called a ranker but may not desire to respond.

The attractions of hitting up and the shame of being hit up are reflected grammatically, for while the instigator is described in the active voice as "banging" or "hitting up," the respondent is left objectified in the passive voice as "banged on," "hit up," or "sweated." As Harvey Molotch and Deirdre Boden state, "Demands for 'just the facts,' the simple answers, the forced-choice response, preclude the 'whole story' that contains another's truth."[8] The only active verb that describes an action of the respondent other than "claiming" a gang, is an action associated with losing face with respect to upholding a "hard" masculine identity: "ranking out." There is no verb for not claiming an involvement in a gang when one is in fact not involved in one. *This highlights how "hitting up" marginalizes young men who do not claim a gang in such an environment.*[9] Below, I examine the skills and dangers of hitting up. Skills include emotional control, knowing where to go, knowing how to dress, and knowing what to say. Dangers include the known and the unknown, violence, and ranking out.

Skills
Emotional Control

For many young people, to be *told*, "Where you from!" has a raw, intimidating power. Tom recalled a time when he was "ten to twelve," visiting a nearby swimming pool.

> I went out there walking, and I had a big BK on the tongue [of my shoe]. At the time British Knights, BK tennis shoes, were real popular. BK stands for Blood Killer. I had those on, and as I walked out, I just hear, "Ah, Blood, look at this little dog! Whoop di whoop" [a phrase used to index threatening language]. And all of 'em turn around, and I stopped, and like, it just looked like everybody in that whole park was staring at me. I was nervous, man. I had butterflies in my stomach; my heart was racing real fast. He's like, "Hey, little nigga, where you from? Where you from?" And when I turned around to talk, I couldn't even talk. You know how you get so nervous, it's just like it tried to come out, but it couldn't come out. My voice was real squeaky, and I remember them *laughing* at me. Then I was like,

"I don't gangbang, I don't gangbang." They said, "Ah man, leave that little nigga alone. He look like he about to cry." I *was*!

In this story, although Tom was not locally competent enough to know not to wear BK tennis shoes to the pool, he did know the meaning of "Where you from." The reason for Tom's description of his shoes becomes clear in that it foreshadows Tom's terror when he heard, "Ah Blood." Here he presents a shame narrative, recounting an incident in which he was "*before the community without being part of the community* in any recognizable way."[10] Through Tom's dramatic, colorful narrative style, we hear how he sensed his intimidation viscerally, in the "butterflies in my stomach" and "my heart racing real fast." As if clarifying the nature of the confrontation, one of the men in the group "banged on" little Tom. Tom, in describing his response, presents his voice as something separate from himself: he tried to speak, "but *it* couldn't come out." As Jack Katz states, "Shame . . . recognizes its provocation by a vividly sensed inability to respond";[11] Tom's shame was exacerbated when the young men laughed at him. Finally, he was able to utter the response recognized as appropriate in this instance, even though it was contradicted by the evidence of his tennis shoes, and the instigators dropped the matter, apparently out of sympathy for his tears.[12]

After recounting this incident, Tom told how he had walked out of the park but had started running as soon as he was out of sight of the pool. Once he arrived home, his cousins asked him what was wrong, but according to Tom, "I couldn't even talk." One of his female cousins sat down with him in a bedroom and gently solicited his story, helping him to release the shame he felt over being unable to speak and running away. As young people become older they must learn to control such fears, lest they be left vulnerable.

Knowing Where to Go

Being "hit up" is an ever-looming possibility on the horizons of experience for young people in the inner city.[13] As Shawn described it, "Wherever you go, there's always somebody walkin' up to you wanna know where you from, what you claim." To avoid being "hit up," young men in this locale make detailed cognitive maps of "safe" places and places to avoid.[14] Those who have no such map may be reluctant to leave the house. Brad, an eighteen-year-old African American who had attended military school for two years, tells how he faced such a situation after his return to the neighborhood because he was no longer current on the "rules":

"I used to be scared of my neighborhood. I didn't wanna go nowhere, because of the gangs and stuff like that."

"You knew about that street life before you went to military school."

"Yeah. I'm saying, since I left for a certain amount of time, I didn't know the rules because the streets change every day. There's certain things you have to do, and you don't do, and I didn't know them at the time, so I was scared. It took time for me to learn the rules of the street again."

"Can you give me some examples, what are some of the rules?"

"Like basically, know which street to go down, which street not to go down, who to talk to, who not to talk to, where to go, where to ride your bike, stuff like that."

"Did you ever make a mistake?"

"Nah. I stayed in the house."

Those who did know the "rules," or rather the social and geographic "boundaries," could be quite specific about the places they avoided. Eric, a nineteen-year-old Latino, described such a place in terms of street boundaries, though he did not give it a name, instead simply referring to it as "beyond": "Like over there, like Central and Twenty-third. I don't go over there. That's like a—whatchamacallit, what should I say—that's beyond. I don't really go there at all. If I go there, I don't really try to show my face to nobody. I'll just like hide if I go with my friend or something."

Richard, a sixteen-year-old African American, explained his quite complex cognitive map, judging the safety of an area by contextual cues, such as the number of children playing in the street, and relying on his street smarts to negotiate his way through areas that were borderlines between gang turfs:[15]

"When you're going home from school, are there any places you avoid? Is it tricky negotiating the trip home?"

"I always try to avoid walking through any alleyways. I try to avoid walking on streets where there are three or less people."

"Avoid that?"

"I avoid that. If you ever walk down a street and there's only two or three people outside, most likely the reason that they went inside the house is because they're scared to come outside. If you walk down the street and it's just empty, that's not a good sign. So if you see a street where the kids are outside playing cans or hollering at each other from across the street, things like that, that's good, very good, 'cause that shows signs of life. That means that these people aren't afraid of the area around."

"What if there aren't kids playing, but there's groups of young men hanging out on porches?"

"Um, well, that all depends."

"Let's say Friday afternoon."[16]

"If it was Friday afternoon and I was *deep* in Central territory, no, I wouldn't do it. I wouldn't walk down that street. I would care less. If I was on Cole, and the next street was Rand, and that's like at the crossroads between the Blood and Crip neighborhood, I wouldn't worry about it, because I would know I'm so close to the boundaries, they wouldn't wanna start nothin', because all you'd have to do is be like, 'Well, I know this person.' It's not too hard to find out who is who. And since I know how to talk, I know who people are, let him through."

Richard drew upon four sources of knowledge in safely negotiating his way through the city. First, he avoided some places, such as alleyways, as a rule. Second, he read the gestalt of a street as provided by contextual cues, such as the number of people outside or the presence of children playing. Third, he drew on his knowledge of gang boundaries, knowing that a rival gang "wouldn't wanna start nothing" on a dividing line, since it could quickly escalate. Fourth, he drew on his personal relationships with people in the neighborhood and could refer to his acquaintances as a way of defusing tensions.

Knowing How to Dress

Wearing the "wrong" clothes in the "wrong" area was often described as a precursor for being "hit up." In the following conversation, Ernesto, a Latino who worked over thirty hours per week at a Latino grocery store and bred pit bulls in his spare time, told of such an instance of mistaken identification. Once when he was coming home after a day in school, he met with an attack that he attributed to his baggy clothing:

They put mace on my eyes. They came up to me, they told me, "Hey, fuck Eighteenth Street!" They probably thought I was Eighteenth Street, probably confused me. I used to dress with baggy clothes, not these jeans, [but] Ben Davis [pants]. They probably confused me. It was two guys, they came up to me and then they just told me, "Where you from, homie?" I said, "Nahh, man, I don't gangbang." "Why you dressed like that?" "'Cause I want to, man." They just took out like a little black bottle man and sprayed it in my eyes. It was right there by the Sports Arena, right there.

While Ernesto is Latino, Shawn, a Belizean, faced similar challenges with African American gangs. Shawn, with whom I stayed in contact over the years, visiting at his house and inviting him to my wedding, claimed an affiliation with the Crips, known for wearing blue. He encountered a difficulty when problems with his father made it necessary for him to live with his sister, who resided in a Blood neighborhood, where gang members were known for wearing red. In one of our early interviews in 1997, he discussed walking down the street in her neighborhood and having to rank out when he was called to account for his clothing, but being attacked nonetheless.

"I knew there was gonna be some trouble now, 'cause they had on red. As soon as I see that that's apparently tellin' me I gotta brace myself."

"Mm hmm. How many were there?" I asked.

"There were four or five of them. So he walked up to me, he was like, 'Blood, where you from?' I said, 'I don't bang.' He was like, 'You look like you bang to me, you havin' all that flu,' which is blue. And uh, I was like, 'Nah man, I don't bang.' I said, 'Would I be in your neighborhood, would I be in your territory if I was bangin'?' He was like, 'I don't know, but it seem like you bangin' to the fullest.' And so his homeboy took a swing at me."

While these incidents occurred outside school, they were just as liable to happen inside school, especially to a new student. Regardless of whether students were correctly identified by their antagonists as gang members, such occurrences were typically interpreted as good reasons for placing restrictions on what students could wear at school. But although clothing was specifically referenced in these narratives, it alone was insufficient to specify gang involvement, as we saw in chapter 3. Young people working within the context of a staging area, like a school, will find ways to index markers of affiliation or disaffiliation, whether or not these are dress related.

Knowing What to Say

"If you live here long enough, you know that question by heart, and you know what to say," according to Tim, a leader of Central. Conversely, if you haven't lived "here long enough," you may not know what to say. Oliver, a fourteen-year-old Latino, turned the question on me.

"Well, what would you say if somebody were to come up to ask you where you're from?"

"I'd say UCLA."

"Ahhh, tsk! UCLA, you just like a little bitch." He laughed mockingly.

I laughed with Oliver. "What should I say?"

"What do you wanna say? You can't say UCLA."

"What would you say?"

"Just say 'Nowhere.'"

"Nowhere?"

"Yep."

"And do they accept that?"

"Yeah. Or tell 'em you don't bang. Sometimes they will leave you alone. Sometimes they'll sock your ass and jack you for your money. They'll do it."

Responding in such an incompetent manner, Oliver implied, would diminish my masculinity. Moreover, "You *can't* say UCLA"—it simply is not a locally recognized possibility.[17] When I asked Oliver what he would say, he advised how someone in my position should respond, with "Nowhere," or "I don't bang," although these responses were also not without risks.

I was not the only person in this setting who might have had some difficulty in understanding local expectations. Antoine, an eighteen-year-old African American, told me about some of the bewildering experiences he had had after arriving from out of state: "When I first came out here, it seemed like I always had on the wrong colors and stuff. People would ask me like, 'Where you from?' I was like, 'Louisiana.'" I chuckled, and Antoine continued: "They were like, 'Huh?' So I guess they tried to bang on me, but I wasn't knowing. I was telling them where I was from. They thought I was tryin' to be funny about it." In this classic description of a breach of local expectations, Antoine's understanding of a "normal" and "natural" way to respond to this prompt contradicted what would be expected, eliciting my laughter.[18] He went on to recount how his cousin had schooled him in the local ecology, telling him, "Man, there's Crips and Bloods out here."

The standardized quality of the ritualized exchange that ensues when one is "hit up" is practically as obdurate as a script, which any locally competent member can easily cite and explicate. In the excerpt below, Richard, a sixteen-year-old African American whose insights appear repeatedly in this text, provided a sense of this script as he saw it.

RICHARD: If you walk down the street with a black and red suit and this is a Crip neighborhood, it would be labeled not so much as disrespect, but not enough respect. So that would be a person that would be confronted first.

RG: In what way? How would they be confronted?

RICHARD: If the person was, I have to say, between the ages of fifteen and twenty-five, twenty-six, first, gang members would hit 'em up, you know, finger stuff. And if they didn't respond to that, they run after 'em. "Hey cuz, where you from?" You know what I'm sayin'?

[The person would respond], "Well, I don't bang."

[Then the instigators would ask him,] like, "Whachu got all this on fo'?"

"I'm goin' to work."

"Nah, cuz, I heard you's from this, I heard you from that."

And if the person gets upset or gets angry, and shows a willingness to fight back, that's when the situation becomes violent, because the person that's doing, I guess you could say the interrogation [he chuckles], already knows and can read the emotions of the person that's being taunted.

Richard begins by making a point that wearing the "wrong" colors can lead to being "hit up," since it shows "not enough respect." Such a "mistake" does not necessarily lead to being "hit up," as one may be hit up even when wearing the "right clothes," but it does increase its likelihood. Richard then brings up another necessary variable, age. Some young men spoke of being hit up at a very young age, but this was rare.[19] It was also rare to be hit up once one was visibly past adolescence.

Richard mentions hand signs as a precursor to verbally hitting up. Once the finger signals fail, the verbal prompt is given, and in his example Richard provides the default response of one claiming not to be in a gang. Since the claim is contradicted by the clothing, the hypothetical respondent must account for this. Richard describes how violence may erupt in the potentially volatile space of the "third turn"[20] as the respondent becomes angry and the instigator who is conducting "the interrogation" reads his emotions.

Those who are familiar with the ecology of the inner city and are accustomed to the possibility of being "hit up" are not helpless. Rather, several young men I spoke with had devised useful verbal strategies for defusing the threat and humiliation that it posed. Though the most common response is "I don't bang," or "Nowhere," it has drawbacks: it makes no positive claims for the self, implying that the only ecologically recognized alternative to gangbanging is nothing. Such a response may be just as likely to lead to violence as the claim to membership in a rival gang or the accusation of being a "ranker." Some young men, however, described following up this response with a diversionary tactic. Below, Richard recounts how he turns the tables.

> I get it almost every day. "Hey, where you from? I heard you bang over here, I heard you bang over there." I be like, "Dang, I don't gangbang, *man!*" He be like, "Well, where you from, where you used to be from?" I was like, "I never gangbang. I just moved out here from *Detroit*. It's kinda cool, but you know what I'm sayin', there ain't no females around here, you know where some at?" Now generally, men will be men with the gang crap, if you change the situation, you change the subject of the matter. If you're talkin' about women, you know, obviously they're gonna respond. *[vernacular style:]* "Well, check this out. See what you do, you go down over there on hunred fo-teen and Highland. You say, 'Whooolie who whoola' and Chantell come out, you ask her to talk to her homegirl." You know what I'm sayin'? 'Cause even though we don't get along, you know we have to live together.

As is evident, Richard, who, like most of my consultants, had been placed in special education classes, was a master of wordplay.[21] He continued, "Now if you can maintain a level head and you can know how to talk—I mean you have to really know how to talk your way out of situations—then you don't get messed with. That's why I don't get messed with too much, 'cause I use the skills that I honed so well." He laughed, and cogently added, "My lying tactics, to avoid confrontation."

In the above segment, he used three such tactics. First, he stated, in an outraged, assertive way, "I don't gangbang, *man!*" Only when the instigator continued to prompt did Richard resort to his story, "I just moved out here from Detroit," since if he had said this immediately he would have been seen as incompetent, as shown above. Third, Richard ingeniously used his purported status as an outsider to inquire about where he could find a "female." Thus he changed his potential antagonists' focus from thanatos to libido.

Buck, a sixteen-year-old African American, told me another method for turning around the threat of "where you from": "Most times now, I got an easy way to get past the gangbangers. All of 'em have soft spots, so if they ask where you from, I tell 'em the church I go to, 'Westminster Church of Christ,' and they'll just sit there like, 'Oh, I wanted to jack him, but he said 'God.' Don't matter who it is. Say, 'Man, I'm banging for God.' So if you say anything having to do with God, they gonna bow down, like, 'All right, all right.'" Buck also told me that he had been robbed four or five times and lost about $900 in jewelry; such tactics were learned at a price.

Being "hit up" is a frightening prospect. However, as one becomes older, and has, as many of my consultants reported, "heard that so many times," the question begins to lose its drama and sting. The following two eighteen-year-old African Americans, known for their academic intensity as well as their quiet dignity and composure, both expressed a loss of patience for this practice, which they had come to see as juvenile, and refused to allow their identity to be determined through gang rituals that they viewed as onerous and perverse. Jerome, who had only recently moved to the inner city after coming to maturity in the suburbs, spoke of how he had responded the one time he had been "hit up." It had worked for him, but as he stated, it was risky enough that his girlfriend had been quite upset.

"Has anyone ever asked you, 'Where you from?'"

"Yeah, I've been asked that," he nods.

"What happened?"

"It just happened once. I was over here, going to catch the bus, and I was in a real bad mood, so I did something I shouldn't have done. Two guys came up to me, and one of them asks me, 'Where you from?' I was in a bad mood, so I just kept walking right past them. He started to come after me, and he asked me again, 'Hey, where you from?!' I just turned around and pushed his back hard against a parking meter, so they left. I didn't hear anything more from them, and nobody's asked me since. I told my girlfriend about it and she was mad at me. She said, 'What if they'd had a gun? They could've killed you.' I know that, and I wouldn't do it again. But that day, I was just pissed."

Finally, consider the following account from Brad, who simply lost all respect for young men who played with gangs and could no longer take their challenges seriously: "I used to be scared when they'd ask the question. I used to say, 'Nowhere.' Now I just look at 'em and be like, 'Get outta my face.' I've been asked that so many times, I'm pretty much used to it. I don't care what they do to me. It doesn't affect me no more. My heart used to be pumping when people asked me that question. But now it doesn't bother me. You get used to it."

Note that neither Jerome nor Brad responded with the status-diminishing response of claiming to be from "nowhere." Instead, both denigrated the very basis of the threat, refusing to be forced to account for themselves in gangs' terms. Such actions diminish the relevance of gangs in such an ecology.

Dangers
The Known and the Unknown

Gerald Suttles notes that it is commonly overlooked that young people in the inner city know each other.[22] As mentioned above, to demand "Where you from" assumes that the other is unknown but is of an age and an ethnicity to be potentially knowable. However, someone who is already well known does not have to worry about being "hit up" in his community, as Everett stated:

> "Have you ever had anyone ask you where you're from?"
>
> "All the time. That don't bother me, 'cause you know it happens so much. Now, most of the time, when I'm around here, it's like never because everybody know me already, everybody know I don't gangbang."

While being known in one neighborhood may provide safety, it may have negative consequences in an adjacent neighborhood. Frank, an eighteen-year-old who did not affiliate with a gang, felt safe with the members of the Eighteenth Street gang who congregated on his block. However, he had to be wary when going outside his neighborhood, since rivals of Eighteenth Street might have seen him and associated him with their enemies:

> "Since we live here so much, the gangsters kind of know us. So they kind of socialize, and if they see us, they're like, 'What's up.' We live here. But if we go to a neighborhood where they don't know us, they'll stop us and they might shoot, because now they're crazy."
>
> "Is that Eighteenth Street too?"
>
> "No, over there is like BMX. We don't really go through like small streets neither, 'cause you never know who comes out of it."
>
> "So why would they shoot at you? You've never been in a gang, and you don't ever gangbang."
>
> "'Cause sometimes gangsters pass through your block. Since that's Eighteen's block, they'll probably see you. If you pass through their block, it'll be like, 'I seen that guy over there, and that Eighteenth Street,' and they're gonna think you from Eighteen now. That's what happens. Some reason, they'll put you in the mix. And that happens kind of a lot too. And that's why we kind of take care of ourselves and just watch our backs."
>
> "Watch your back, so you would go out with your brothers or your friends?"

"Just watch what street you go to. Don't get into streets that look like they have gangsters on them."

In the ecology of this neighborhood, where little action is to be found in the form of youth programs or other diversions besides what young people create, Frank speaks of how simply walking through a neighborhood can take on the characteristics of a gamble. Frank fears going to BMX's block because he surmises that members of that gang have seen him on "Eighteen's block" and thus put him "in the mix" of those involved with gangs. When I provide one local meaning for "watch your back,"[23] Frank gently corrects me, telling me that he means "watch your back" in terms of avoiding dangerous places.

Instigators may also "hit up" respondents whom they know well, as a means of daily harassment. In this case, the instigator harasses the respondent by continually invoking the contrast between their identities, juxtaposing "gangbanger" to "nobody." The respondent is reminded on an ongoing basis that while the questioner is from "somewhere," he is from "nowhere." As Frank noted, "In the afternoon [after school] I used to pass through there, there just used to be like gangsters. And I'm living in that block right there, living for four years and they still be messing with me. They like, 'Where you from,' telling us a lot." As Goffman claimed, "If the victim still declines to join the battle, the aggressor may goad him with increasingly unpalatable acts, in an apparent effort either to find his ignition point, or to demonstrate that he doesn't have one."[24] Through such tactics, instigators demonstrate not only the local salience of gangs but the local *righteousness* of gangs.

In the inner-city area around CAA, each standard high school was perceived as dominated by two gangs along racial lines: one Latino gang and one African American gang. As Steve, a Latino consultant, succinctly stated, "Every school's divided into two. See like one [side is] is run through the Hispanics, like Eldridge is run by Venice. But through the blacks, it's run through the Bloods."

CAA was rather notorious as a "gang-owned" school, and "hitting up" was the primary way such ownership was demonstrated. New students at CAA were hit up as a matter of course by members of Central. As Lamont, an eighteen-year-old African American, clarified, such school-based interrogations took on a matter-of-fact, "natural" quality.[25]

"The most I ever had somebody ask where I'm from is when I got to this school right here. Most people were like, 'Where you from, whoo whoo

whoo.' I wasn't used to that. So I kind of got used to it up here, got used to the more petty type. That's how it is, so you gotta get used to it."

"Take me back to that. What was it like your first day of school here?"

"My first day here, like for everybody, if you're male, for a female, you get asked too. I got sweated a couple times as I was leaving school."

Not all students were able to negotiate this intimidating trial. Marco, an eighteen-year-old Latino and a member of Vernon Locos, told how he had "had to learn the hard way" when he encountered members of the Eighteenth Street gang at Liberty High School. For such students, getting "kicked out" connoted an act committed by the local gang, not school administrators.

"I got kicked out [of Liberty] 'cause I have gang problems."

"What do you mean, gang problems?"

"I was getting chased by Florencia a lot. They was trying to take me out. They just told me where I was from and I told them. And then he goes [Cholo voice], 'You know what? We're gonna leave you right here today. But we kickin' every fools that's from somewhere, we kickin' them out of this school, 'cause this school belongs to us.' I tell 'em, 'All right. Just let me finish the day today and I won't come back.' So they just let me slide that day. Came back next morning, next morning before I even got in school they put a gun on me. I was barely gonna cross the street so I could go into school."

Following this incident, Marco dropped out. Such a reason for dropping out was not uncommon in this area.[26]

Prompting Violence

Part of the attraction of "hitting up" is that the respondent doesn't know what level of violence may follow his response, and often the instigator doesn't know either. Asking the question is thrilling, as the "wrong" response may lead the instigator to explode in a way that even he has not anticipated.[27] The following sort of incident recounted by Ben was quite common: "I was walking with my sixteen-year-old brother, just walking down the street to catch the bus. And these guys come up to him, right, and then they ask him where he's from. You know how they do, right? He says um, 'Four-Deuce Crip,' right. And then they just start beatin' on him."

Here the likely purpose of the "interrogation" was to punish a rival gang member. Yet a literal "hitting up" can follow the prompt regardless of whether the respondent claims a gang. Consider Terry's account of how the instigators transformed his negative response into a precursor of violence through a bit of clever wordplay: "It was me and my friend walkin' down the street. We went to pick up a friend at middle school, and then it was like, 'Where you all from?' We was like, 'We don't bang.' They was like, 'Y'all about to.' And they hit us, pushed us in our backs and then we just started fightin'. And then like a whole group of their gang came and tried to fight us, but the police had come, put everybody against the wall."

Thus claiming a rival gang is a sufficient but not necessary condition for violence after one is "hit up." Further, many young men speak of being "hit up" as a precursor to robbery, as Buck mentions below, describing a situation already alluded to by Shawn, Oliver, and Richard:

"Did you ever have anyone ask you where you're from?"

"All the time."

"When's the first time you remember that happening?"

"Eighth grade. I was at the bus stop, and I had on red shoes. I was in the wrong neighborhood too. They asked me where I'm from, and then I got jacked. I used to have something bigger than this [necklace]. I had a chain bigger than that. Every three months I got jacked. I got jacked like four, five times a year. All the jewelry I wore cost more than $900 altogether, the bracelets, the watch, the rings, chains."

"And they would start to jack you by asking you where you're from?"

"Ask me where I'm from. If I say I don't bang, they still want to get they knife. I'm not going to just give it up if they just have fists. I can run from a knife or fists, but not if they got a gun."

As we have seen repeatedly, Buck begins his narrative by speaking of wearing the "wrong color," in the "wrong neighborhood." In such cases, demanding "Where you from" can be understood as a way of "constructing a subjective moral dominance" over the victim, common in stickups.[28] As if justifying being placed in the shameful position of giving up his belongings, Buck explains that he will not allow himself to be victimized "if they just have fists" and that he can run from a knife but that he can't resist or flee "if they have a gun."

Consultants also spoke of more serious assaults following the challenge "Where you from." For instance, Johnnie told of being hit up in which he delivered the same response as Buck and Terry but with more frightening results: "They come outta nowhere. Niggas on bikes. We turn around, ping, started runnin'. And they caught up to me. At this point in time, I was, fuck it, I wasn't in no bangin' mentality. I could care less about the hood, fuck that, this my life. 'Where you from, homie?' 'I don't bang.' I just said it like that. So after that, then they shot at us. That was kinda eerie. I didn't wanna go back." Johnnie could recite many stories in which he figured as a "gangbanger," but in this instance, by ranking out he disaffiliated himself. Whether or not his assailants knew of his previous involvements, their question implied they did not. The shots were simply inexplicable to Johnnie.

As eerie as Johnnie's experience was, the occurrence of violence without the demand "Where you from" seemed especially random and unpredictable. Frank told me of an incident in which "the guys that shot me, they didn't ask me, 'Where you from?' They just came and shot at me. And so that's why it be hard for people to walk on the street without taking care of their back."

Ranking Out

Though certain young men claimed to be gang members, they weren't gang members *all the time*. Young men who affiliated with gangs engaged in many activities, in a class, around a dinner table, or at the movies, where their gang identity was irrelevant. Gang members might also strategically disavow their membership in a gang by ranking out. Even Tim, a recognized leader of Central, could mention times when he'd "ranked out on his hood" and expressed disdain for those who *didn't* rank out, especially in dangerous circumstances. According to Tim, a young person he "banged on" "was from one of my rival gangs. He was about to say 'Yes,' or some stupid answer. I coulda shot him 'cause I *[high pitched]* had the gun right there. Wouldn't nobody be stupid enough to say 'Yeah,' if you see the gun and someone asks if you from—are you from this place?—but some people are."

Four years later, I spoke with Billy, another leader of Central, who provided me with a similar justification for ranking out.

My friends way over there, and I'm way over here. And if I ranked out, who gonna know? My friends ain't gonna know I ranked out. My friends ain't gonna go over there they self. *If I feel this fool gonna take my life over a street, I'm cool, I ain't gotta claim that street just for five minutes.* Just for a second. When you get back to your home, then you know where you from. But you can be stupid and try to tell 'em where you from, and let your life get took, that's on you! But I'ma be the smart guy. Shit. I'm tryin' to survive! I'm tryin' to see mo' days. I'm tryin' to see stuff I ain't never seen before. I'm tryin' to have things I ain't never had before. Go places I ain't never went. I'm tryin' to live right now. I wanna be here for a long time, and I mean a long time. Right now, I rank out for five minutes, for a second. I rank out. Okay.

While Billy repeats Tim's insight that claiming a gang can be stupid, especially when one is faced with a gun, he also notes that his friends would probably not know that he had ranked out, since they would not go into an area where they would have to rank out themselves.

Nevertheless, many young men "in the hood" define a "ranker" as tantamount to a coward, unwilling or unable to defend his affiliations, and hence his masculinity, or a "punk," the term for an object of homosexual predators in prison. Such a term applies to anyone who does not claim a gang affiliation when he or she is hit up, regardless of any "real" affiliation with a gang. Jaime, a twenty-year-old Latino, noted disdainfully that many attempted to pose as a "badass" by looking "all gangstered out" but that when push came to shove, few, if any, were consistently able to "hold their heads up":[29] "They kicking it or whatever, and some big fools from somewhere else or whoever comes and hits 'em up, 'Where you from?' They gonna straight out be like, 'Nah, we ain't from nowhere.' Rank out, straight out. 'We ain't from nowhere,' put their heads down. I know what I'm telling you 'cause I seen it. Any motherfuckers, they'd slap 'em. Like 'Bam!' slap 'em. They ain't gonna do nothing, man. They just all gangstered out, all bald headed, looking criminal."

Below, Earl, an eighteen-year-old African American who had been evangelizing as a born-again Christian for the two years prior to our interview, had discussed with me intimate details of his sex life, his methods of manufacturing and distributing illegal substances, and even the possibility that he had murdered a rival gang member. However, the only topic he was wary of mentioning on tape was "ranking out."[30]

"There was a lotta times when stuff went down—there was times, man, when I even rang—I even say this on the tape—I even ranked out on the hood once."

"Ranked out, what's that?"

"When somebody asked me where I was from, I told 'em I wasn't from nowhere, once, once. And that's no lie."

"When was that?"

"This was like, I'd been in the hood for a little while. I'd been in the hood for like a year. I ranked out on the hood. 'Cause some Dodge City

Crips had asked me where was I from, and I remember I told 'em nowhere. Nigga pulled up on me in a car, asked me where I'm from, and they look like they heated [i.e., they had guns]. I told 'em, "Nowhere." And I admit, man, I got heat from the homies by that."

"They found out about it?"

"Yeah, 'cause I told 'em, I talk to 'em. I got heat from the homies, but I believe I got what I deserve."

"What'd they do?"

"They gave me like a warning."

"Which means—"

"I remember the big homies, they was like, they was tellin' me that 'We should jump you, nigga.' [He laughs.] That was basically it. 'We should take yo' head off. You don't *ever* rank out on the hood.' I was scared as hell."

In this case, Earl was on the other side of a gun held by someone like Tim. Yet unlike Billy he didn't present such "ranking out" as "cool" or "smart" but rather as an act so shameful he hardly dared to mention it. For such a transgression of neighborhood loyalty, Earl stated, "I got what I deserve."

Yet an ostensible gang member may find ways to respond to the challenge "Where you from" without ranking out and without claiming an affiliation, as David demonstrates:

I was up at this gas station right here on Main. We went to get some air in our bikes. I had on all blue like I got on right now. Shit, he just drove over to us. They was like, got a big-ass gauge [shotgun] on me. That boy be like right in my face [*menacingly*], "Where you all from?" I was like, "Nigga, there's Blood all around here, right? That's right." I think fools didn't shoot me because my homeboy that I actually hang with, he was one. Every time I see that market there, that's what I think about, that shit.

In response to the challenge, David referred implicitly to the common-sense knowledge that "there's Blood all around here, right?" In other words, although he was wearing blue, he got away with it by implicitly asking, "Would a Crip be so stupid as to be caught here?" Yet in retrospect he considered that it wasn't his quick wit but his affiliation with a (nonpresent) Blood that had saved him.

Another variation on ranking out was presented by Roger, a rather hard-core tagger, who spoke of ranking out as a strategic measure to employ at a new school when your crew is still small. Once a fair number of members have joined, however, they may begin to "claim": "If I was the only one from GC right here, and I had lots of enemies, and they was to tell me, 'Where you from?' I would tell 'em 'Nowhere' until I get a lot of fools in. Then if I get fools in, I just keep it fool [quiet] until we get deeper than them niggas. We'll fuckin' come out on them. That's what we did at Jamison High. At Jamison I used to be from BBC and nobody like BBC; it was full of enemies. 'Where you from?' 'Nowhere, nowhere.'"

Hitting Up as a Resource

Consider Tom, who cried like a baby when Bloods mock-challenged him over his BK shoes, yet cut a formidable figure once he came of age. A large Belizean man, standing over six feet tall and weighing at least 250 pounds, but he was compact for his size, earning the nickname "Tank" among his friends. Below, he tells a story of how he "did being" a Crip by wearing blue when he went to visit a cousin from Avenue Pyroos, whose gang, a precursor of the Bloods, wore red:[31]

I was coming from there, and my cousin was from Avenue Pyroos, and I was walking to his house, which was a big mistake, because my favorite color was always blue, even before I got into the gangbanging thing. I just always wear a lot of blue. I know you see me come here with a lot of blue on all the time. So this guy came up to me, and was like, "You all got on blue, where you from? Whoop di whoop." I said, "40s Crip." He's like, "This is Avenue Pyroos, right here." Like that, we got into it [a fight]. Then when I got to my cousin's house, I told my cousin, and he's like, "I'ma handle it." I'm like, "No, it's cool."

Usually, say you're my cousin, and I'm from 40s, and they see you walking through the 40s hood, and they be, "Where you from" you be like, "I don't bang," or "I'm from such and such a hood." You guys don't get along. But if your cousin tells them, "Tom's my cousin," then they be like, "All right. We're gonna give you *a pass*. We'll leave you alone." And if they don't, then you go back to your cousin and tell your cousin when they have their meeting or whatever, and that person gets *disciplined*. "Why you beat up my cousin, man? He told you he my cousin!" And it goes like that. So that's what my cousin was thinking when I told him. But I didn't tell him anything. I don't know. I kind of felt like I was invincible *[he laughs]* or something.

Tom, looking for a fight, wore blue to visit his cousin. Tom found this violence ("we got into it"), but after he arrived at his cousin's house his cousin was disappointed to find that Tom had been in a fight. Tom's cousin wanted to stick up for Tom, telling him, "I'ma handle it." Tom said that such "handling" could be justified as "discipline," punishing a fellow gang member by fighting with him within the gang. Yet Tom had not asked for the "pass" before entering his cousin's "turf." Still, Tom's cousin might have found a use of "discipline" as a resource for revenge against Tom's attacker, even though they were in the same gang. (As Shawn, another Belizean, stated, "family comes first.") When Tom said, "No, it's cool," he was admitting to his cousin that he had in effect been looking for a fight and did not want his cousin to exercise "discipline." Tom knew he could have obtained a pass, but he didn't get one; he knew what his clothes meant in his cousin's neighborhood, yet he still went. We can see this as a clear example of using gangs as a resource for (1) creating action, (2) showing off for a cousin by affirming to him that one can get by on one's own (perhaps even be "a man"), (3) reifying geographic gang boundaries, (4) reifying local meanings of dress, and (5) building a reputation among one's peers as a badass. If one has a thorough knowledge of the possibilities for performing identities in this local ecology, the anticipation of being "hit up" can create the same sense of action as actually "hitting up." Others who choose to take "the pass," however, can apparently rest assured that their kinship ties will override their gang ties.

Gangs as a Resource

The lives of children growing up in the ghetto have been likened to flowers blooming in the cracks of a sidewalk.[32] This chapter shows that although gangs may appear to have the intransigence of concrete, young people creatively use them as resources to flexibly work the possibilities of gang/nongang affiliations. The challenge "Where you from" can provide gangs with the most powerful sense of permanence, yet a "ranker" may simply make his gang disappear. Knowing how to work these alternatives in the appropriate circumstances comprises tools for molding identity in this ecology.

All young people growing up in such a neighborhood, regardless of whether they are "in" a gang, must be resourceful in using such tools to negotiate everyday life. To summarize, hitting up, for the instigator, is a tool to (1) demonstrate gang membership; (2) create a local ecology in which young people must commonly expect to present an identity answerable to gangs; (3)

establish and maintain the importance of friendship and kinship ties, gang boundaries, and dress as a gang signifier; and (4) provide a ritual prelude to ongoing harassment, a robbery, a fight, or a shooting. For the person anticipating being hit up, it is a tool to (1) strategically contextualize where and when a gang identity is revealed; (2) demonstrate street wits and smarts in providing a response to this prompt; (3) invoke the strategic importance of friendship and kinship ties, gang boundaries, and dress in order to anticipate, interpret, and manipulate an interaction; and (4) avoid the possibility of ongoing harassment, robbery, a fight or a shooting. In short, through hitting up, young people have found ways to imbue an inner-city environment with action and excitement without the encumbrance of expensive gear, by holding each other accountable to the nuances of local knowledge.

Such an interaction ritual is also powerful in invoking emotions that legitimize violence, in two ways. First, it provides a recognized script to accomplish the shame and rage necessary for violence. Violence rarely simply happens.[33] Rather, people draw upon an embodied sense of how emotions work to create interactions for violence to emerge naturally as "gang related," often by insulting another's masculinity.[34] Like a stickup, the script for hitting up quickly accomplishes this, yet with heightened uncertainty. Second, the aggression of hitting up and shame of being hit up are cyclical and self-reinforcing.[35] "Hitting up" is a ready resource for a young person looking to create action. A young person who is hit up and does not claim a gang affiliation is shamed and practically negates his identity by claiming to be simply from "nowhere." Such humiliation is infuriating, and "hitting up" then becomes an available way for a humiliated victim to deal with his rage.

We should not overlook that many may hit up others in order to avoid being victims themselves. To protect one's turf, in fact, whether in games of sport, the military, or a "neighborhood watch," is considered by many a highly honorable act.[36] Although gangs are commonly demonized, we should never lose sight of the fact that with a slight shift in perspective we can see the ways of gangs not only as familiar but as close to home. Indeed, one might consider the violence that non–gang members accomplish through the assessments, judgments, and provocations that may ensue when one asks where another is from. To be from an inner-city area is a stigma many find hard to escape.[37] To impose such a stigma, through dehumanizing representations of gang members as merely criminal, contributes to gang violence. We may well find further ways in which gangs are both a source of tension and a tool to manage it.

5

Affiliations

There are many different aspects of identity and situated ways to present them. Chapter 4 probed the variable, contingent ways in which young people may perform gang identity by hitting up. The skills and dangers involved in this situated interaction ritual provide a lively means to escape the oppressive, alienating institutional routines found in many inner-city environments, such as the school and classrooms of chapters 2 and 3. This chapter explores some of the many types of affiliations that ostensibly provide a basis for hitting up.

In the area around CAA, young people have many different options for the types of groups with which they may affiliate and how they wish to affiliate with them. Some who may be seen as gang members explicitly deny that their social group is a gang, instead calling it a "clique," a "bisa crew," or a "tagging crew." Others who might be seen as gang members simply "kick it" with the local gang socially, without engaging in violence or criminality to gain respect. And many young people in the community associate the term *gang member* not with monstrous and terrifying thuggishness but with poverty and problems related to family, school, law enforcement, and employment. Most young people, even in an area seemingly saturated with gangs, choose not to affiliate and pity those who do.

Not only is a young person's decision to "rank out" or "claim" a gang contingent on a strategic reading of the immediate circumstances, but the more general level of commitment to the gang also changes. As Elijah Anderson showed in his book, *A Place on the Corner,* one's place in a social group is determined through social interaction. One cannot simply claim a place; the claim depends on what others will allow.[1] While the accounts in this chapter are one-sided, they often allude to such contested dynamics: even as a consultant situates himself with a specific social identity vis-à-vis local gangs, his account and reputation often suggest that others see that identity differently.

Below I offer a typology of young people's accounts of the social groups that they create and affiliate with; while such typologies may be convenient, they present analytical dangers. One grave mistake is to use such categories as a basis for explaining or describing actions.[2] They are better appreciated as a spectrum of *resources* that young people may draw on for molding identity in this locale, much as young people in locales with less alienating institutional opportunities might draw upon hockey, violin playing, or horseback riding as resources for molding the self. Through hard work, one may come to be seen as a hockey player, at least during certain seasons. But that "hockey player" identity is always contingent on one's performance, injuries, competing interests, and so on. So it is with gang membership.

The chapter will begin by examining how some young people in this study were involved in sporadically organized social groups (cliques, bisa crews, tagging crews). Such members engaged in certain distinctive activities on a sporadic basis: clique members prided themselves on partying and picking up girls; bisa crew members earned props based on their dancing and clothing styles; and taggers garnered local respect through their graffiti. Such groups often have rivals, but rarely do these rivalries result in serious violence. In fact, members of such groups often have predetermined ways of resolving disputes: clique members may compare their conquests and rapping skills, bisa crews may hold dancing contests, and tagging crews engage in battles to determine which crew can write more graffiti or place it in especially challenging spots, as discussed below. Such events may nonetheless give rise to further disputes.[3]

Other young people talked about being part of a gang, but the level of commitment could be quite variable. At one end of the continuum was Marco, who would go into a neighborhood claiming a gang to which he did not belong, knowing that it was antagonistic to that neighborhood, merely in hopes of starting a fight. Marco was not a "wannabe" or "hook"– a pejorative term, which none of my consultants would use to describe themselves, denoting a young person who wants to be and acts like a member of a gang that does not want to claim him as a member. Marco didn't seek to be in a gang; he merely used the rituals of gangs to accomplish a personal agenda. Other young people "kick it" with gang members, hanging around socially without participating in violence, while some claim to only "kick it" but are often implicated in violence. Some are members of a gang but no longer "bang" the way they used to, and some gangbang but have difficulty managing their ties to the gang. On the other end of the continuum are those who "bang to the fullest," who are understood by other young people as not easy to love and as typically impoverished. Finally, I will look at accounts from those who speak of ways of avoiding gang membership.

Sporadic Social Groups

Many inner-city neighborhoods lack programs and organizations that might spark the interests of young people. Even if some such programs are available, a young person may not be aware of them or may lack the transportation or money to pursue them. Hence, many teens meet their social and recreational needs through a variety of informal, sporadic social groups. Some studies term such groups "gangs,"[4] yet, as one CAA teacher noted, most are "just young kids assimilating with one another." Such groups are remarkable for their creative expressions of group affiliation and their efforts to publicize these expressions. They typically spend considerable effort in finding a dynamic, exciting name and advertising it on clothing and perhaps public places, such as walls and school desks. Such crews and cliques are as sporadic and variable as the whims of those who create them. Table 3 provides a sampling of some of the cliques and crews young people at CAA claimed at the time of the research, with the pseudonyms of the young people who told me about them. Depending on their energy and enthusiasm for developing *communitas*, such groups may develop their own distinctive styles of dress, language, handshakes, and interests.

Cliques and crews may be defensive responses to the more notorious, institutionalized gangs in the neighborhood, such as Bloods, Crips, or Eighteenth Street. "Claiming" NSP, STD, or BBC when one is "hit up" may offer a refuge and an alternative from more demanding, long-term involvements. Many studies of gangs, as well as residents of inner-city communities, recognize a clear distinction between such sporadic groups and hard-core gangs, which are larger, more lasting, more "corporate," and sustained in inmate prison cultures.[5] Members of sporadic groups also clearly distinguish themselves from hard-core gangs, while acknowledging that gangs often recruit from their groups or pressure their members to join. While hard-core gangs are often presented as especially violent, members of sporadic groups may engage in rivalries with similar groups, and the altercations that occur during such rivalries may involve limited physical violence and small weapons, but rarely weapons with deadly force.

"Cliques," typically composed primarily of African American young men, are usually focused around relationships with women, according to members, and their names, like Niggas Straight Pimpin' and Too Many Hos, often refer to sexual relations with women. The other two varieties of such sporadic social groups at CAA were composed primarily of Latinos. "Bisa crews," whose members are referred to as "cowbangers" (a variation of "cowboys"), are exclusively Latino, since they draw upon identities affiliated with Mexi-

TABLE 3. *A Partial List of Cliques and Crews*
at CAA at the Time of the Research

Acronym	Clique Name(s)
AV	Alliso Village (Latino, Charlie)
AVK	Alliso Village Kings (Latino, Charlie; no apparent relation to the Almighty Latin King and Queen Nation)
—	Chaos (African American, Lamont)
CCT	Culver City Thugs (African American, Lamont)
GFC	God Father Criminals (African American, Lamont)
GNP	Grand Niggas Pimpin' (African American, Brian)
NSP	Niggas Straight Pimping (school authorities claimed it stood for "Niggas Starting Problems") (African American, Lamont)
STD	Slippin' Through Darkness, Strictly The Dope (African American, Ken)
TMH	Too Many Hos (African American, Terry)

Acronym	Crew Names
BBC	Been Born Crazy (Latino, Ken) (When this crew died out, members split into DC, GC, and Triple C)
BMN	Banda Marquis Negro (bisa crew, Angel)
DC	Don't Care (Latino, Juan)
FA	Fuck Authority (Referred to as "Farm Animals," "Fucking Animals," or "Fucking Assholes" by GC) (Latino, Ken)
GC	Going Crazy (Latino, Ken)
MF	Madres with no Future (Latino, Frank)
NC	No Control (Latino, Mel)
PM	Proper Models (Latino, Johnnie)
PS	Proper Skills (Latino, Oscar)
SOK	Still Out Killing (Latino, Roger)
Triple C	Crazy Creations Crew (Latino, Juan)
WAI	Wrecking All Interstates (Latino, Juan)

can towns, music, dance, and clothing styles, and their members are more likely to be recent immigrants than taggers are. "Taggers" find their primary identity through their expression of identity in the adventure of inscribing their group and individual monograms in public space.

Some young men are involved in a clique that outsiders perceive as a gang but that members insist is not gang affiliated, as Lamont says of his clique:

"How would you respond if someone were to ask you where you're from?"

"I would respond that I'm from nowhere. When my buddies ask me, I would be like NSP, Niggers Straight Pimpin', but I never was from a gang. I don't gangbang now. Those were cliques back then, they weren't gangs. . . . Gangs are like Eight-Tre Gangster, Central, Bloods and Crips, stuff like that. I don't consider myself a gang person."

Note that Lamont did not "claim" when was hit up by a stranger, for then he would be asserting that he was "down for his hood" and would in effect be putting his sporadic group on a par with more established gangs. Lamont's group was confused with gangs, however, and he resented being kicked out of his prior school for what school administrators claimed was "starting a gang." He disassociated his group from such a stigma, stating instead that they were primarily friends who would look out for each other: "But it wasn't like being in a clique as in, like, being violent or anything. It was supposed to be like a clique where you can get girls. They said it was called Niggers Starting Problems, but it was Niggers Straight Pimpin'. Like pimpin', we were pimpin' females, in other words. Tell you the truth, all we were was a group of buddies that hung out with friends, and we had each other's back, that's it. They took it the wrong way."[6]

One of my consultants was involved in a bisa crew. While cliques focus on relationships with women and taggers focus on graffiti, cowbangers primarily focus on dancing Ranchero style (although many who dance this style do not consider themselves cowbangers). When they go out to dance, they typically dress like cowboys, with boots, cowboy hats, jeans, dress shirts, and sometimes sweaters. Sometimes young Latino men involved with other types of social groups or gangs will also don such attire to appear respectable, especially for an event such as a *quinceañera*.[7] Bisa crews also have rivals, according to Angel.

You dress nice, go dancing Ranchero style. It's a song. Back in the day, it used to tell the news, like if I die, they make a song about how I loved, how I lived. They used to tell the whole town, and sing songs about the person. . . . Kick it, go dancing.

We used to have enemies, other bisa crews. They didn't like us. Some of my enemies, four of them found me. I went at it with them right there. First time we went at it was after I got in. That afternoon, they said, "Let's go to Fedi High School, we're gonna go fuck Fedi." "Why, what?" I ask. I'm new to the crew. I don't know who the fuck are the enemies. "Let's go, so you can know," [they said]. "All right then." I just got to that point where I didn't care. I went inside first, to prove to them I was down for the thing. I went inside the school, and I was the first one who went up to this fool and said, "Where you from?" He was like, "Fedi Cartell." "Is that right? Fuck Fedi Cartell." We socked his ass. We jumped that fool.

Although Angel described his bisa crew as mostly interested in dancing, he did talk about learning who the enemies were and proving himself to his friends. Note that he said he was down not for his hood but for "the thing." He nonetheless described "banging on" an enemy, in a ganglike manner, though without weapons.

As dancing is to bisa crews, writing graffiti is to taggers. Tagging is a recreational activity growing out of middle school or sometimes elementary school friendship groups.[8] Taggers are usually Latinos who do not wish to join a gang and who enjoy the risks, excitement, and expressive possibilities of writing graffiti. A tagging crew begins with a group of friends who choose to give themselves a name. While gang names in this area typically denote streets (30s, 40s, Eighteenth Street, Central, etc.), tagging crews' names are expressive, proclaiming a strong opinion (i.e., "Fuck Authority") or a state of mind ("Goin' Crazy"). They refer to themselves by their acronyms (here, FA and GC), rarely the full name, and they delight in creating new referents for the acronyms (see table 3), as well as negative referents for the acronyms of enemies (such as "Farm Animals" for FA).

A tagging crew's raison d'être is to tag. Tagging is done through "missions," usually conducted between 9:00 and 11:00 p.m. A tagger may "go bombing" (tagging) solo or in a group. Each tagger typically has a slow tag and a fast tag, used depending on the situation. Slow tags are done "to look nice," while fast tags are done merely to let it be known that a wall has been tagged. Slow tags may be done by artists who are in effect designing graffiti murals. They often ask permission to tag a wall, and they may work on it for days. If their work is "nice" they may achieve some renown, and their work will be respected— meaning it will not be covered by other taggers—at least for a while.[9] Taggers take a great deal of pride in their slow tags and practice them for hours in blank artists' journals. They pass these books among themselves, and the artwork there is often quite impressive, full of multicolored surreal patterns and variations. Fast tags, on the other hand, must involve at least three elements: the tagger's nickname (usually three or four letters, like Wrec, Fuel, or Dove), the tagger's number (usually three digits long), and the acronym of the tagger's crew. These are also practiced in sketchbooks, and these typically energetic, adventurous young people take pride in their invented name, number, and style. If the tag is part of a battle (discussed below), then an extra symbol representing the battle will be displayed. Juan, a sixteen-year-old Latino, explained a difference between those who practice slow tags and those who practice fast ones: "The tagger that doesn't want to destroy stuff just goes to a wall and writes on it. They want it to look beautiful. And a tagger that wants to destroy stuff, he goes, crosses out people, makes it look nasty, and then puts his stuff on it."

Taggers pride themselves on "can control": being able to achieve a smooth coat of paint with a minimum of drips. Taggers often have idiosyncratic and stylized ways of holding their cans. They may push the button with their middle finger, index finger, or thumb. They also must find a way to carry the can as they run between tagging sites so that the "little ball" inside will not bounce too much. One consultant found that the back of his pants under his waistband was the best place to manage this.

Taggers take solace in such skills in order to manage the considerable and obvious risks. Of course, tagging is illegal, and especially with the rise of "broken windows" policing, emphasizing the façade of public order over all else, taggers break numerous public ordinances, including trespassing, defacement of public property, and violation of curfew.[10] While both fast and slow taggers take pride in the mere act of tagging, these are far from the only skills involved. Management skills are necessary to attract and organize members, maintain a group, and strategically plan "bombing runs." Skills in shoplifting are important, as many taggers steal their materials.[11] The possibilities for self-expression and action are potentially infinite, expanding far beyond the basic act of tagging.

Some might say that taggers are simply thrill seekers, but such an explanation is far from sufficient, since tagging involves many nuanced skills. One of the most exciting aspects of tagging involves imagining the expressive possibilities, but nothing compares to the thrill of running the streets under cover of darkness, dealing with whatever may come, whether enemies, angry property owners, or the police, and showing others the tag at a later date, a mnemonic for the good times that were had.[12]

Leaders of crews will monitor walls to ensure that younger members are "putting in work." If not, the leader may assign them a mission. If the younger member does not perform the mission adequately, he may be disciplined (punched) by the leader. The more work put in, the more prestige a tagger has in his crew. Work that is especially dangerous, such as tagging freeway signs or the outside of the girders of bridges over freeways (referred to as "heavens"), is especially valued.

A tagging crew must have enemies. Enemies are created through "beefs." In exploring "beefs," we begin to see the highly structured and ritualized nature of some inner-city conflict, as well as the indigenous ways to resolve it. A beef can be created in a number of ways. The most common way is for one crew to "cross out" another crew's tags. Leaders will often explain, "We gotta go down [i.e., fight] with them because they crossed us out." Another way is through disrespect or fights that may erupt between members of rival crews. Once two crews "have a beef," members must fight their rivals on sight. This is why taggers may "hit up" strangers by demanding, "What you write." If the stranger claims a rival crew, the two must "go at it," usually only with fists. Typically, however, rivals are not strangers—they often know each other from school and live near to each other—otherwise they would not be interested in tagging the same walls.

After a beef has endured for a fair amount of time, leaders may decide to "squash the beef." To do so, the crews must "battle." Rival crews become quite excited about a battle, as it channels action into a highly structured ritual, combining the thrill and chance of a gamble with the rules and formality of a sport.

As in many forms of action, leaders must decide on the stakes before a battle begins. Usually, they will choose a certain number of "krylons" (small cans of spray paint), acrylics (fat ink markers), and perhaps drugs (typically a set quantity of marijuana), as the bounty for the loser to provide to the winner. The extent of the stakes depends on the pride and prestige of the two crews battling. The winner of a battle is the crew that has tagged more often within a prespecified area for a prespecified length of time. If tags occur outside the immediate vicinity, such as in another city or even country, they are documented with photographs. Winners of battles are determined by judges, experienced taggers who will drive through the area and also consider the photographs laid out on a table. If one crew has more photos, their victory is perceived as self-evident.

At times, taggers struggle to enlist the support of their friends in their exploits. Below, Roger, a sixteen-year-old Latino known locally as Fuel, worked especially hard to muster the enthusiasm of his friends to fight a rival tagging crew, FA:

> Roger excitedly told me they were probably going to be in a fight after school. He told me that first he had fought with one of the rival taggers, and then he and his enemy had both gotten one person to back them up, but now they are going to meet them deep. "We're gonna take pictures!" he

said, pulling out two plastic film canisters from the pockets of his pants. As Roger's friends came out of class, he approached them to enlist them in his plan, bouncing among them with the film canisters. "I don't know," some said, hesitant, but Roger persisted, hovering, badgering.

Roger presented the prospect of taking pictures of the fight as too much for his friends to resist. Still, they did resist him, both by moving subtly away from him and by offering excuses, like "I've got to work," or "I wanna be with my girlfriend." Depending on whom I talked to and when, Roger and various combinations of friends were "members" of GC (Goin' Crazy), BBC (Been Born Crazy), Triple C (Crazy Creations Crew), DC (Don't Care), or SOK (Still Out Killin'). Clearly, Roger and his friends delighted in finding new names for themselves, new meanings for old acronyms, and new acronyms for their "enemies." Who was in the gang at any time or place was never certain; the only certainty was that the name of their "crew" contained a "C" (SOK was an old crew of Roger's that had disbanded). I marveled at what such creative energy could accomplish if schools knew how to channel it.[13]

Sometimes such tactics to enlist the support of friends took on the character more of a threat than of an enthusiastic enlistment. In one taped interview excerpt, Roger presented Ken, a sixteen-year-old African American, with a forced-choice question and indicated that the preferred response was a practical obligation ("some stuff to do"): "You gonna be right there, homie, or no? You got some stuff to do. You gonna stay with us too? Right there on the corner? It's gonna be you, me, Frank, Case's gonna come to school. Doggie I don't think is gonna come, fool. Damn!"

Despite such efforts at coercion, members of tagging crews did not face substantial difficulties in avoiding violent confrontations. To Roger's description, laced with bravado, of engaging in a drive-by shooting, Ken responded: "I haven't done none of that yet, and I *won't*. I'm down to fight, I ain't down to be like, I'm just gonna kill you, shoot you. I'll be like, 'Come on, we gonna fight right now. Come on, come on.' If I get my ass whipped, I get my ass whipped." Below, Juan provided the excuse he would offer in his tagging crews when his friends wanted him to engage in violence with which he was uncomfortable: "Every time that the EKs used to be like, 'We gonna go rumble such and such crew,' I used to be like, 'Nah, I can't go, I gotta go with my dad to here,' because I know that they're gonna have weapons. So I just used to avoid it. I used to be like, 'Hey, I gotta go with my dad to such and such place.' And they just be like, 'Oh, all right then.' They used to come and pick me up at my house, and I always used to tell 'em, 'Oh, I gotta go somewhere.'"

Teachers at CAA were aware of the existence of sporadic social groups and were dismissive. As Mr. Dolan stated, "Where I used to work, they had gangs that popped up every day. They had Tiny Toons, the Baby Ballers. There's a gang here called the Parking Lot Pimps. You can't have respect for all that stuff; it's too much. They just come up with a name all of a sudden and poof, they wanna tag it everywhere and say 'Hey, this is our gang.' They're here today, gone tomorrow."

Students at CAA with experience in more hard-core gangs were often dismissive of taggers' antics:

> As Roger ran among his friends trying to enlist their support, Johnnie and Alek overlooked the scene from the ramp to a classroom, leaning against the handrail.
>
> "What do these little punks think they're doin'?" Johnnie wondered aloud.
>
> "Who is GC anyway?" Alek asked rhetorically, and they laughed.
>
> "Some of these fools just started taggin' two years ago," Johnnie said, dumbfounded. "Now we got all the little guys gangin' up, tryin' to be somebody. Shit."
>
> They shook their heads.

Members of more hard-core gangs at CAA asked the taggers to avoid fighting at school, lest they attract too much attention from the police.

Varieties of Gang Involvement

Invoking the relevance of a gang is a strategic, situated event for young people in the ecology around CAA. Below, I will explore the variety of ways in which such young people refer to their involvement with gangs, along a rough continuum from lesser to greater degrees. As we will see, there are many ways to be involved with gangs. Diego Vigil posits four such varieties: regular, peripheral, temporary, and situational.[14] In the analysis that follows I present seven, but such varieties are in no way exhaustive or mutually exclusive. There are potentially as many ways of being a gang member as there are gang members. One young person could embody every variety at different times, or represent himself as embodying different varieties with different people. Marco's choice–claiming, in rival territory, a gang that isn't his just to provide himself with opportunities to fight–is especially idiosyncratic. These accounts, like any accounts, should not be considered in terms of a correspondence to "truth."[15] Rather, they should be understood as situated, strategic, and contingent.

Claiming a Gang One Doesn't Belong to in Order to Create "Action"

Marco told how he sometimes claimed membership in a gang in order to antagonize members of a rival gang, start a fight, and create action. Yet Marco was in no way affiliated with the gang he claimed: "Sometimes I be missing fighting, and just be going to different neighborhoods and just saying that I'm from Eighteen [Marco was ostensibly a member of Vernon Locos] just so I'll be getting in a fight, picking a fight." In our interview four years later, Marco reflected on how "crazy" he had been to assume a false gang identity:

> "You told me before that you used to go into a neighborhood and claim a gang just so you could get into a fight with somebody."
>
> "That was crazy. I used to go to neighborhoods to go fuck around with them fools 'cause I woulda had nothing to do! That's *exposing yourself.* Know what I mean?"

Being a "Wannabe" or "Hook"

Many gang studies, like Daniel Monti's, have defined *wannabe* as someone who hangs around with gang members and wants to be part of a gang but has not been formally accepted.[16] But Monti's definition of this term differs from the one used by my consultants. In Monti's analysis it carries more positive connotations, indicating young people like Jaime or Carlos (discussed below), who "kick it" with the gang ("experiment," in Monti's terms) but are not "from" there (have not "made a full commitment").[17] For my consultants, however, *wannabe* had a highly pejorative connotation and was used to describe those who acted as if they were from a gang even though they were not accepted by the gang. Thus they were actually the reverse of young men like Jaime and Carlos, for while the former "kicked it" with the gang but did not formally "claim" it, a wannabe claimed a gang he did not "kick it" with. The term *wannabe* was considered derogatory and was used to refer only to others, never to oneself. As Donald, a fourteen-year-old African American, stated, "He tries, he says he's a gangbanger, but he ain't. He say, 'I'm from Watts and like.' He'll just say, 'I like the gangbangin' better.' But he ain't. He don't gangbang, he just claimin'." This is the classic depiction of a "wannabe," someone who is "just claimin'." Oliver, a fourteen-year-old Latino, reiterated Donald's definition, making clear its derogatory significations:

"Do some people say they're in a gang but they're not really?"
"Yeah, there's a lot of people like that, the wannabes. They'll say they're from a gang and they're not from there."
"How come they do that?"
"'Cause they're stupid."

Another term for a wannabe is a *hook*. Doogan spoke of it in our interview as a deeply insulting term to which he had to respond with physical violence: "He came up to me, he was like, 'I heard you was from some pussy-ass gang called blah blah blah blah blah.' I looked at him, and I was like, 'What?' He called me a 'hook.' 'Hook' meaning you ain't really a gangster, you a fake. So that made me upset. So I reacted like any other person would've reacted [by fighting]."

One young man at CAA, Joey, was explicitly and disdainfully referred to as a wannabe in three separate interviews. Although Joey did not wish to be interviewed, it was surely not a term he would use to refer to himself. Antoine, an eighteen-year-old African American, spoke about Joey during his interview with me:

"I always see him around school. He just tryin' too hard to fit in, and it's not workin'. It's like he make everybody laugh at him and stuff, 'cause he tryin' too hard to like be cool with everybody and fit in. It seem like he the type where he don't know which crowd he wanna hang around with. And he think he hard, but he's not hard. It's like he's playing a role that he ain't."
"How does he do that?"
"He's saying, 'Cuz,' 'Central this' and 'Central that.' I heard he wasn't even from Central. And he claimin' it, like he's from it, so he can get hurt like that, like real bad, by them gang dudes, man. He has friends who's in it, but he's not from it, so he shouldn't be claiming it. He's a wannabe."

Juan, a sixteen-year-old Latino, similarly stated about Joey: "A lot of people don't like him, because he just be buggin'. People don't like him really because he's like a wannabe Central. He's always claiming Central and this and that."

With wide, serious eyes, Antoine told me that being a wannabe like Joey "can be really dangerous!" This was exemplified for me one day in Ms. Mates's class when one young man pointed at Joey and declared, staring at him hard, "If you was to get shot, they wouldn't have any idea who done it, so many people wanna get you." The class fell into a deep silence.

Eventually Joey was transferred to another school.[18] When I asked staff about this, they revealed that they too had no love lost for Joey.

Mr. Dolan, Mr. Merritt, and Bill were standing around in the yard talking about a local basketball team. I mentioned that I heard Joey had been transferred.

"For instigating a fight," Merritt said.

"He had it coming from someone," Mr. Dolan said.

"I always told him to stand in the back of the line," Bill said. Then, grinning, he added, "and to keep looking behind himself." The group laughed.

"Kicking It" with Gang Members without Being a Member

Jaime did not fully consider himself as a gang member; rather, he embodied the locally recognized niche of "kicking it" with the gang. His friends were in the gang, and he hung around with them regularly. When the "big homies" wanted to jump Jaime into the gang, Jaime accepted, but he redefined the incident as a fight, saying, "They just wanted to throw down with me."[19]

"If they're gang members, and I'm with them and I ain't from nowhere, they go see the other big homies, and like they gonna wanna jump me, 'cause I'm with them, even though I don't want to."

"Did they try to do that?"

"Yeah! Hell yeah, they try to do that. Actually they did it once, and I was like, 'Fuck it, you and him.' And it was three of 'em that jumped me for like sixty seconds. But like I'm telling you, they didn't take me down. They didn't really harm me, so I didn't really sweat it. Like fuck them still, they just wanted to throw down with me. That's what they wanted. They such punks, they wanna get three of 'em with me. Fuck it, go at it."

"Yeah. So they jumped you. After that, did they think you were in the gang?"

"They used to say that, but I never claimed it or nothing."

"Hm."

Carlos, like Jaime, "kicked it" with gang members but disavowed actual membership:

"I still hang around with them, but I never get into Eighteenth Street now. I hang around but I'm never from that gang."

"Yeah. So how did you first get into Eighteenth Street?"

"I'm not from that gang."

"You're not?"

"I kick it. My brother's in it, and the homeboys go to my house, we kick it. We go to parties and that."

"So when people ask you where you're from, what do you say?"

"I kick it with the Eighteenth Street."

"You kick it with them?"

"Yeah."

"Yeah. . . . So if you say you kick it with them, that's not the same as saying that you're from Eighteenth Street."

"Yeah, yeah, but still basically if they don't get along with Eighteenth Street, you still gotta go down [fight] with them."

"Uh huh. Yeah. So what does that mean? Do you do things for Eighteenth Street?"

"Nah. We don't do a thing. Like if you kick it, like if you wanna get in, you gotta kick it first."

"Uh huh."

"But like I got brothers, I don't gotta get in; I don't really gotta get in."

While Carlos seemed to be ambivalent about his gang involvement, this was only because I, as the interviewer, was not aware of the niche into which he fit himself in the local gang ecology. My question "How did you first get into Eighteenth Street?" betrayed this ignorance, of which he quickly disabused me. He then defined "kick it" for me as the specific niche that he embodied: "We go to parties and that." Kicking it allowed him to reap the social benefits of associating with gang members without having to "pay the price" by participating in violence. Still, he stated that when Eighteenth Street's rivals would ask him, "Where you from," he would say he kicked it with Eighteenth Street and then might have to fight ("go down with them"). Apparently his brothers in the gang didn't expect any deeper involvement from him and protected him from that.

According to one of the administrators at the school, this practice was common. As Mr. Merritt stated, "They'll affiliate with a gang and wear the clothes just to try to be safe, because that's what controls their neighborhood, but many won't actually participate in any violence. Kids sometimes get hassled by the cops on their way to or from school, but the more experienced cops are better and know what's going on."[20]

Still in a Gang but No Longer Gangbanging

A number of young men claimed to be involved in a gang but said they did not need to "prove themselves" by becoming involved in dangerous activities. Chris, for example, stated: "I don't really bang like I used to. But everybody around here is from Central. So everybody around here know I'm from Central, so I ain't gotta prove myself to nobody."

While Chris may not have had to prove himself, at times in class he faced criticism, from peers not affiliated with gangs, for continuing to claim. His status with his gang-affiliated peers was also subject to challenge, as in the following incident.

> Chris mentioned that the Vice Lords were in Mississippi. "Vice Lords are in Chicago," Louie corrected. "But they in Mississippi too," Chris protested. Tim came to his defense and said that Chris was right but that the Mississippi Vice Lords weren't as violent as those in Chicago. Someone mentioned they were an old-time gang. Chris said they were a real gang who used their fists instead of guns.

Each of these claims of knowledge was status imbued and subject to affirmation or denial by the others.[21] Chris, who had been criticized and mocked a number of times already in this exchange, made a claim to knowledge by stating that the Vice Lords were in Mississippi. He was quickly corrected by another student who claimed the Vice Lords were in Chicago, as any gang researcher would know. Chris's claims were substantiated by Tim, however, whose size and reputation provided a solid check on validity.

Chris attributed his diminishing involvement with the gang to the strong influence of his mother. As he stated, "When I stopped goin' to school, that's when she [his mother] started puttin' like a tight squeeze on me." This process of gradually withdrawing from a gang without being formally "jumped out" is quite common. Below, Joe, an eighteen-year-old Latino, spoke of how this might occur.

> "Did you get jumped out?"
> "No, I never got jumped out. But um, as you get older and the homies get older, they understand that you have priorities. Like if you have a kid, shit, they understand, you can't fuck around anymore. Let's leave the drugs, fighting, and all that to the younger generation."

"Kicking It" with a Gang but Still Caught Up in Gang Violence

At this point on the continuum, young men might preface their comments to me with "I'm not gonna lie," since it was evident to my consultants that I, as an outsider, could see their involvements as culpable. As Tom said, "I'm not gonna lie, when I was younger, I was influenced by people to join a gang. And I did." In the following protracted tale, abridged here, Tom spoke of how a former rival had held him accountable for things he had done in the past. Although Tom now kept his involvement with the gang to a minimum, his prior level of involvement necessitated that he be answerable for his past actions:

So we were getting some fast food. It was me, my cousin, and two of my friends. They were getting something to eat over there and I saw this girl walk by. I went outside and I was talking to her. A guy drove by in a white car. I can't remember him exactly, but he said he remembered me. I did something to him that wasn't right or whatever. Like first, when they passed by, he was yelling out the window, like, "Hey, I know you from somewhere." And then they hit the light and they turned around. He got out the car and he was like, "Yeah, I remember you, you did such and such." I'm like, "Well." I didn't remember this guy, to tell you the truth. He had his reasons. I'm like, "I don't know what you're talking about." He was like, "I know you. You were from such and such. Whoop whoop di whoop." I'm like, "Man." He's like, "You denying it?" I was like, "I ain't denying nothing. I don't know what you talking about, though. You talking about something way in the past." He was like, "Whatever, man," and we just got into it. He hit me right here under the eye. We started fighting, and then his friends hopped out. We was at the corner for like a cool five or ten minutes. So then my cousins came to the corner because they realized I was gone a little bit too long. It was like a big thing right there on the corner. I didn't get arrested, though, because I told them it was just self-defense. Stuff like that doesn't need to happen. I admit, I probably did do something to him a long time ago. I'm not saying what I did was right, or what he did was right, but what I did to him was back then. All I'm trying to say is, if I wasn't into what I was into back then, that wouldn't have even happened to me. I feel it's stupid, man.

At this point Tom's friends, who were still part of the gang with whom he "kicked it," sought further revenge. Tom then described the rather painstaking steps he took to avoid playing a role in this and to step out of his gang's cycle of escalating violence.

> My cousins were like telling me that we need to go shoot them up, because it's a rival gang or whatever. [But to me] it's not that important. Nobody died. Nobody except me and my cousins and my homeboys got hurt. I got a little scratch under my eye, and that was about it. It was just the principle of it. I had to go through a lot, because they were saying, "You're acting like a little punk right now. You ain't doing what you supposed to be doing." It's just like I feel that I'm older now. When we were younger, it was cool, because we didn't have to worry about going to jail or nothing like that. But now you got to worry about going to county jail, you gotta worry about going to state penitentiary. You gotta worry about keeping your life. It's hard enough for people to survive on this earth without getting shot at, just by trying to get a job and take care of themselves, then try to get a job, take care of yourself, and worry about getting shot too?

Here Tom described an intragang struggle over his affiliation with the gang. While he wanted to lessen his involvement, fellow gang members tried to promote his participation through insults, no doubt because his size and courage made him an asset when confronting a rival. Tom's account also struck at the logic of why most young people tend to age out of gangs. The first reason is the threat of punishment as an adult. The second reason is the increased responsibility one faces as an adult and the fear that getting shot will interfere with one's ability to find a job and take care of oneself. Often the gang literature fails to mention this clear recognition by locals, whether they are gang members, ex-members, or nonmembers, of the tragic *stupidity* of gangs' rituals of violent retaliation.[22]

Knowing how demeaned a young man like Tom can feel to be called "a little punk," I picked up on this topic, and he described a fascinating intragang conflict resolution strategy: the friendly fade.

> "Like, how did you respond, right there."
>
> "When they called me a punk? We had it out. . . . I took it personally, but it was only for the fact that he disrespected me. As far as me being worried about anybody else calling me a punk, or anybody else wanting to fight me, I don't have to worry 'bout that, because I have respect. They know I'm not really a punk. I told 'em they always gonna be my friends, they always gonna be my cats in my heart. I ain't always gonna be with them, 'cause I'm

my own person now. . . . So when he called me a punk, we had our words. We was yelling back and forth. They were like—I didn't wanna fight him, but it was like, 'You all just need to take a *friendly fade*. Y'all hate to fight, and you want to be friends, but just get the animosity out, basically.'"

"Take a friendly what?"

"Fade."

"Fade?"

"When they say, 'Take a fade,' that means fight. Basically, at first I didn't wanna do it, but he kinda got me upset, so we did. We fought in the street. It was like, five minutes, a cool five minutes. After that, we was all friends again. That's just how we do it. If we have any anger or animosity toward each other, that's what we do. We go in somebody's backyard. Or we'll go right there in the middle of the street to forget about it . . . We did that, we fought, and my cousin was like, 'Fuck that. They did this to me. I don't know about you, but I'm gonna do what I feel I wanna do.' I was like, 'Do what you gonna do. As long as you don't throw me in there I ain't got no problems with it.'"

Like pseudopsychologists, other gang members recognized this as an opportunity to effect a ritual that would allow Tom and his antagonist to displace their rage. They were thereby able to use violence to avoid violence. Although Tom made no effort to actually dissuade his gang from its violent agenda, he had at least managed to excise himself from participating, thereby gradually disaffiliating himself from what he saw as an aspect of the gang that was especially dysfunctional for him at this time in his life. Such stories were not uncommon: a number of other consultants told similar tales of their dilemmas and difficulties in lessening their gang involvement.

Gangbanging but Having Difficulty Managing It

Some young men become strongly involved in gangs but then experience difficulties and conflicts with other gang members. One young man, Kelly, an eighteen-year-old African American, always seemed attentive to the emotions of others, cheering up students who felt down and enlivening interactions with his friends. Once he told me of the dishes his grandmother made for large family gatherings, including collard greens, rice and beans, and sweet potato pie. Unfortunately, Kelly was experiencing a number of personal difficulties that arose out of his involvement with Central. Mr. Ross, a teacher in whom Kelly would confide, expressed to me some of his concerns.

Mr. Ross told me that Kelly had said he wanted to go to college, and Mr. Ross had been incredulous. "You think your homies are gonna let you go to college?" He said that Kelly hadn't been to school since he'd been beaten up with golf clubs.

"With golf clubs?" I asked, shocked.

Mr. Ross shook his head with dismay. "He was gettin' too serious about school, so they had to cure him of that."

While I'm uncertain if Mr. Ross knew exactly why Kelly had been beaten up, it was common knowledge that he was having difficulties abiding by the strictures of gang membership. As sometimes happened, Kelly refused to be interviewed.

Another young man, Shawn, saw himself as a member of a Crip gang but had difficulty managing this status since he had to live with this sister in a Blood neighborhood. After he found a Crip from another, compatible set, in bed with his girlfriend, Shawn's rival began spreading rumors that Shawn was becoming a Blood. Subsequently, Shawn had difficulty getting backup from his gang members to retaliate against this rival. Thus, while Shawn was still with the Crips, his ties to his set were becoming strained, as we will further explore in chapter 7.

Banging to the Fullest

At CAA, hard-core gang members made little effort to conceal themselves and were well known as gang members by school staff and students. As I sat next to Billy in Ms. Camp's class, he pulled out a green knit glove. I told him the motto of his gang. He smiled back, and we gradually came to know each other over the course of the following months. As he told me in our interview, "Like for me, I ain't even gonna lie to you. I'm kinda like in the middle of this gang stuff."

So much ink has been spilled on the dysfunctional dynamics of gangs, their violence and ruthlessness, that the association of hard-core gang members with crime and violence constitutes "what everybody knows."[23] Like all myths, this one has some basis of truth, as the prior chapter makes evident. But overlooked is a whole other set of significations around the term *gang member* for those who actually know gang members and interact with them on a daily basis. I was taken aback in hearing their accounts, which constituted a subaltern discourse far more nuanced and complex than the hegemonic discourse on gang members as violent thugs.[24]

Gang members often showed themselves as caring, warm people. For instance, as I was speaking one day with Ben, a young man who thoroughly disdained gangs, about our efforts to find him a new transmission, Tim, a leader in Central, overheard and offered, "What, a transmission?" Ben told him how his transmission had died on him, and Tim shook his head sympathetically, offering some suggestions in a kind and reassuring manner.[25] I knew from interviewing both that neither was in touch with his biological father and that both had tenuous family circumstances—perhaps they knew they had more in common than superficialities revealed.

Furthermore, young men with histories from different, even antagonistic gangs could come together in a common cause. For instance, when a new Latino student at CAA was going to be jumped by five or six young men from the Eighteenth Street gang because he wouldn't say where he was from, Shawn from Crips LAF, Marco from Vernon Locos, and Joe from Florencia Trece backed him up and stood up to the Eighteenth Streeters at CAA, so they backed down and left the new student alone.

Many hard-core members of Central whom I talked to were from poor families, had histories of extreme trauma, and had been marginalized in multiple ways.[26] At no time did they act more like gang members than when they were "hitting up." But while "hitting up" may create drama and action, much of the everyday life of a "gangbanger" is suffused with the ordinary boredom of poverty. Consider how Ernesto, an eighteen-year-old Latino who lived with gangs throughout his neighborhood, answered my question about gang recruitment efforts:

"And then once you're older than thirteen or fourteen, and you're still not in a gang, do they stop trying to recruit you? Do they lay off?"

"Yeah, they stop. But they be asking you for money, like, 'Whassup fool? You got money I could borrow?' 'Cause sometimes they used to stay over at friends' houses, stay there like for five or six days sometimes. They didn't have no money to eat. So they used to come up to me. I used to lend 'em like two or three dollars. So I used to tell 'em, 'Why you don't come into my house? Wanna eat something?' I just treat 'em right there in my house. It was cool, man, it was cool."

Such association of gang members with homelessness was common in this neighborhood.[27]

While the condition of poverty is often mentioned in studies of gangs in the context of entrepreneurial efforts to overcome it, many "gang members" are simply desperately poor.[28] As Earl told me, "We ain't goin' to clubs and all that kinda stuff. We gangbang, all you do is kick it at the spot with the homies and that's it. Sometimes y'all might go someplace, but most of y'all be broke. Most of the niggas is broke and they don't have nothin'. Maybe like two of 'em got a car." Or consider Doogan's statement about young men he had come to know in his African American gang: "It's not always easy caring for everybody who's in the gang. Most people that I know had more bad luck than anybody. They had it rough, really rough. Some of them have no fathers."

Many gang researchers have noted that the gang lifestyles involve a great deal of boredom.[29] Steve, a twenty-year-old Latino, commented about his gang life, "I kept doing the same things over and over." Shawn, a twenty-year-old Belizean, stated, "The only thing I could kill was time." Joe, an eighteen-year-old Latino, told me, while describing his frustration at not being able to move freely about the city, "You get tired of it." And Malcolm Klein notes, "It's a boring life; the only thing that is equally boring is being a researcher watching gang members."[30]

"So why do young men join a gang?" I asked Doogan.

"Because there's no hope," he responded. "There's no hope in the ghetto."

Aside from the boredom and alienation of school, the boredom and alienation of gangs themselves provide another powerful motivation to make something out of nothing.

"Yo, I'm Not into That": Avoiding Gang Membership

Diego Vigil and others such as Terry Williams and William Kornblum note that even in the roughest neighborhoods only about 10 percent of young people are gang members.[31] While this study contends that such numbers would be impossible to arrive at, since "gang membership" is situated and variable rather than an obdurate fact of identity, some young people took pains in our interviews to differentiate themselves from gang members. For many, the best evidence that they weren't gang members was plainly apparent in their everyday embodiment, "the way they carried themselves," as we saw in chapter 3. Ben, for example, a young man from a Central American country, had the sort of body–somewhat chubby, naturally curly hair–and carried it in such a way that he could not be mistaken as a gang member. Other consultants had to resort to more explicit tactics in avoiding gangs. Terry, a seventeen-year-old African American, had to be assertive in rebuffing gang members' recruitment attempts.

"I just didn't like it over there. I didn't like the people that was over there."

"How come?"

"There's a lot of gangbangers and stuff over there."

"What kind of things did they do?"

"Like always wanted you to like join their gang and kept askin' me, do I want to."

"What did you do?"

"I just keep goin' to school. I used to go to Sixty-fourth Elementary School."

"So did they do that every day?"

"It went on for about three weeks."

"Tell me about it."

"Like the third day I moved in I was on my way to school. Then they asked me, they're like, 'Where you from?' I was like, 'I don't gangbang.' They're like, 'You wanna be from—' somewhere, I forgot what was over there—the place where I went to school."

As the interview continued, Terry told me that he managed to avoid becoming involved in a gang by leaving whenever he noticed a nearby gang-related event.

"Do you know many guys that gangbang?"

"Yeah."

"Are you friends with them?"

"I know 'em, but I don't like hangin' with 'em."

"Uh huh. How come?"

"'Cause they like, I went out with one once, and then some car passed by and [they] said somethin', then he started throwin' up his gang signs, whatever, and I just turned around and left. So that's what made me stop hangin' with people that gangbang, period."

While Terry was able to avoid gang involvements by simply ignoring gang members or leaving their company, Eric, a nineteen-year-old Latino, had to resort to more strenuous resistance to avoid being jumped into a gang. According to him, his sister, a person he complained about throughout the interview (see chapter 7), enlisted her friends to forcibly drag him to a park in order to jump him into her gang:[32] "She'd force me, like pull me, and I'd be like, 'No, I don't wanna go.' Only one time one of her friends dragged me over there to the park, and they wanted to jump me in the gang, but I just ran." He laughed. "They got distracted with something else . . . and I just ran. They didn't see me. I went home and locked the door."

Some informants discussed actually being jumped into a gang but not adopting a gang identity. Frank, an eighteen-year-old Latino, told me about such an incident that occurred when he was nine years old. Exactly what happened is unclear, but Frank was sure that "two kids just started hitting on me" and that his interpretation of the event differed from the interpretation he attributed to them: whatever they might think, as far as he was concerned, he wasn't jumped into the gang; he never kicked it with the gang and had nothing to do with them.

> "Where I used to live I think they jumped me in a gang; I don't know, I'm not really sure."
> "They jumped you into one?"
> "Uh huh. But I really didn't ever claim it, so I consider myself not in a gang. I was just like nine years old or ten."
> "You were nine years old."
> "Yeah. They just took me to this friend's house and then two kids just started hitting on me. And I was little. I didn't know what to do so I just, they just hit me and they just, they just told me I was from the gang but I never claimed it, so I consider [myself] to be not from the gang."

Another consultant, Ernesto, an eighteen-year-old Latino, talked about another imaginative way of avoiding gangs. According to Ernesto, he followed his father's advice to make up a gang to claim in order not to be bothered by local gang members. Yet he could not simply choose an arbitrary name; the name had to make sense locally. "He told me, 'It's not worth it, if they tell you one day, Where you from, just tell 'em, make up a story that you used to be from a gang and you didn't like it.'"

> "Oh, so that's where you got that idea."
> "Yeah, I got that idea, told 'em, 'Man, I used to be from this gang named Harpee's.' I make up some gang they get along with. 'Cause if I say, 'I used to be from this gang, Eighteenth Street,' they don't get along with it, they gonna jump me. [They said,] 'Oh man, all right, it's cool, man, it's cool.'"

Such accounts of being jumped into a gang but not claiming it, inventing a gang, or claiming a gang in which one is not a member are overlooked by most gang studies, since they would be discounted as "noise." Gang questionnaires, in fact, insist through their formatting on young people's lack of any sense of creativity or nuance in their affiliations with gangs, using such Manichean wording as "Are you now or have you ever been a gang member?"[33] Yet such accounts as these are not rare; nor were they elicited through any special "digging."

Young people who were not affiliated with a gang tended to have other commitments and looked down on gangbanging as silly. For consultants in 1997, these involvements included riding dirt bikes and playing the trumpet (Leroi), playing video games with friends (Donald), playing basketball (Terry), working nearly full time at a local retailer (Ben), going to parties (Oliver), working in his father's grocery supply business (Pete), and fixing up his van (Eric). In 2000, such interests included working on the hydraulics and accessories of his car in a car club (Brad), producing music with a nonprofit organization that taught young people such skills (Everett), having fun with friends and girls (Antoine), kickboxing and modeling at a semiprofessional level (Jerome), playing basketball and other sports competitively (Buck), helping out around the house (Brian), and, for the young women, working in the fire department's Explorer's program (Esmeralda), performing gymnastics and dancing competitively (Tammy), and taking care of her baby (Maria).

Those students with less serious involvements, such as Donald, Oliver, and Brian, were young (Donald and Oliver were both fourteen, and Brian was sixteen) and seemed to me at risk of becoming involved with delinquent activities. Donald and Oliver, for example, fought each other at school, and Brian told me of frequently running away from home temporarily by aimlessly spending hours on the bus when his family members were fighting. All of the other respondents were eighteen or older and spent the majority of the interview excitedly discussing their personal interests. The following excerpt from Everett's interview shows some of the enthusiasm and energy of these consultants, in striking contrast to the rather morose tone of many gang members. Note that these involvements had been made possible only through the concerted work of caring adults.[34]

"What are some of your plans now?"

"At first, my plan was just to be like a rapper. But then, as I got more into it, I met a lotta people, I started learning a lotta stuff. Maybe I'll rap a couple years, and then when I'm rappin', I'll start like a nonprofit organization. I was in a nonprofit organization, that's how I learned how to do recording engineering, at a studio called World Impact. It has a $30 fee. After you pay that, you don't pay nothing else; you go to the studio as much as you want, as long as you want. They give you piano lessons, guitar lessons, audio."

"That's great."

"That got me into engineering. When you look at all the buttons, you might think, 'I don't wanna do it.' But like once you learn everything it's kinda simple. You just gotta have a good ear. So I thought about that, then I thought I might as well start a small record label for youth. Because I noticed a lotta young kids with talent out there. Not to make money off little kids, just to do like promotions, stuff like that. Just to start entertainers off young and then later on help them get big. Anything really to do with music. I'm not a good piano player, but I can play some chords. Guitar, I never really got the hang of it. I played the drums."

Throughout my fieldwork, I found that the more students were involved in hobbies and other activities, the less they were involved in gangs: they simply didn't have the time. The principal at CAA justified the school's clubs and activities in this way, stating that after a full day of school and work, students would be "too pooped to pop." Those who were lucky enough to have such opportunities provided to them by adults often saw gangbanging as ridiculous. At times, I practically insulted a consultant by asking about gang membership, as when Oliver recounted how members of a neighborhood gang had tried to get him to join.

"And then what'd they say?"

"'Oh, well, if you ever wanna get in, you can come over here to me, I'll court you in.'"

"Yeah. How come you don't wanna get into a gang?"

"Why, you want me to get into a gang or something?"

"No, I'm just wondering why you don't want to."

"Tsk! I don't *wanna* get in a gang."

"How come?"

"'Cause I just don't want to." He laughed.

"Why not?"

"I don't know. You tell me. You wanna get into a gang?"

"No." I laughed.

"Then," he scoffed, "why don't you wanna get into a gang?"

"Well, I don't live around here."

"So you can get into a gang where you live at. There's gangs all over the world."

"Yeah. I'm not into it."

"I'm not either. Yo, I'm not into that."

Who Claims You

Gangs mean something different to each young person involved with them, and teenagers vary in the ways they may invoke and adopt a gang identity. Cliques, bisa crews, and tagging crews afford their members the opportunity of practicing and demonstrating certain skills—with women, dancing, or "can control"–to earn the respect of peers. Such groups create symbols of in-group affiliation, including clothing, language, handshakes, insignia, and even enemies. As with high school football teams, ritualized battles with such enemies strengthen, at least sporadically, collegial ties.

More long-term gangs may seem more fixed, but as we saw in chapter 4, young people use them as a resource just as they use sporadic social groups. This chapter shows how young people continuously negotiate their relationship with the neighborhood gang and how gangs afford spaces for mitigated involvements. Many young people merely "kick it" with the gang, avoiding violent pursuits. Even for hard-core gang members, the gang is merely one aspect of their identity. Many of those seen as deeply involved in a gang are recognized in the community as deeply troubled, impoverished, and homeless. "Leaving" a gang is often a gradual, unmarked process, consisting of a drift to non-gang-oriented activities, often necessitated by jobs and child rearing. As we saw in chapter 3, the embodied transformation that this involves is a difficult and overlooked process in the life course of some inner-city teens. The use of videotape, analyzed by teens' reflexive commentary, would be an appropriate step for future research to unpack this elaborate and nuanced process. Meanwhile, those who stay out of gangs are often involved in other activities and see gangs as silly.

Out of the tool kit of culture, gangs are a vital tool for molding identity.[35] Yet it is not only young people in the neighborhood who play such games. In fact, for years our media and our laws have demonstrated that many who live outside the neighborhood are every bit as fascinated by "who's in" and "who's out" of the gang as those in the neighborhood. A vital difference, however, is that when one talks to residents in the neighborhood one finds different affiliations for different individuals, depending on whom one asks. One also finds, as Elijah Anderson did, that such categorizations are always interactionally situated, subject to demonstration or refutation on any particular occasion.[36] In fact, even in the one-sided accounts found in this chapter, one finds evidence for a loose, fluid, contestable gang identity: Lamont claimed to be in a clique while his teachers claimed it was a gang; Angel had to "prove he was down" for his bisa crew; Roger had a hard time compelling his tagging crew to rumble, even with his camera; Marco claimed a gang to which he did not belong; Joey, known as a wannabe, would never admit to being one; Jaime was jumped into a gang in which he was not a member; Carlos kicked it with gang members but wasn't really in the gang; Chris was in a gang but no longer gangbanged; Tom took a "friendly fade" rather than participate in his gang's violence; and those who were in the gang were typically described by their peers, not as monstrous, predatory, or thuggish, but as "poor," "hungry" and "hard to love." *It would seem then, that conceptualizing gang identity as fluid and contingent is the rule in the inner city, not the exception.*

What each of these statements of affiliation shows is the work of young people to create social groups that sustain their interests, inciting their passions and motivation. If we hope to reduce gangs, we need to work just as hard as gang members to find activities that sustain their involvements. Such programs are not "antigang programs," as if gangs were somehow the default and the program merely interceded. Rather, gangs arise in areas where young people have few other activities. In some neighborhoods, a child may simply be at a loss to find *something better to do.* The following chapter will focus on how those with something better to do must exercise skill in providing justifications and employing methods for avoiding violence.

6

Violence and Nonviolence

It takes a lot—it's a lot harder than they say. If you walk away
from a fight nowadays, it's almost like you're committing a sin.
So it's really hard to walk away from fights.

—Doogan

Where there is only a choice between cowardice and violence, I
would advise violence.

—Gandhi

The most powerful challenge another can make is to one's *face*—how
one sees oneself in relation to community.[1] Especially when one's identity is vulnerable, one may be prone to defend it physically. In an ecology where everyone's identity is vulnerable because of the marginalization and alienation discussed in prior chapters, not fighting to defend identity may pose a great risk, as
Doogan states above. Indeed, if we feel we have been "deprived of our rightful
place in the world," it is hard for most of us not to consider fighting to regain it.[2]

Specific skills that are useful for starting a fight involve knowing how to
antagonize another person, manipulating him or her emotionally through tangible, believable threats to face.[3] These perceived threats create the interactional
grounds for the highly charged dynamics of reciprocal humiliation and rage
that give rise to fights. Skills for avoiding fighting in such circumstances involve
substantial personal discipline in managing one's emotions and redefining the
situation so that it is possible to live with one's face/identity, even as the moment
may have transformed it. The risks are manifold and painfully obvious, threatening the most foundational basis on which one is granted a place in community. For both males and females this basis is respect, and for males such respect
is especially entangled with notions of masculinity.[4] Questions such as "What
are you?" and "What will you be?" always loom on the horizons of a violent
confrontation, providing the very stuff of human drama, fascinating to one and
all, impossible to turn away from. The alternatives are stark, ranging from being
tough, cool, and hard on one hand to being a wimp, pussy, or bitch on the other.
Such dynamics seemingly leave little room for middle ground.

We might gain a glimpse into the ever contingent, situated dynamics of a fight from my experience one morning at CAA, when a group of students crowded around the window behind the teacher's desk, and a stack of books was pushed from a shelf to the floor. Suddenly, the two fourteen-year-olds whom I had been tutoring, Oliver and Donald, physically confronted each other. Oliver is Latino and Donald African American.

I reached down and picked up the books. Oliver, who was in front of the row of books, politely pushed them together so I had room to replace the stack that had fallen. Suddenly, Oliver and Donald were chest to chest taunting each other, and I was between them. I was confused about what was happening.

"Come on," I said. "What's goin' on? I was just working with you guys last week. You guys are friends, let's not have this," and by lightly touching their chests I moved them apart.

But Donald was resolute and kept coming in, taunting. "Let's go, let's go. What, you afraid? Come on, motherfucker, right now!"

"Okay, right now," Oliver said.

"No no," I said. "Come on now."

Oliver looked in turn reluctant, disgusted, and courageous.

Donald, on the other hand, was raring to go. He backed up, chest puffed up, arms swinging menacingly, and danced in the space between the teacher's desk and the rows of students' desks. "Let's go, muthafucka. Right here, right now!"

Oliver, in what I saw as reluctance but a desire not to lose face, rose half-heartedly to the challenge. "Okay, let's go!"

"Come on, what are you doing, Donald?" I said. I felt as if I should give someone my glasses, for Donald was summoning a sort of energy that seemed bent on destruction and unstoppable. Suddenly Ms. West, the no-nonsense teacher's aide, simply put her arms around him from behind and carried him from the room.

"Now what the fuck was that all about?" the teacher said, pulling out a discipline slip.

"I was trying to put the books back on the shelf," Oliver said. "And I asked him to move so that I could get the books arranged."

"That is the stupidest reason for a fight I ever heard!" the teacher said, and put the slip away. "I'm not gonna write it up."

"Why you not gonna write it up?" someone asked.

"Because there's no point to it. Oliver didn't do anything."

"That's right, I didn't," he said, and went back to work at his seat.

The next day, I asked Donald, "What happened between you and Oliver yesterday?" He smiled, and quickly mumbled something about books falling and me picking them up, Oliver pushing him and calling him a nigger, and them going at it.

Although I was literally right in the middle of this situation, I did not hear what Donald reported, although I cannot confidently refute it either. I observed nine such instances, and none were ever any clearer than this. At CAA, as in schools, prisons, and other settings throughout the country, a "zero tolerance" policy is in place whereby anyone who engages in a fight, for whatever reason, is immediately subject to severe discipline; in schools this typically means suspension or expulsion.[5] Hence, the teacher in this instance was taking a risk in not writing up the "fight," an option he surely would not have taken if he had heard Donald's side of the story. But Donald had been taken from the room, his perspective wasn't included in the decision, and he chose not to pursue the matter further. While no punches were thrown and the two boys hardly touched each other, no one at the time, myself included, doubted that a fight had taken place.

What mattered more than the reasons for starting the fight, the steps we took to intervene, or the teacher's decision not to write up the event was the powerful challenge to face signaled in that moment of confrontation. Donald especially but also Oliver dramatically enlarged the space they were taking and issued loud challenges marked by harsh insults and strong glares. Through this highly charged, totally believable *performance*, both signaled that their most prized possession, their place in community, was at stake and that neither would or could back down.

There is a robust sociological literature on fights, but most studies analyze stories of fights rather than fights observed firsthand.[6] Thus the situated, emotional, embodied dynamics out of which fights are born are utterly lost, and what is left is a narrative analysis.[7] One highly influential study that bypasses such limitations is Elijah Anderson's work on what he calls "the code of the street."

According to Anderson, who provides an eloquent and detailed portrayal of the code of the street in his book with the same title, "The code is not new. It is as old as the world, going back to Roman times or the world of the shogun warriors or the early American Old South." Anderson states that such a code, also familiar from gangster movies and Westerns, is an organizing principle for violence in the inner city. Fights are central in Anderson's analysis, since the "real meaning of the many fights and altercations that 'hide' behind the ostensible, as a rule seemingly petty, precipitating causes" is that a child's cumulative interactions with face-threatening situations "ultimately determine every child's life chances." In fact, the message "If you mess with me, there will be a severe physical penalty—coming from me. . . . must be delivered loudly and clearly if a youth is to be left alone" and consequently "is essential for a child's well being—and perhaps even for his physical survival."[8] According to Anderson, inner-city residents recognize a clear distinction between "decent" folk, who abide by mainstream moral values, and those of the "street," who do not. Yet even the "decent" must be able to "code-switch" when dealing with those of the "street."[9]

Anderson's "code" is a convenient encapsulation of the dynamics of face and identity that arise in fights between young people. Indeed, one might well see both Donald and Oliver as following "the code," for Donald did not back down when he was apparently insulted by Oliver, nor did Oliver back down when he was faced by Donald. Yet Anderson overlooks another type of challenge, which, as Doogan states, may well be more difficult than following the code: nonviolence.[10] While the skills of manipulating another's emotions through antagonism are considerable, not much skill is involved in allowing one's emotions to be manipulated and simply following the dictates of "the code," although it is usually impossible to discern just who is the manipulator and who the manipulated. Responding to an insult with aggression is kids' stuff; learning how to walk away is the work of adults.

This chapter first explores accounts of confrontations in which young people follow the code. Then it probes young people's locally rational reasons and strategies for walking away from a threatening confrontation. Finally, it briefly explores how "street" young people often perform a "decent" identity but how the "decent," who have less experience and fewer social ties for appearing "street," as well as more to lose, typically refrain from performing the role of "street." As this exploration makes clear, the crude practices of retaliation pale in respect to the nuanced skills of walking away, and fortunately a "decent" performance of identity is available and achievable for all.

The Data Set and Definitions

In each interview I asked about fights experienced and fights walked away from throughout the person's life. I recorded a total of ninety-three stories of fights and forty-one accounts of "walking away." Respondents varied greatly in loquaciousness; some spoke for over a half hour about a single fight episode, while others limited their description to a few lines, despite my efforts to solicit as complete an account as possible. I also directly observed fifteen instances of fights, six of which I categorize as "play fights," since the participants were laughing and smiling at the time, even though these could become quite rough.[11] In one instance, two young men who were chasing and grappling with each other crashed through a locked gate on a six-foot-high chain-link fence, only to arise laughing and somewhat surprised. The gate was badly damaged.

The data set is limited to fights experienced; I omit all fights witnessed secondhand unless the protagonist became directly involved. I also omit fights involving gangs, drugs, or guns, for these features often overshadow the fights themselves, occurring within an ecological framework that deserves attention in its own right.[12] Hence, I limit what is to be considered a "fight" to an aggressive physical engagement, understood as a fight by my consultant, that does not involve gangs, drugs, or guns. "Walking away" is similarly dependent on the definitions of my consultants and does not include instances involving gangs, drugs, or guns.

Violent Retaliation

According to the accounts below, walking away from a fight creates an overwhelming oppressive burden, weighing one down with shame and humiliation. One simply *has to* fight, since not to fight is to be disrespected: verbally stripped of one's masculinity and stigmatized as a "punk," "pussy" or "bitch."[13] Consider, for instance, the following exchange I had with Oliver, the same young man who faced Donald above, who told me how he and his friends were occasionally harassed in middle school.

"They would go over to us and like try to punk us. You can't go let a punk say that, you feel like a little bitch. You know, getting punked this and that by another person, then the whole school thinks you're a little bitch."

"They think you're a little bitch?"

"Yeah," he laughed.

Such "punking" included both short- and long-term physical and/or verbal harassment. Oliver spoke of a powerful motivator to fight: "The whole school thinks you're a little bitch." In my sample, people were most commonly motivated to fight in response to continued, long-term harassment (twelve cases) or offensive words (nine cases).[14] In the following excerpt, Antoine, an eighteen-year-old African American, reiterated these elements of the code in his description of a fight.

"We all playin' basketball, right? So I'm just doggin' 'im, I'm usin' him all day. I'm makin' shots on him, scorin' on 'im. So he gettin' mad. He started trying to bang. I never knew he was a gangbanger. . . . He just kept going on it, picking at it."

"What did he do? What did he say?"

"He tried to lie and switch it up and say, 'Oh I've seen you in such and such hood.' I was like, 'You ain't seen me nowhere.' I tried to walk off. But sometimes you just have to fight, you know! Me, I didn't know what he had on him, a gun, a knife or nothing. So he just kept on trying to fight me. So I have to stick up for myself. 'If you wanna fight me, come on, man. I ain't fittin' to sit up here and let you punk me.' So he got up in my face and he swung on me. So I just slammed him on a car [chuckles]. I just started chokin' him out. All his friends were laughin' at him. And they told me, 'I see that you ain't a punk.' So they just wasn't gonna mess with me, period. I had to stick up for myself and I had to fight. But you know, I don't like fightin', period."

"Right."

"This was in front of a lot of people, so you can't just punk out here. If so, they'll be like, 'Oh, so I know he a punk now, so I can just punk him every time I see him.' So sometimes you gotta stick up for yourself. So I stuck up for myself and I told him, 'Come on then.'"

Antoine described a scenario common in seven separate fight tales, where a contest (such as a competition over gymnastic flips) or a game (usually basketball) led to a confrontation. According to Antoine, his adversary, humiliated by Antoine's basketball skills, concocted a gang rivalry as a justification to fight ("he started trying to bang"). Although Antoine didn't know if his rival had a weapon, he was highly conscious of the crowd watching the interaction and was determined not to be seen as a "punk." His story validated the code of the street, as did the onlookers, in whose eyes Antoine claimed to have earned respect ("They told me, 'I see that you ain't a punk'"). His rival, meanwhile, was humiliated by the audience's laughter.

Later in this interview, Antoine's good friend Charlie, also an eighteen-year-old African American, joined the interview, and agreed wholeheartedly with Antoine:

"If you let somebody disrespect you, you a punk, simple as that."

"Yeah," said Antoine.

"You ain't *supposed to* let nobody disrespect you," said Charlie.

Such is the moral authority of the code, prescribing the ways one is "supposed to" act. If one does not, the myth goes, one will be punked over and over again. For example, Jaime, a twenty-year-old Latino, told how walking away from fights led to greater violence than simply standing up and fighting.

"Have you ever walked away from a fight?" I asked.
"Well, it's hard to walk away from a fight here."
"Here at this school?"
"No. Here in this area, period. 'Cause if you turn around, they gonna come right back on you. They might even hate you, to tell you the truth."
"They hate you because you walk away?"
"I mean, 'cause, you already gonna have a scar there, they already gonna be talking shit about you. When you turn around, they might just get back on you, and that's that." He laughed. "You know, you might as well know what happens after that."

According to the code of the streets, if one does not stand up to an antagonist one will continue to be harassed indefinitely. As Oscar, a nineteen-year-old Latino, claimed, "I never walked away from a fight. Basically what I think, you walk away, they gonna call you a bitch for the rest of your life. You backed off. You scared. They keep bugging you. They still bring stuff up. Really, I never backed off a fight." He offered this on the basis of his firsthand observations of how walking away affected the identity of an adult who sometimes hung out with his group: "We got a friend, he kinda old, we still bringing that stuff up, then he be feeling bad, and he sometimes just go home."

Such episodes may also lead to intense, long-term self-recrimination. In his short story "On Violence," David Nicholson describes the humiliation he felt when, as a ten-year-old recent immigrant to Washington, D.C. from Jamaica, he refused to participate in a staged fight despite pressure from his peers. As he states, "I'd done nothing to Furman. He'd done nothing to me. And besides, one of us might get hurt." He notes, "It is a terrible thing to be condemned by others as a coward, but it is even worse to condemn yourself as one. For that reason," he adds, "I brood about that time in the alley more often than is probably healthy."[15] Such a tale exemplifies how a response to violence, in one small moment, may have long-term consequences for how one perceives, accounts for, and presents identity.

Walking Away

In the above instances, as in Anderson's analysis, invocations of "the code" are unproblematic: one's masculinity is forever compromised if one walks away from a fight. But the "code of the street" was reinforced by many of my consultants even as they provided evidence to the contrary. Such an unquestionable assumption is called an incorrigible proposition: it cannot be proved wrong since it is such a part of "common sense" that members continue to believe it even when faced with contradictory evidence.[16] Many young men with whom I talked had an intact reputation for masculinity even though they told of numerous instances in which they had "walked away." In each case, the unquestionable authority of the code was preserved through justifications for not following it. Still, such "exceptions" accumulated into a substantial number of tales (forty-one), both with and without bystanders. Below, I examine the skills involved in summoning good *reasons* for walking away and the nuanced *methods* of doing so.

Good Reasons to Avoid a Fight

In my interviews, I could count on every young man to tell me that anyone who walked away from a fight would be punked for life. I could also count on almost every young man to tell me about a time when he had walked away from a fight. He was able to walk away without losing respectability because of "good reasons." Many in this context would consider that fighting despite such good reasons would be stupid or shameful. For instance, sometimes the odds are not equal, as when the protagonist has backup (friends who will assist him), is much bigger and stronger, or is seen as a member of a gang. At other times the consequences of fighting are not worth the risk, as when one might lose a job, be expelled from school, or risk harm to family members. Another good reason is that the matter is not significant enough to fight over, such as a perceived foul during a basketball game. Finally, one would be seen as a punk for "hitting a girl."

Unequal Odds

One vital aspect of inner-city teens' accounts of fights is "backup."[17] Often seen as a motivation to join a gang, backup consists of friends who will provide assistance in case of a fight.[18] Having no such friends or seeing that others do have them is a "good reason" not to fight.[19]

Ernesto, a sixteen-year-old Latino, recounted an incident in which he had avoided a fight without humiliation because the antagonists were especially large and intimidating. Though he had told me about fighting a co-worker at the grocery store where he worked, and fighting in school, he was also adept at walking away from a challenge when necessary. Once, as he was riding his bike after school, two men approached him and demanded, "Hey, man, gimme your bike." Ernesto ducked into a liquor store, and, in his words,

> I was acting stupid like if I was looking at the candies and shit like that, and they came up and just took it from right there. The man that works in the store said, "Hey, they stole your bike!" I came outside and I saw 'em, they had my bike. I was like, "Man, fuck it." I wasn't gonna fuck with them 'cause they were big! [he laughs] They were kinda buff. They didn't have no shirts, man, and you could see they were buff, like they barely came out of camp [prison] or something. I thought, "Man, I ain't fucking with them. Fuck them. Take the fucking bike, man. Fuck the bike."

Having a personal item stolen is a clear way to be "punked" and led to fights in five accounts. Such episodes of "jacking," typically signaled by the mundane request "Give me ____," are intended to "construct a power asymmetry" and "make a fool of the victim."[20] Yet in this case Ernesto saved face, since it made sense locally for him to not confront multiple "buff" assailants, as his account makes clear. Also, he showed some street smarts by not handing over his bike when he was first asked for it but providing a cover for his victimization so that he would have as little interaction with the thieves as possible.

Other consultants also spoke of "backup" as a good reason for potential antagonists to avoid a fight. Terry, an eighteen-year-old African American, understood a young man's reasons to stop harassing him in these terms: "I started hangin' with my cousins. When he saw that I had people that go to this school, he started leavin' me alone."

A third form of unequal odds that provides a good reason to avoid a fight is intimidation by the other's gang connections. Ernesto's bike wasn't his only loss to local predators; he also told of losing the weight-lifting equipment he had placed outside the door of his house. In this case, his justification for not fighting was not the size of his antagonist but his apparent gang connections: "One time I had some weights. I had 'em outside the door of my apartment, and some fool got 'em. It was some gangster, so I said, 'Fuck it.' I saw him go get 'em. He got 'em and he put 'em in his car, and I was gonna go tell 'im something, but I left there. I didn't wanna get into no problems. Fuck it, man, he got it already. [If] I'm gonna go up there, talk shit to him, then he's gonna come back and try to do something."

Carlos, the eighteen-year-old Latino who "kicked it" with members of Eighteenth Street, mentioned each of the above justifications for not fighting in his story of a fight that never materialized. First, he mentioned the large size of his opponent, though he portrayed himself as undaunted by this. Then he described how the opponent realized that Carlos had gang backup and left the scene.

I was in Jackman [High School]. I was with a lot of girls in the [lunch] line. I thought it was a lady's folder, of one of my friends. I was gonna start writing "Eighteenth Street" and all that, when that fool was from Thirty-eighth. That fool was from Thirty-eighth, and that fool told me, "Whachu wanna do," and all that. He said he was gonna throw down with me. I told him, "What's up?" And then we went out. That fool was big and tall. He was like two years older. . . . I'm like, "Oh well." And then when one of my homeboys saw that he was gonna throw down with me, he was like, "Let's go down, let's go down, me and you." He [the antagonist] like started running.

"I Don't Wanna Burn Myself around There": Consequences of Fighting

Young males also spoke of not wanting to fight to avoid negative repercussions, such as losing a job, being kicked out of school, or bringing harm to family members.[21] Consider the following excerpt, in which Jaime, a twenty-year-old Latino, told of being accosted by a drunken gangster while he was taking out the trash at the printing company where he worked.

I was out in the alley putting trash in the bin, and this gangster walks up to me. I didn't even know him or nothing. He's like, "You got any money?" I'm like, "Nah, I ain't got no money." "Lemme check yo pockets," he says. I'm like, [high pitched] "What?" "Lemme check yo pocket." I go, "Man, I ain't got shit," and I just talked to him. I coulda straight out beat him up. I'm like, "Nah, I ain't got shit, man, it's cool." You know? Try to avoid him and shit. "Lemme check your pocket." I had money in one pocket and my pager, so I'm like, "Look, man, I ain't got shit." Put my hand in my pocket, took it out of my pocket, ain't have shit. In my other pocket I had my pager and my money. He was like, "Lemme see your other pocket." I'm like, "Nah, man, get away." He had a bottle. He was actually drunk. He had a beer bottle. I'm like, "Man," I was like, "Come on, man, it's cool." That's the way I was telling him. I was actually acting like a punk, but it was for the best for me, 'cause at my job I don't wanna lose, I don't wanna burn myself around there.

Jaime, a tough young man who had been kicked out of six high schools for fighting before entering CAA, told me elsewhere in his interview that he had very little respect for punks. Yet in this excerpt he admitted to being one, because "it was for the best for me." As his tale continued, he told how his quick movements had allowed him to get past his drunken assailant and inform the boss of trouble. From that point on, he made sure not to go to the trash bin unaccompanied and always carried a long metal rod that his manager told him he could "throw through the heart" of the assailant if he bothered him again.[22]

Anderson offered such accounts as instances of what a "decent" person must be prepared to face. According to Anderson's analysis, Jaime would be "code-switching" in this instance, using street smarts by showing the assailant only one of his pockets and then moving quickly to get back into the shop. Yet Jaime had also been kicked out of numerous high schools for fighting, had taken drugs, and "kicked it" with gang members, all characteristics that would certainly fall on the "street" side of the decent/street dichotomy.[23] Above, Jaime tells of acting "decent" in order to not lose his job, but later, with his boss's permission to arm himself in the alley, he relishes the potential opportunity to do great harm to his assailant. Thus Jaime shows, not how he is "decent " or "street," but how he skillfully and contingently performed "the code." Jaime may speak of himself as "punked" in this instance, but like Ernesto he had a good reason, as well as a vow not to let it happen again.

Another potential consequence of fighting was to be kicked out of school. Although the deterrent effect of disciplinary expulsions has been extensively criticized,[24] some students cited this factor as a good reason to avoid a fight. Donald, a fourteen-year-old African American, told me, "I try to avoid it. You hear people talk. People like be watchin', they be tryin' to have you fight. . . . I didn't wanna get suspended or nothin', or kicked out, miss school and everything else." Similarly, Brian, a sixteen-year-old African American, stated, "In junior high, people talking mess, trying to bag, I just walk away, because I know they gonna wanna fight. People call names like, 'Scared, chicken.' I don't even care. I never cared. They don't punk me. They know I ain't scared.

I don't need to be kicked out of school." And Buck, another sixteen-year-old African American, told me, "I was in junior high, and I had straight A's and everything I wanted. This boy tried to pick on me. I was like, 'Man, I don't gotta fight you.' He had bad grades; he didn't have nothin' goin' for him. I was like, 'I ain't about to fight you.' I had everything. I had all of it. I had good grades, science fairs."

In these excerpts, both Donald and Brian referred to the pervasiveness of the code, represented through taunts of others at school; as Donald stated, "You hear people talk," and according to Brian, "People call names." While Donald simply did not want to be suspended, Brian claimed, "I never cared," taking the rare moral stance that the code did not interest him. For Buck, a student labeled as "gifted," school was too precious of a resource for him to miss, and the actions of the young man who wanted to fight him were understandable by virtue of his bad grades. If more inner-city students could be inspired by such an outlook toward school, zero tolerance policies for fighting might have some teeth. At CAA, however, Buck lost this perspective; he was known for humiliating and infuriating a teacher at the school by stealing her teaching manual.

A third good reason to avoid the consequences of a fight has to do with family members. Charlie, an eighteen-year-old African American, mentioned this as his only possible reason.

"Do you ever remember a time when you walked away from a fight?" I asked.

"Once. The only reason I walked away from that fight was I had my little niece with me. It wasn't that the guy was older or anything like that, it was that I had my little niece with me, and she was kinda young. I didn't wanna like put her in that kinda environment."

Angel, an eighteen-year-old Latino, offered a similar justification, in light of threats of a fight wrought by a bisa crew rivalry.

Me, my lady, and her two sisters are at the movies in Huntington Park. Me and an enemy bumped heads with each other. He was like, "What's up?"
"Shh, homie."
He was like, "Fuck BMN."
"Wha?"
"Fuck BMN."
[clicks tongue] "Whatever, *esse*. I don't care. I ain't from there no more."

"What? You straight punk ass bastard."

"You know what, *esse,* you wanna get down with me? Because of the crew, I'm not getting down. But if you have a little personal problem with me, just let me know."

He wanted to get down because of the crew. I used to be from BMN. I used to put a lot of work into it. He was like, "Fuck BMN. Fuck this. Fuck that."

I said to my lady, "You know what? Let's go. Fuck that. Let's go to another movie theater." I just let him talk his shit. He got mad, because he was talking shit, I wasn't paying attention to his ass. Like my lady said, "They know you ain't no punk. They know if you want to, you can whoop his ass." I got down with him once at Eldridge. He's taller than me. "Let's go." We went to another theater. I wasn't gonna let this fool ruin our little night out. Even though I had paid already, I said, "Let's go."

After Angel distanced himself from his affiliation with BMN, his antagonist called him a "straight punk ass bastard," a likely response to "ranking out." Angel then reported changing the topic of the encounter from "gangs" to "a personal problem." When the antagonist continued, Angel turned to his lady to propose leaving, and she affirmed that this did not entail a loss of face to his antagonist, since Angel had "already whooped his ass" previously. Although Angel's evening out was compromised, his skillful interactional moves left his honor intact.

"Nothin' but a Game"

Many young males, in the inner city or not, become quite passionate when playing basketball. The excitement of the sport, the physical labor required to play it, the fouls that may be committed intentionally or inadvertently, and the fact that one's reputation is often on the line as one plays this very public game often lead to fights. Since the game is known to be so combustible, many young males can foresee trouble and know when to back off and how to deescalate confrontations. As Chris, an eighteen-year-old Cherokee/African American, explained,

My homeboy T-Faith, we was playin' basketball, and he jump up, went to grab my shirt. I grab his shirt, I said, "Look, you can raise up off me, homie, I'm tellin' ya 'cause I didn't hit you." He was like, "Well, cuz, who hit me?" The guy don't know. "I didn't hit you." I'm like, "Man, it wadn't nothin' but a game. It's a contact sport, you gonna hit regardless." So then he went to push me an' I pushed him back. I was like, "You know what, cuz? Ain't worth me gettin' kicked out of school no more and goin' to jail for you." I jus' turned around and walked away. Later on that day cuz come up, he was like, "Man, you know what? You got some big-ass balls to do dat."

In this case, Chris was playing basketball with a friend who suddenly grabbed his shirt, thinking Chris had hit him. Chris responded that in a contact sport like basketball "you gonna hit regardless," but T-Faith didn't accept this reasoning and pushed him. Chris, not one to be punked, pushed back but continued his explanation, invoking the prospect of being kicked out of school or going to jail. Through extensive reasoning and toleration of some physical abuse, Chris left the scene of the threat with his honor intact.

If a crowd is present at a basketball game, such a resolution of conflict may be more difficult to arrive at, as was apparent in Antoine's story above. Terry, facing similar pressures, ended up fighting despite his better judgment.

> "We was playin' basketball and then he elbowed me in the lip, so I bled. And then I just walked off, and then everybody was like, 'Why you let him do that?' I was like, 'We just playin',' so that's why. I was like, 'Forget it, fool, we was jus' playin'.' Then everybody was like pressurin' me, and I was like, 'Forget it.' so I just—"
> "So everyone else was pressuring you?"
> "Yeah, so I just told him to go outside; we started fighting."

In this case, Terry was unsuccessful in using the same justification for not abiding by the code that Chris was able to use: "We just playin'." Also, while Chris practically boasted of reducing the tensions that could lead to a fight, Terry resorted to fighting as an acknowledged surrender to pressures from the crowd. Here we see that for Terry, "the issue . . . was not one of being seen positively, but one of folding oneself into the cultural fabric of the group so as not to be subject to its devastating gaze."[25] Unable to muster his wits to avoid violence, he had to depend instead on his physical prowess for maintaining face.

A Young, Weak, or Female Antagonist

One final reason for young men to avoid fights is fear of being perceived as a punk if they do engage in violence, an explanation possible if their antagonist is considerably younger, weaker, or female. Below, Buck, an eighteen-year-old African American, spoke of being hit by his girlfriend at school.

"When I was at high school one time, my homegirl was mad at me for some reason. She slapped me in front of everybody. I wanted to just hit her back, but I was like, 'Cool down.' Everybody was saying, 'He's a punk if he hits her back.' I was like, 'I know.' Then she hit me again, so I was like—"

"In front of everybody?"

"In front of everybody! So I just sat there. I just walked away. I was like, 'All right.' I go to my class. And then the next period came, I couldn't take it, so I told my counselor, 'Could you send me home? I'll come back tomorrow. I just need to cool down.' She sent me home."

In this case as above, a crowd was present and the narrator spoke of being attacked by the assailant. Yet while Chris was concerned he could be kicked out of school, Buck spoke only of the gender of his assailant. Although one may face increased pressure not to punk out in front of a crowd,[26] here the crowd exerted a moral force in the opposing direction. While Anderson does not mention such instances, they are clearly cases of upholding the code of the street without violence.[27]

Good Ways to Avoid a Fight

More interesting than a young man's good reasons for avoiding a fight are his ingenious *ways* of doing so. In the face of an antagonist, perhaps with a hungry crowd eager for action, how might one back away, and what are the consequences? While this is the topic of innumerable conflict resolution programs, young men in the inner city have their own techniques that are not based on special training. As this discussion moves from rationalizations to descriptions of methods, the relevance of the code diminishes. In fact, many of the young men spoke unapologetically and even proudly of practices that directly contradicted edicts of "the code," such as "Don't back down," and "Don't snitch."[28] In this section, I examine skills for avoiding a violent confrontation, including backing down; conversational techniques such as complimenting ("sweet-talking") the antagonist or switching the topic; making the fight into a contest; telling an authority figure ("snitching"); and avoiding the antagonist.

I observed at least one situation in which a student explicitly backed down. Ken and Gerald are both African American; Ken was sixteen and Gerald eighteen. Ken was a member of one of the school's tagging crews, and Gerald had established a solid reputation on the basketball court. The following scene occurred under the basketball net.

When Ken made fun of a young man on the court, Gerald said, "What are you saying this to him for? It's like you think you can play basketball just because you made a shot yesterday. You can't rap or play ball, so you best shut up." Ken shook his head; Johnnie put a hand up as if asking Gerald to back off, and another player said, "Ahh," as if asking Gerald to go easier. There was a momentary, powerful pause, as we knew Ken could take a swing at Gerald, but instead he laughed slightly and said, "I know I can't play ball, I never said I could. Come on."

Such incidents happen on a daily basis, but they seem to pass without notice and are never mentioned in interviews. The moment began with Gerald coming to the defense of another young man by ridiculing Ken's basketball and rapping skills and telling him, "You best shut up." What's fascinating about this incident is the collaborative work that other young men do to defuse Gerald's attack.[29] Johnnie diminished the tension by raising his open palm toward Gerald, and another young man vocalized a calming "Ahhh." Ken then provided an "offering," acknowledging the truth of Gerald's attack, and thereby cooled down a potentially violent confrontation.[30] One week later, Ken brought Gerald a silver scorpion that Gerald had lost on the basketball court, showing how a young man may "get cool" with another in a way that does not involve fighting.[31]

A second short-term way to avoid a fight is through conversational techniques. Many young men enjoy telling of their quick use of wit to avoid trouble. Below, Jerome, an eighteen-year-old, told how he had avoided a scrap in the days when he was younger and smaller by complimenting the fine taste of his older antagonist.

There was one time when I was a freshman, there was a guy whose girlfriend was in class. I knew they were going together. One of his friends said that I was flirting with her. I was like, "Okay, I flirt with his girl, whatever." He [the boyfriend] comes up to me, he's this big football player, a big senior. He's like, "You lookin' at my girl?" I was like, "You know what, you have a very cute girl. You have a *fine* girl. Let me tell you that. I'm not flirting with her, I'm not trying to disrespect you in any way at all. I'm just complimenting you. Your girlfriend's hot." He was like, "Oh, thanks, man." And it was fine. I woulda gotten my ass beaten then [*laughs*]. This dude was big.

A third immediate way to respond to a potential threat is by turning the fight into a contest. While seven consultants told tales in which an athletic game became the scene of a fight, Chris told of an instance in which he and his friends managed to create a contest out of a threat during a football game: "We was playing, and there was about like five or six big ole heavy-set Mexican dudes walk up, they was like, 'That's my ball, that's my ball.' We was like, 'Nah, man, that ain't your ball.' My friend was like, 'We can play football for the ball. Whoever win, game is twenty-one, and if we win, it's our ball, if we lose, it's your ball.' I was like, 'Okay, cool.'"

A fourth way of pacifying a threatening situation was through "snitching." For example, Bix, a sixteen-year-old Latino, told how he had resolved a menacing situation by simply telling school administrators about bullies who had stolen his money in a high school locker room.

> I thought I was gonna get punked because I saw all kind of big kids. They stand at the end of the hallway when you walk out of the locker room. You gotta go through that to get outside of the locker room. They'll pocket check you right there. Take your money or take whatever they want. I thought they'd beat me up. I just got punked in the locker room. I got jacked for my money. Oh man, I felt like a little punk. Some other kids got jacked too. That was only one day. I snitched on 'em and they got caught, so they went to jail. Two out of the four of 'em went, and they didn't do that anymore.

According to Anderson, "The code of the street is actually a cultural adaptation to a profound lack of faith in the police and the judicial system, and in others who would champion one's personal security."[32] Yet in this and in five other instances, young men spoke of resorting to persons of authority in school, whether security guards, teachers, or administrators, and receiving a definite respite from their worries, with no ill effect on their reputation. In interviews, young men also spoke of many times when their families had called the police to report violence that had been done to them. Such individuals often faced threats from those who claimed that "snitches get stiches."[33] Those who take the risk to snitch are exercising an important weapon of the weak, and they must take care that they report to the right people and that the charges stick, lest they face retaliation.[34]

Nonviolence, Violence, and Identity

As contingent, situated, and fluid as invocations of gender, race, ethnicity, nationality, or gang membership have been shown to be, it is also important to consider the barriers to certain invocations, which give these identities the sense of being fixed. For those limited by a lack of experience, tradition, social ties, or bodily practice in carrying off a believable performance of a gender, race, ethnicity, nationality, or gang membership, such alternatives are pointless to consider.[35] Elijah Anderson discusses predispositions to perform a nonviolent or violent identity (decent or street) as fluid and performative, at least for those who are, in some fixed sense, "decent." For Anderson, the decent must "code-switch," enacting a street persona when confronted in order to be safe.[36] This section explores how the findings of the present study are the reverse of Anderson's, in that it was much easier for "street" young people to adopt a "decent" persona than vice versa.[37] In other words, I found that the "decent" face more practical, moral, strategic, and embodied limitations to being "street" than the street face to being "decent." To illustrate this, I will present brief portraits of two individuals: Darin and Ben.

Darin

In the area of this study, many hard-core gangbangers at CAA were also respected as decent kids. One large, intimidating local gang leader, Tim, who spoke of "hitting up" strangers with a high-caliber rifle in chapter 4, later became a sales representative for a large telecommunications firm, as discussed in chapter 2. Another notorious gang leader, Darin, whom the principal of CAA acknowledged as a leader of Central, and who brought significant problems to her school, later became an assistant to a local city councilperson. Ms. Reynolds, CAA's principal, spoke of how Darin's efforts to assert control over the school had prompted many local residents to substitute the name of the local gang for the name of the school, changing it from "Choices Alternative Academy" to "Central Alternative Academy." "I mean, the school was known as Central High School," she told me. "They had taken ownership of it to that extent. Darin didn't beat 'em up personally, but he intimidated them with his friends. And all they had to do was stand on the corner, and these kids had to pass by them. Just think of the fear many of them had, with these Centrals across the street, on the corner, and they have to go to the bus stop. What are they gonna do to me? Are they gonna rob me? So they were intimidated."

Mr. Griffin, the director of a local community center, was familiar with Darin's exploits:

"Darin and his Central pals used to beat up all the kids from outside the neighborhood. I asked him, 'Are you fighting?' 'With everything I can get my hands on,' he said. 'With chains, baseball bats, anything we can get our hands on.'"

Mr. Griffin told me how Darin knew CAA was supposed to be a neighborhood school, so he "and his Central pals" were beating up anyone who wasn't from the hood.

"Sounds like he needed some negotiating skills," I said.

"Oh, he had those." He told me this was a kid who was on the board of the community center and went to meetings, and he wanted the school to benefit this neighborhood, so that's how he did it.

Such narratives epitomized Darin as a street thug: an acknowledged leader of a local gang who intimidated students in order to "control" the school. Darin was also a prominent—perhaps *the* prominent–neighborhood drug dealer. Yet his character was not so easily summarized. Consider Mr. Griffin's account of Darin in a separate interview. Here he provided a portrait that does not fit easily into the "decent"/"street" dichotomy, for he knew Darin personally.

"Like I said, we've had some young folks who were very near and dear to us. For example, with one of the young men, Darin, it was a thing where he was close to the point—not close—here is a guy who's been arrested several times for selling drugs. Somebody comes to me and says, 'You know what? You are the only person this guy will listen to.' It was a guy who was working with one of the gang programs, and I didn't even know Darin. He would hang out at my organization and come to these planning meetings and stuff. I knew the young people respected him a *lot*. He was only fifteen, but there was like all this awesome respect he had, even though looking at him, you wouldn't see that. He didn't come in like, 'I'm gonna kick your butt' kind of guy. This guy writes poetry. So for the next year or two, I got to know him a lot better. Obviously, at one point he had to live at my house because there was some stuff going on in his neighborhood where he couldn't go home. His mother asked if I would shelter him, and I did. So he hung out a lot with my family, both here and up north, and then he got a good job, working for the councilperson. She wanted to promote him to the downtown office. And right on the verge of that promotion, on the verge of him applying to college—the condition of him going to college would be that it would not be in this city. I didn't care if I had to take a second mortgage out, or a third."

"You were going to help—"

"Oh yes. Whatever it took. And actually, my family was. People in the family said, 'Whatever it takes.' These are particularly older people in the family. But he wasn't gonna do that. So he gets arrested for selling drugs. Little write-up in the paper about the councilperson's deputy arrested. It was on page 2 of the local news section. They found out he was a clerk later on. And even though they offered him his job back once the trial was over, he was so embarrassed by that. He told me, 'I just feel like I let you down. But it was like, that's what I had to do. I kind of had to let you down, because I wasn't ready to do that. That's not me.' It was a lot of other self-deprecating stuff, kind of like whether or not he *deserved* those kinds of things. So it was hard, and he went back to what he knew."

In the course of my fieldwork, consultants often switched between "street" and "decent" modes in our interactions. As we will see in the methodological appendix, in my first few days at CAA, Chris and Kelly tested me, playing a vicious version of the "dozens" (or "bagging") and repeatedly referred to each other as "nigga" in my presence, compelling Mr. Merritt to apologize to me.[38] Yet later, when Chris and I were alone in the room and he rapped for me, he was the model of decency, never criticizing me for my awkward references to popular culture. Kelly, whom many spoke of as "having difficulty managing" his membership in Central (see chapter 5), often expressed compassion for others, noticing, "You look like you feel down today. Whassup?" Other students, like Richard, who initially presented me with a quite "decent" front, officially introducing himself to me as a gallant, self-mocking sort of an ambassador, later told me of numerous "street" experiences, such as gangbanging, using drugs, and getting around drug tests, and was in prison when I returned to CAA. In sum, no matter how "street" a young person might be, "decent" was always part of his or her repertoire of identities. But was "street" part of the repertoire of identities of the "decent"?

Ben

Ben, an eighteen-year-old Belizean, spoke of many ways of avoiding violence. For instance, he told me that looking like a gang member led to more problems than not looking like one. In fact, when I interviewed him he wore the vest of the local retailer where he proudly worked. Below, he told me how he avoided conflict on the street.

I asked, "So you don't feel like not being in a gang constricts your lifestyle at all or limits you in any way?"

"Nope. . . . If you look like you from one, then they're gonna mess with you. Like me, *[he chuckled]* the way I look, nah. Nobody's ever asked me, 'Where you from' or asked me, 'What you lookin' at?' 'Why you starin' at me like that?' or somethin.'"

"Yeah."

"I'm just, you know, I just walk down the street and mind my own business."

According to Ben, it is looking and acting like a gang member ("if you look like you from one") that may lead to difficulties, not the converse.[39] Ben had lived his entire life in the area around CAA, one of the most violent areas of the country at the time, and had never become involved in a fight. When I asked him how that was possible, he responded, "I just leave everybody alone. I just don't, you know. I try to get people to not look at me as a bad person, somebody against them. When that happens, something's going to happen to you, watch."

Such an account runs contrary to "the code." As Anderson states, "Young people who project decency are generally not given much respect on the streets. Decency or a 'nice' attitude is often taken as a sign of weakness, at times inviting others to 'roll on' or 'try' the person."[40] Yet Ben, decent by anyone's standards, beloved by his mother and the teachers at CAA, walked the streets at will and had never been jumped. Despite working full time, Ben often experienced car problems and walked miles through some of the most notorious neighborhoods without incident. I saw how Ben walked, and while he did not exude an air of toughness, he did not seem especially "nice" either. Rather, he appeared as a serious young man going about his business, staying out of the business of others.

To Steve, a twenty-year-old Latino member of the Eighteenth Street gang, young men such as Ben lived in a prison: "Oh, but see, Ben lives that life. We call it the prison life, prison at home. You can't live in your home if you scared to come out. I mean, I'd rather go to jail, stay in your cell all day. It's like most fools here, everybody's stubborn, 'Fuck this.' Everybody's stubborn and most of 'em ambitious. You gonna wanna go out. You see people, you gonna go out and talk to 'em. That's nature, that's logic. That's why most everybody's in it [gangs]."

Yet despite Steve's comment, the contrary actually seemed to be the case: often those in gangs, or those who fight, became prisoners in their own homes. Consider the following statement from Emily, whose large tattoos on her arms and reputation testified to her bygone status as a hard-core gangbanger.

> "We went to check into another school. You know, we had to go to school. We checked in, and the first day we checked in, you know how they test you first, to see what classes to give you. Me and my sister were barely walking in to get tested, and here comes all these fools from Florence [Florencia]. And they're like, 'You fuckin' bitches, get out of our school.' They started chasin' us. So they chased us all the way home and we lost 'em. Since that day, like they would be downstairs and we lived upstairs. They would be downstairs, sitting there, like waiting for us to come out."

"Mm hm. Wow," I said.

She sighed. "We couldn't. We couldn't do nothing. We were like prisoners in our own home. Until finally my dad said, 'Oh well, go stay with your aunt in Hawthorne until we move,' until him and my little sister move."

Steve's logic dictated that he had to avoid certain neighborhoods, Emily and her family had to move because of rival gangs, and both Steve and Emily were terrified of the police. Ben had no such fears. In the divergent ways in which Steve and Ben understood Ben's behavior, we can see how "the code" can bias one's interpretations.

> "Are there places you don't go when you walk to school?" I asked Ben.
>
> "I don't go?"
>
> "Or you avoid? Places that are scary?"
>
> "No." He laughed.
>
> "No?"
>
> "Nah, I just walk straight, that's it. I just walk straight down the block."
>
> "Uh huh."
>
> "I walk everywhere, man."

When I visited Ben's house, a group of men on the porch across the street watched me hard and let me know they were watching. It was a haunting experience but one that Ben knew how to manage by sticking to his own business and not putting on airs of trying to be tough. When I interviewed Ben four years later, little had changed. He still worked at the same job and visited CAA on occasion. While he still walked wherever he wished, he was loath to take the bus, since, as he stated, "Too many things happen on the bus!" Prior to our interview, Ben had been held up twice at the same bus stop, by the same man:

"He just walked up to me, sat next to me, said, 'What would you say if I told you I had a gun, and told you to put your stuff out on the bench there.' I took my wallet out, stuck it on the bench. He opened it, took out the $6, and just left. Second time, he just walked up. I just couldn't believe it. The bus just passed right by, and he came out right from behind the bus. I'm like, 'Jeeze, is this guy following me or what?' Like eight or nine o'clock at night. As soon as I saw him I just pulled it out. I don't *[pause]* like *[pause]* to hassle stuff. I just pulled it out. 'There's nothing in there, so.' 'Well, I'll take your bus pass.' He took my bus pass."

"But he left you with the rest of your wallet," I said.

"He left me with my wallet, of course, yeah. And I had some bus tokens in there which he didn't find. The bus pass was up in a week anyway so I didn't care. As long as nothing happened to me."

Such events are certainly not unique to the inner city. One could only imagine what might have happened if Ben had tried to appear "tough."[41]

Reportoires of Identities

In sum, none of the young people I met suggested that following the code of the street led to greater safety. In fact, young people often informed me that *not* following the code led to safety. As Ben stated, "If you look like you're from one [gang], then they're going to mess with you." Moreover, "looking like he was from one" was simply not among Ben's repertoire of identities. On the other hand, as the interviews in this volume testify, I never met a gang member who wasn't "decent." As Tom, a former hard-core gang member, stated regarding violence and gangbanging, "It's not cool at all, man. It's pointless. You could get this easy money, you could get these nice big cars, and you could get these females or whatever. But it ain't worth it, though. The consequences—you always gotta look over your shoulder. You can't trust nobody. Everybody's saying they're your friends, but it ain't like that. If that's what you wanna call somebody who don't gangbang, a square, it's better to be a square." And from watching how Tim, one of the most notorious gang members at CAA, acted with Ben on numerous occasions (see chapter 5), I had no doubt that Tim respected Ben, who would never be mistaken for a gang member.

In the inner city being "punked" is a matter of definition. If one has good reasons to avoid a fight in terms of local expectations, one can walk away from a threatening situation without losing face. Rather than being punked, being able to use such good reasons is simply smart. Such smarts are displayed not only in good reasons for avoiding a fight but in the ingenious ways of doing so. These tactics are much more common than many depictions of inner-city life might lead us to believe, and many young people take pride in their ability to draw on them as a resource in their everyday lives. Hence, despite claims that the facework of inner-city young men is routinely and manifestly violent, this analysis shows that the efforts of such young people to avoid violence are often quite subtle, creative, and mature.

One's face is always on the line in a violent confrontation. Few can be the "baddest" or the "hardest," and many would not want to be; such a stance cannot be sustained indefinitely. The 99.9 percent of us who aren't, in the inner city or elsewhere, must find ways to respond other than through brute force when we have been slighted, insulted, or challenged. Invoking good reasons and strategies to avoid the use of force without losing face constitutes an important set of survival skills. Our leaders would do well to study the ways young men in the inner city deploy these skills, with a view toward defusing dangerous world conflicts.

Even the most hard-core gang leaders were adept at behaving decently, but many young people accustomed to acting decently all their lives were far from adept at behaving in a "street" manner, and carefully avoided such a presentation of self lest it lead to unnecessary danger. The following chapter will probe further into the skills of avoiding violence, especially in terms of how they involve refined practices of emotion management.

7

Avoiding Retaliation

In the moment of righteous indignation experienced when one has been wronged, one faces a crucial moment of choice, to decide to accept and live with the wrong that has been done (to "lump it") or to retaliate.[1] It is worthwhile to appreciate this gap between cause and effect, at least to recognize the myriad possible outcomes, as the consideration of how to respond after perceiving a wrong is far from academic.[2]

While a focus on individuals who abstain from retaliation may be rare in the criminological literature, scholars of law and society have found that the modal response to disputes is to "lump it," leaving a social situation with a dispute unresolved, even in inner-city areas, where, as Elijah Anderson has argued, "the culture of the street does not allow backing down." As Sally Engle Merry notes, on the basis of her classic ethnography of conflict management in an inner-city area, "Ultimately, the only resolution of disputes occurs through avoidance, the 'exit' of one or both disputants from the neighborhood."[3] Even studies supporting the "code of the street" thesis note that "reliance on street justice may deter would-be perpetrators from attacking because of fear of retribution."[4] Furthermore, "Violent retribution, and residents' fear of it, may serve as a form of social control—perhaps *preventing* some types of crime in the community."[5] As yet such conjectures are purely hypothetical, for few studies explore how young people in the inner city manage to "lump it" when faced with a perceived injury. Felstiner, Abel, and Sarat's observation that "social scientists have rarely studied the capacity of people to tolerate substantial distress and injustice" remains as pertinent today as thirty years ago.[6] Such a capacity is fundamentally based on one's ability to manage one's emotions in the midst of a dispute.

Emotions and Disputes

Aside from a few remarkable exceptions, criminologists have mostly overlooked the emotional dynamics of disputes.[7] In the literature on emotion management, on the other hand, much of the richest data focuses on how workers *intrapersonally* manage disputes.[8] Arlie Russell Hochschild developed the notion of emotion management to reveal how individuals attune themselves through "surface acting" and "deep acting" to the rules and ideologies of private and public life. Hochschild was especially concerned with the emotive dissonance and alienation wrought when emotional *labor* is compelled by an employer, and one must attune one's feelings, like it or not, to the demands of the workplace.[9] This chapter, on the other hand, focuses on how emotive dissonance may also result from the everyday phenomenon of emotion *work*, when young people must restrict their desire to retaliate because of structural constraints.[10] Such emotion work involves considerable skills to manage a dangerous situation.[11] Young people struggle to attune their actions and emotions to the demands of social structure by "lumping it," or in local terms "sucking it up," even as they express the fantastic desire to indulge in righteous retaliation.[12]

What constitutes an omission for criminologists certainly does not apply to studies of dispute resolution, which view the management of parties' emotional dynamics as central to mediation and negotiation.[13] A number of studies have focused specifically on how various socially entrusted troubleshooters manage the emotions of clients involved in disputes. Austin Sarat and William L. F. Felstiner show how divorce lawyers must manage the emotions of their clients in order to help them focus on resolving the case and moving on.[14] Others have shown how deputy U.S. marshals must manage the anger and grief of prisoners as they are taken into custody.[15] Yet, as with studies in the sociology of emotions more generally, the focus is disproportionately on the workers, in terms of how they must manage either their own emotions or the emotions of those with whom they are charged.[16]

Few studies have gone as far in examining the emotional dynamics of crime as Jack Katz's pioneering book *Seductions of Crime*. In his discussion of righteous slaughter, Katz invokes the sensation of "wetness" to exemplify the experience of humiliation, and such images as water boiling over, or of the cartoon character Yosemite Sam exploding in rage, to illustrate the felt dynamic by which "rage constructs and transforms humiliation so quickly and smoothly that talking and writing about the process can very easily become artificial and obfuscating."[17] Katz's more recent work analyzes road rage using the metaphor of dominoes, exploring the interactional moves of conflicts as both parties struggle to make the final avenging move and not be left with a "domino" they cannot play. At that point, drivers are left only with an "imaginative solution to conflict," a pent-up frustration that may be transferred to other individuals or inanimate objects.[18] One remarkable and frightening aspect of many of the following accounts was how readily each respondent had access to guns and considered using them to imaginatively redress his conflict. Other analysts of violent confrontations stress how violence often involves avoiding shame and protecting one's honor, yet for the most part they overlook the ambivalence experienced when retaliation might threaten social ties.[19]

It is commonly underappreciated that the code of the street is a discourse, albeit the most obvious, most accountable discourse in the area in which this study was conducted.[20] According to Anderson's code of the street, one must retaliate against insults to gain respect, which ensures safety. Such "insults" not only are affronts against one's person (such as a "bump" in a "staging area") but also may be affronts against one's family (most infamously, one's mother) or one's friends (commonly one's crew or gang). But if the insult is coming from a family member or a friend, or if one foresees that retaliation may harm family and friends, what then? Does one retaliate against that which, according to the code of the street, should be defended? Such a fundamentally ambivalent situation is not easily managed in a discourse as Manichean as the code of the street.[21] Yet young people find ways to live with such ambivalence, and as they do they come to terms with an identity that supersedes notions of "decent" or "street": adulthood.[22]

Avoiding Retaliation

In each of the five cases below, the consultant was speaking from within the midst of a struggle with a challenging dilemma and expressed an emotionally charged need to talk about it.[23] The narrator was beset by a burdensome grief and rage over what had occurred months before or was troubled by an ongoing, intractable situation that continued to haunt him. While other respondents also spoke of difficult situations in their lives, the following circumstances are notable for being fresh and still heavily laden with emotion.[24]

Since each story was still very much in play, none of the young men were certain whether they might retaliate. I was able to follow up with three of these men, Steve, Ben, and Shawn, four years after our initial interviews and get a glimpse into their acceptance of ambivalence. Four years later, Steve and Shawn seemed to consider their issues resolved, while Ben still wrestled with difficult circumstances. Of the two young men with whom I was unable to follow up, Ernesto had resolved to "lump it," while Eric had decided to move away but to retaliate if aggressions continued. Their ages ranged from sixteen to twenty at the time of the first interview. Steve, Eric, and Ernesto considered themselves Latino; Ben and Shawn were from Belize but were often perceived as African American.

Steve

Steve had lived his whole life just blocks from CAA and claimed that he had been involved with the Eighteenth Street gang for nearly that entire time, since he was six. Although he still "kicked it" with many gang members and wore slightly toned-down gang-style clothes, he claimed that he hadn't really banged since he was fifteen, when many of his homies had either died or gone to jail. He is a good student and a superlative artist, having won a number of prizes in local art shows. When I interviewed him on his twentieth birthday, he spoke of his gangbanging days.

"So what kind of things did you do when you messed around with gangs?"
"Well, typical thing is to go shooting, go robbing, selling dope, riding, jumping people, stabbing people. All that stuff, stuff you always did since you was little."
"Uh huh. How old were most of the guys in the gang?"
"I was the youngest one. Till today I think I was the youngest one in Eighteenth Street. Most are something like thirteen, twelve; I'm the youngest, I was only six. Now they consider me as an old one, as a veteran."

The issue eating at Steve during our interview was that his girlfriend of two years had aborted her baby because his longtime male friends had told her that the sister of one of them "liked" Steve. One of his hopes was to be a father and raise a family, and he was deeply hurt by this news: "I didn't think she was gonna tell me she had aborted it. I didn't see her for like two, three weeks. And when she came she gave me that news. I was like, 'Maaan.' She told me, 'Hey, your friend told me this and that about—.' I go, 'Oh man.' I said, 'Dang. Well.' See, I wanna shoot them but I can't, 'cause I know they mom. See, we all grew up together." As in many of these interviews, Steve clearly presented structural constraints early in his tale of non-retaliation, as a foreshadowing justification for not retaliating. In this case, having grown up with the young men whom Steve believed had brought his girlfriend to abort their baby, and knowing their mother, provided a locally justifiable "good reason" for not shooting them. As he continued, he struggled to express his emotive dissonance in a narrative full of pauses and doubts.

"So I don't know."
"Uh huh."

"They come here to this school."

"They do?"

"I can't staaand seeing them. Ooooo. I already told them, I better not see, y'all better not pull another thing, not even raise ya voice at me, Imo shoot you. I don't like it. That was that. That's what's getting me mad right now. I'm not even talkin' of goin' back. Who knows where I would've been right now."

"Yeah."

"So I don't know."

"Yeah. So you still feel like you could use a gun to solve a problem?"

"That's what, that's what I'm tryin' not to do," he laughed.

"Tryin' not to do." I laughed.

"That's what I'm really trying not to do. I even, I even took 'em outta my house."

"Took the guns outta your house?"

"I give 'em to my neighbor," he chuckled. "'Keep my guns for me.'"

"Uh huh."

"That's what I'm really trying, I'm trying to find out another way. I know it ain't gonna really do nothin' 'cause when I pass by they giggle. I don't know if they gigglin' toward me. But whatever. It's like I told them, I go, 'Oh, when I pass by I better not even hear you, 'cause I'm gonna snap at ya, and I don't give a fuck how many babies you all got or where you from, I'mo shoot you.' It's hard."

"It's hard."

"It's hard. Yeah."

"So how long have you felt that way toward them?"

"For like the last three months."

"The last three months. Wow."

"It got, that got to me, it got to me."

"So it's not like that feeling just goes away."

"Uh uh. It got, that gots me. It gots me real good."

While the code of the street states that inner-city residents must fight for respect, in his dilemma we see Steve trapped by lines of honor wherever he turns.[25] For his girlfriend to have a child was a great honor, but she aborted it, which was not only a dishonor but a disappointment. To add to this, he was dishonored by his friends' rumor-mongering, which he felt had led his girlfriend to abort the fetus.[26] He was also unsure why they were giggling when he passed, but if they were giggling at him it was a further dishonor. When he said he didn't care "where you from," he was referring to their common gang identity with Eighteenth Street (see chapter 4), a primary structural factor that inhibited him from retaliating, along with knowing their mothers. To avenge this loss of face he was tempted to use his guns against them, but he guarded against his rage by placing his own guns out of reach and avoiding looking at the friends who had caused his grief. With no commitment to deep acting and little desire to surface act, Steve at least controlled his environment in case he might lose control of himself.[27]

Four years later, when Steve happened to visit CAA to talk to Mr. Martin, the school plant manager, we revisited this dilemma.

> I asked Steve how his grandmother was doing, and for a moment he stopped his squinty-eyed smile and told me she was doing fine. I told him that there was one thing I wanted to ask him about, and we dropped our heads and turned away from the group around Mr. Martin to create a bit of private space. I asked him about the guys who'd told his girlfriend that thing where she'd aborted her baby. "What eventually happened with that?" He said he still thought back on that sometimes, and it still made him angry, but not as bad as before. He tried not to think about it. He wasn't in touch with those guys anymore who said that, but he said that if he did see them, he would still be mad. He said that for what they did, he developed the practice of keeping his friends and his girlfriend separate. "You notice how you don't see me around with her a lot, I don't talk about her," he said. I nodded. He told me he liked to keep it separate, just to keep things straight.

Steve clearly showed how he had been able to come to terms with the wrenching ambivalence of this situation, spatially and temporally separating his time with his girlfriend from time with his friends. While his earlier effort to distance himself from his guns had been reactive, one might now notice how his efforts to avoid conflict were proactive, involving a separation of different types of relationships. Furthermore, instead of retaliating violently against those who had disrespected him, he had come to earn respect through other means. When I knew him at age twenty-four, he was working two jobs, as a roofer and a fast-food manager, and was also the sole caregiver of his grandmother. When he hung out with his homies he never smoked or drank and could always be counted on for a ride home. As Joe, one of his friends confided to me, "I got nothing but respect for him." Despite living in one of the roughest neighborhoods anywhere, he earned respect not by engaging in violence but by taking care, as a veteran of Eighteenth Street.[28]

Eric

Eric, a sixteen-year-old, large (six foot two, over two hundred pound) Latino, was well versed in nearly all of the conflict management strategies discussed by Merry because of his efforts to manage the profound difficulties posed by his sister, Daisy.[29] He and his mother had kicked her out of the house, had had her arrested and sent to juvenile hall, had moved, had reported her to the police, had tried to ignore her, and had tried to sue her. We might also see Daisy and Eric as engaged in an increasingly high-stakes game of dominoes in which both sides resisted holding the last piece.[30]

Daisy, nine years Eric's senior, joined a local gang at age twelve. (Eric had four other sisters, one older and three younger; he was the only boy; all were raised only by his mother.) According to Eric, Daisy then began to physically abuse their mother, steal her money, and pressure Eric to join the gang when he was six years old. In response, the mother evicted her from the household. To retaliate, Daisy, then fifteen, threw a Molotov cocktail at her family's living room window, which shattered against the security bars and set fire to the couch and draperies. Her mother had her arrested and she served three years in juvenile hall. When Daisy was released, she went back to the gang and during this time had three children with three different fathers. Once when Eric and his uncle were at a local mall, they were jumped and viciously beaten by members of Daisy's gang. Eric then began to take boxing lessons to learn to defend himself. When he was fourteen, Eric's mother had saved enough money to move the family, but he was horrified to find that his sister had followed them, moving into an apartment behind theirs. As he related, "One time I was outside fixing the car, and I saw my little nephews playing around. I'm like, that's my sister's kids. What are they doing there? . . . I told my mom about it."

Three weeks before the interview, Eric reported Daisy to Child Protective Services. As he stated, "The house looked like a garbage house." According to Eric, they put her on "checkup," saying she had a "60 percent chance of losing her children." He then purchased a truck and began to work on it diligently, fixing it up in hopes of driving it to school, but two weeks after he had reported his sister he heard people outside his window whom he could only assume were members of Daisy's gang, hitting the truck a number of times with a sledgehammer. He spent much of the interview elaborately describing the truck to me,[31] and experienced such emotive dissonance when it was damaged that he became physically ill.

It's a V-8, a standard. It's a nice truck. . . . And I got it like fixed up. I dropped it a little bit and I put a nice steering wheel on it, and I got some nice vents on it, and I have, you know, some nice sounds in it. . . . I already have finished sanding it down completely, so I had washed it. . . . It's only been primered for two days, and then bang bang bang, and then, oh man. Shh. . . . I went to my friend's house. I said, "I'mo bring it to school." And then this happens, and I'll be like—I got sick from Monday to Wednesday.

When Eric called the police to report the incident, he became further enraged that they wanted to see his driver's license, asked how he was able to afford the truck, and even checked under the hood to see if parts were stolen.[32] As he stated, "Oh man. I didn't call 'em to ask me where I got the car, you know." Afraid he might lose his temper, "I just went inside the house and that's it," in order to manage it. Eric had seen the need to learn such techniques; he was the only young person I spoke with who had sought professional help to manage his emotive dissonance and control his rage.

"How did you learn to control your temper like that?"
"I went to counseling actually."
"Oh, you did?"
"Yeah, I was in counseling."
"Yeah. When was that?"
"Maybe like two or three months ago. Like before I would just get mad and I would just start breaking things and doing things. So I was like, I'm gonna go to counseling. I gotta stop all this."

Eric's skills allowed him to "think slow" and remain in control rather than lose himself in anger. Drawing on his training, Eric noticed his feelings of anger and went inside to cool off, but he did not give up in seeking a formal means of retaliation. With criminal charges blocked, he decided to sue his sister for damages.[33] Meanwhile, he and his mom had packed their boxes and were ready to move out of state. Yet he had his doubts that this would be effective, confiding, "You know my sister always say that she's never gonna stop bothering my mom." Faced with this stalker, he reasoned that if she followed them out of state he would try to kill her.[34]

"I don't know, man, I just feel like, like I said, I wanna kill her, you know. I bought a rifle. It's a nice rifle. You know those seven-millimeter rifles? Have you seen 'em?"

"No."

"You know how big those bullets are?"

"How big?"

"About this long. Seven millimeter. I just barely bought it, 'cause I have money saved up in the bank. . . . I had to go with my mom and take out money, 'cause I couldn't go by myself, you know."

"Did she know that you bought that?"

"No, I haven't told her. I don't wanna tell her, or she's gonna tell me something, you know." He laughed. "I bought that rifle 'cause I'm thinkin' about it already. You know, it has everything. It doesn't need nothing. It's got a big telescope. It's round and big. It's a Crosman telescope that is good. I've gone to the shooting ranges, like over there in the mountains, you know. I've been to the mountains, and I will shoot something like very far from it, and it'll hit it, like maybe as far as from right here to that pink place over there. I'll hit a soda all the way over there, and it'll blow up. Splash! You see the soda go like that, and like hey, I shot it. And I would just go and shoot and shoot and shoot. I took my uncles, you know. . . . Like my other uncles and my dad's friend, and we took a lot of guns, like, you know, other guns. We were shooting, practicing how to shoot."

"Do they know how you feel about your sister?"

"Yeah, they know about it, you know."

"What do they say?"

"Just," he laughed, "'Don't do nothin' stupid,' you know. 'Try to ignore it.' And I'll be like, 'How can you try to ignore something that just keeps, you know, she keeps doing the same thing over and over and over. I can't ignore it.' So you know, I've been there. I've gone and I've practiced shooting already, and I know I could do it. You know I could just do it, but I don't wanna do it. I do wanna do it, 'cause I want everything to stop, you know. But I'm not sure right now, you know."

Unlike other accounts of retaliation presented in the literature, we hear little about masculinity in this tale, or honor, or a quest for respect.[35] Rather, we see that the antagonist had trespassed upon and destroyed something of vital importance, not just once but repeatedly. For his entire conscious life, Eric's sister had terrorized him and his family. Despite this, Eric's mother and uncles continued to counsel him to keep his cool, reinforcing the structural inhibition that "blood is thicker than water," even as the uncles accompanied him to the shooting range. Perhaps, in teaching him to shoot, the uncles hoped to cathect Eric's rage without intending him to actually make use of such skills. Once the police had tried to get them to talk to each other, but the sister had refused. "What happened to us is like a movie," Eric said, "with all those things she's doing to us." He closed the interview by noting with a laugh, "You'll probably hear about me later on in the news." Still, the steps he had taken to avoid such consequences thus far were remarkable. And after ten years, I have yet to hear about him on the news.

Ben

Ben was an eighteen-year-old Belizean, born and raised within blocks of CAA. He was a model student, raising and lowering the flag in front of the school each day, providing assistance on the office computer and in the school garden. He was also an exemplary worker at a local retailer and often wore his work vest to school. In the past he had had perfect attendance and had been an excellent student, participating in Glee Club, but this changed on his first day at the large local high school.

"I just stopped, stayed home."
"What made you not wanna go? What did you see that day?"
"Everything was too new to me, man."
"Uh huh."
"They didn't have anything. They didn't have any homeroom, they didn't have any classes for me."
"Did they treat you poorly?"
"Yeah," he chuckled, "they kept sending me back and forth."
"The teachers?"
"Yeah. They kept sending me everywhere, man, sayin', 'Go over here to get some classes, go over there.' I didn't like that, so I just didn't go back. I only been out for three months, then I came here."[36]

Ben was the second oldest of four brothers, the oldest of whom was in his early twenties and seldom at home, while the others were sixteen and thirteen. Ben's father had left the family following Ben's eleventh birthday and moved to Chicago. Ben's sixteen-year-old brother was getting involved in a local gang, smoking marijuana in Ben's car on a daily basis, and subsequently was sent to probation camp. According to Ben, his thirteen-year-old brother was following in the sixteen-year-old's footsteps and enjoyed instigating trouble. A few nights before our second interview, this brother had been insulting his mother's boyfriend when the boyfriend, drunk and already acting abusively toward the boys' mother, began to attack Ben's brother. Ben recalled, "I kept askin' her, 'Do you want me to get 'im off for you?' And she keeps sayin', 'No, I wanna handle it.' Then my little brother tried to get 'im off. That's when he started punchin' on my little brother."

Eventually the boyfriend stopped, lying on the floor drunk and exhausted. Ben sent his mom and brother to separate rooms and then called his auntie to come pick them up, leaving the boyfriend lying in their apartment. Ben spoke of a deep animosity toward this man and of the rage he had felt after a previous incident in which the boyfriend had hit his mom. Like all of the consultants in this analysis, Ben engaged in fantasy revenge as a way to manage the emotive dissonance he experienced by being structurally inhibited from retaliating, even considering excuses he could use in court. His manner of speaking was strikingly similar to that of Steve, full of pauses and hesitation, encouraged by the interviewer's use of continuers.

"What were you thinkin'?"
'I was thinkin' about a bat."
"Getting a bat, uh huh."
"Knockin' 'im down."
"Uh huh."
"Beatin' the livin' hell out of him."
"Uh huh."
"I would like to beat him half to death."
"Right now?"
"Not now."
"Yeah. How long did you feel that way? How long did you feel like you wanted to hit him with a baseball bat and smash his head in?"
"That lasted for seven weeks."
"Seven weeks you felt that way."
"Yep. And I even thought about ways how I could be if he took me into court, I even thought about ways how I could get out of it."
"Uh huh."
"Like temporary insanity or somethin' like that."
"Uh huh."
"'Cause that ain't how I usually act."
"Yeah. Yeah."
"I been thinkin' about all that stuff."
"Uh huh."
"Even gettin' a gun and shootin' it."
"Uh huh."

Once, in a similar incident, Ben had hit his mother's boyfriend. Then subsequently, like many victims of domestic abuse, he experienced misgivings, in part because the boyfriend had helped him in the past.[37] In Ben's reckoning of the boyfriend's sympathy margin, his abuse did not quite override his good deeds.[38]

"That time there when I did hit him, it did feel good, but afterwards, man."

"Afterwards?"

"I felt, I felt real messed up. . . . I don't ever wanna do that again. Never."

"How come?"

"Because, the way it makes me feel, man." He exhaled. "That man helped me so much. I shouldn't a put my hands on 'im. But then he did hit my mom and my brother. . . . I do get confused sometimes." He chuckled. . . .

"So um, did you feel like you should apologize or anything for hitting him?"

"Yeah, I apologized."

"And what'd he say?"

"He said it's all right, because he didn't know what he was doin'. He shouldn't a did that in the first place. I talked to him for a long time about that." He exhaled. "He made me late for school too." Again he exhaled. "He's been doin' all this stuff for me, lookin' for insurance for my car."

Four years later, Ben and I shared a three-hour interview over lunch and in my car, which I parked in front of the community-based organization where I volunteered. He still worked at the same local retailer, where he had moved into a semimanagerial position. Ben's mother's boyfriend continued to drink and be abusive and was still in their lives. Ben's feelings toward him continued to be ambivalent, as he remained in control despite his rage for the sake of the family.

Ernesto

Ernesto was a friendly seventeen-year-old Latino who had lived near CAA all his life. In describing how he had come to attend CAA, he told of missing a week at his last high school, when his brother had had a major operation, and then not returning to school for two more weeks. When he did return, he found himself far behind in his work. Discouraged by his failing grades and lack of assistance from teachers, he ended up being "pushed out" like

Ben.[39] As he stated, "The teachers wouldn't help me, and I used to ask them for help with this or that; they didn't care. I was like, 'Fuck it. What the fuck am I coming to school for if they're not gonna teach me anything?' . . . They was giving me fails fails fails fails. Fuck that, man, I ain't going to school for that, man. I wasn't getting credits; what the fuck I was going to school for?"

For six months Ernesto dropped out of school and fell in love with raising pit bulls. He learned the hobby from a friend who sold him male and female all-white dogs with red noses for $100. Much as Eric (a friend of Ernesto's) became devoted to his truck, Ernesto came to devote most of his time to training, breeding, and fighting his bulls, buying them the best food and equipment, and making an estimated $1,000 a year from his efforts. Some of the money went to his mom, some to buy clothes, and the rest to his dogs. "I used to love my dogs a lot, maaan. I don't know, I used to love 'em a lot. . . . Watch, I'mo show you his picture, watch. Yeah, he had a big chest."

Unfortunately, Ernesto lost his dogs when a neighbor became angry that they had broken his dog's leg. Although Ernesto's mother paid the $200 veterinarian bill, the neighbor nonetheless poisoned Ernesto's pit bulls. Ernesto discussed his emotional response to this incident.

"After that I wasn't making no money. I was mad right there."

"I bet you were mad."

"Man I was *mad*, man, I, I was gonna—I don't know—I was gonna do something to 'im, but I kick back right there 'cause—"

"You didn't do anything?"

"Nah, 'cause he knew a lot of them gangsters from right there, from Thirty-sixth. I didn't want to mess with them, 'cause he's gonna tell them, 'What's up? Let's go do something to that fool.' He'll fuck me up."

Ernesto explained his desire for revenge, not out of obeisance to a code, but out of sheer anger. Yet Ernesto controlled this desire out of his knowledge of the neighborhood's social structure. As Jack Katz states, "It is at least as feasible to understand gangs as reducing crime as causing crime."[40] As the interview continued, Ernesto told of his fear for his mother and his fear of what he would do if his mother were hurt.

"Did you think about what you were gonna do?"

"Tsk! Yeah, I think about it. I got my mom right there. I don't wanna fuck with that. They fuck with my mom, that's it. I don't know what I would do. I'll kill 'em, fuck that."

"What did you think you might do to him for doing that to your dogs?"

"I was gonna beat him up, man! I don't know how, but I was gonna go, go up and shoot his dog or something. Kill his dog too. But something held me back, and I'm glad I didn't do it."

"Yeah. Are you glad you didn't?"

"Yeah, I'm glad, 'cause fuck it, it's not worth it, do something like that, get your enemies and shit like that behind you and shit. Man, I just left it like that, fuck it."

Here, "Fuck it" might be considered an iconic statement of emotive dissonance, which Ernesto juxtaposes to structural inhibitions to retaliating. Echoing Duneier's sidewalk vendors and junkies who have given up on mainstream aspirations after numerous disappointments, Ernesto, in saying, "Fuck it," embodies both rage and resignation, neatly encapsulating frustrated desire.[41] Like the others I interviewed, Ernesto indulged in numerous revenge fantasies but took them a bit further by playing them out against a wall.

"What did you do with your anger?"

"I don't know, man."

"Did it make you feel sick, or did you go punch on a wall?"

"I used to punch the wall, man."

"You did."

"I used to punch the wall. It used to fuck with my fingers. Look, you see?"

"Uh huh."

"I used to hit the wall a lot."

"'Cause of this?"

"'Cause of that, man. I got mad. I got—I even cried like one or two times, man. I got mad. They were my dogs. I used to, I took 'em to the shops. My mom spent like more than $1,000 on them two dogs. Took 'em to shops. I got his ears clipped and everything. That's what fucked it up, man."

Instead of inflicting his rage against his antagonist, Ernesto cathected it against the wall, punishing himself as a painful living embodiment of his predicament, borne witness by his scabbed knuckles and the worn pictures of his deceased dogs, which he continued to carry in his wallet, his bittersweet memories helping him cope with ambivalence.

Shawn

Shawn was a twenty-year-old, soft-spoken Belizean who had immigrated to the neighborhood with his father when he was fourteen and who missed his mother dearly. Although his father lived close to the school, Shawn chose to live with his half-sister because of conflicts with his dad. This posed a problem, since many of his cousins and uncles were affiliated with the Crips, while his half-sister lived in a Blood neighborhood. Thus Shawn was especially careful about when he left the house and what he wore.

While negotiating gang territories made Shawn's life difficult, his situation with his girlfriend of two years made it nearly impossible. A week before our interview, he went to see her at 2:00 a.m., partly out of suspicion that she was cheating on him, and found her in bed with another man. This man also happened to be a gangbanger, and he pulled his gun on Shawn.

"And when he pull his gun . . . and he crank it back."

"Mm."

"Which was a nine, nine millimeter. . . . So at the time, okay, we there, it was like, who is this, who is this? He was like, he's from Harlem Crips. And I'm talking, 'LAF, Looney as Fuck.' He was like, 'Is that Bloods or Crips?' I said, 'Man, this is Crip,' know what I mean? He was like, 'Well, what I'm saying. I don't have no problem with you callin' my people from 30s.' So then he was like, 'Who your people?' And I start callin' some of my cousins' names and whatever, which they're older cousins and younger cousins, they stay in their area."

"Mm hm."

"And he was like, 'All right.' So after, I was like, what I mean, 'Whassup?' I was talkin' to her, I was like, 'Whassup? What's this actually all about?' But then again I really care less to hear anyway what was that all about. . . . It's like, they're from 30s, my people's from 30s too. And we figure, my cousin, we already know families comes first."

This is perhaps the ultimate humiliation, not only for a young man in the inner city, but for anyone, anywhere. Yet the situation was resolved peacefully, thanks to their gang ties. For as Shawn told it, rather than firing shots or attacking each other, each wanted to know–in fact, desperately needed to know–the other's gang affiliation (see chapter 4). When they found they were from sets friendly to each other (not all Crip sets are), they started "callin'," dropping names, and finding that friends and relations from both sets affiliated with Thirtieth Avenue Crips. Still, Shawn hoped that his family ties would outweigh gang ties in backing him up when he chose to retaliate against this interloper. He later told me he was unsuccessful in these efforts, as his cousins not only refused to back him up but warned him against retaliating. This dilemma proved increasingly difficult for Shawn, especially when his ex-girlfriend's sister told him that his rival was spreading a rumor among Crips that Shawn had become a Blood, since he lived in a Blood neighborhood. Shawn spoke of this rumor with utmost seriousness and worked to defuse it lest his fellow Crips act on it.

With his plans to retaliate against his rival foiled, he still harbored a resentment toward his girlfriend for the pain she had caused him, and he expressed hopes of striking back at her.

> "Truthfully enough, how could you actually hurt somebody you adore when you love this person? Then again, I look at it and say, well hey, this person, you, you love this person. How could they, how could they hurt you? But I say, the same way how they hurt you, you could hurt them."
> "Mm hm."
> "It was emotional, but in a way, if you can't hurt them emotional, why not hurt them physically."

Four years later, at twenty-four, Shawn was philosophical about this predicament. Having moved on to a steady girlfriend for over a year, taking care of her children as if they were his own (he had none of his own), he remembered the pain of the experience quite vividly and was grateful for not having resorted to violence. When I reminded him of the incident, he responded, "Something just told me to just go by. That's what happened. The question did come on my mind before it happened, just probably listening to songs, or probably seeing a movie. What would I do if I actually ended up in that predicament? I thank God above to know that well, it's not the end of the world. I do live and get the experience. Even right now at this point, it's like everybody goes through their own trials and tribulations, doesn't matter what it was about."

Like most individuals embroiled in disputes, Shawn learned to "lump it." While Steve resolved to live with emotive dissonance by working hard, taking care of his grandmother, and keeping his romantic life separate from his life with friends, Shawn came to terms with his ambivalence by caring for a new girlfriend and her children and moving on.[42] Despite what individuals may say about a "code of the streets," "honor," or "respect," in actual life situations individuals in the inner city learn to live with and abide by what they see as the best decision for a given circumstance in light of its effect on their social ties.

Reconsidering Retaliation

Despite dicta that one cannot back down from a conflict without losing respect, it is important that we consider seriously what members take as circumstances that mitigate the necessity of such measures. An "affront" or "insult" in itself is not sufficient to inspire retaliation. Rather, individuals take into account the effect of violence on their social ties before responding, and they learn to exercise skills at emotion management in order to remain in control.

For those who do retaliate, acts that dishonor or disrespect may retrospectively be deemed an important justification for violence.[43] Yet prospectively, the importance of such "dissing" is far from determinative of violent retaliation.[44] That more tightly knit communities experience less crime and violence is far from an accident,[45] but not necessarily for the reasons we have thought. The righteous grandmother who disciplines local youth and the alderman quick to make neighborhood changes such as adding lights to a local park are surely important in reducing crime through their community involvement,[46] yet they are most hesitant to intervene with those they perceive as most violence prone, such as the young men of this sample.[47] Moreover, when a young person tells of a time when he or she abstained from retaliation, it is rarely the grandmother or the alderman who comes foremost in the accounts. If the antagonist is one's lifelong friend whose mother one knows well (Steve), if he has overwhelming gang backup (Ernesto), or if he is a member of a gang friendly to one's own (Shawn), one may well think twice before retaliating. In the stories here, even when the antagonist had done nearly everything possible to jeopardize family ties, Ben still had conflicted feelings of loyalty to his stepfather, and Eric was more willing to engage in a costly and cumbersome interstate move with his mother than to raise the rifle he had fantasized shooting at his sister.

The case of Shawn is especially enlightening, for it involves such a prototypical situation of revenge against a rival for a girlfriend. Many have shown how gangs play an important role in maintaining community,[48] yet few have provided such an intimate glimpse of the importance of such ties as Shawn. How many individuals, confronted with a similarly dramatic situation, could hesitate as Shawn and his antagonist did, thoughtfully considering the social damage that their actions might wreak, and then simply lump it? Such a tale inevitably adds another layer of critique to the widespread acceptance of the criminalization of gang members and suggests that we should be cautious in our efforts to reduce or diminish such ties in hopes of reducing violence.[49]

Just as the consultants in this study paused before retaliating, we should pause before characterizing the quest for respect through retaliation as a general tendency for inner-city residents.[50] By focusing primarily on violent outcomes, criminology misses the many moments of nonviolence in the lives of even so-called violent offenders. Whether one responds violently "in the end" is not necessarily as important as the many instances, reasons, and strategies by which one was able, in surely a much greater number of instances, to respond nonviolently. Criminologists should begin to take greater pains to capture such nuances.

While Anderson carefully notes that "decent" and "street" are conceptual categories by which members organize and judge their behavior, any resident will act in a nonviolent way in the context of certain structural inhibitions: when, for instance, retaliation would betray existing ties, even if such ties seem strained to the breaking point. On the other hand, victims may be more likely to retaliate and in fact may relish a righteous retaliation if it will reaffirm important social ties.[51] The necessity to preserve social ties dominates such decision making; concerns with "masculinity" and "respect" are important only insofar as they affect such ties. Whichever option is chosen, retaliation or lumping, is ultimately based on an individual's calculus of which might threaten his or her social integration less or enhance it more. The emotive dissonance of "lumping it" is a cost young people are often willing to endure to maintain their place in community.

8

Streetwork

Writing is a shallow reflection of experience. Up to this point, the narrative has moved from case to case in order to build or contradict an analysis. Fortunately, life doesn't work this way. To understand the central theme of this book, that gang or street identity is a strategic resource, we need a more in-depth view of a single individual, following him over time to get a feel for what the variable performance of identity might mean in context.

Joe Figueroa was a nineteen-year-old hired to help enlist and keep track of youth for a federal employment program, and he was also a gang member. Whether Joe was a current or ex–gang member was an open question, and Joe's response depended on who was asking and how they asked (see chapter 4). In *The Presentation of Self in Everyday Life*, Goffman distinguished between a primary and a secondary involvement, using the example of a person driving down a street and smoking, perhaps even carrying on a conversation at the same time.[1] In the case of Joe, it was hard to tell which involvement was primary and which secondary, bureaucrat or gangbanger.

The insights of two classic ethnographies are especially relevant to Joe's strategic negotiations between the world of work and the world of the street. First, Elliot Liebow, in *Tally's Corner*, returned often to the fictional identities sustained by Tally and his friends in their everyday street-corner banter. For the men Liebow shared time with, tall tales of exaggerated exploits were the order of the day. Yet in the contemporary inner city, the money to be earned from drug sales or the dynamic possibilities to arise from gang rivalries may be a way to actualize a fantasy world. The braggadocio may endure, but in contemporary desperate inner-city economies it may be based more in fact than in fiction.[2]

Second, Ralph Cintron's *Angels' Town*, a lyrical, magisterial work strangely overlooked in much of the deviance and gang literature, repeatedly asks a question that strikes at a key existential issue for the marginalized: "How does one create something out of nothing?" He spends many pages, for instance, painstakingly describing a wall in the room of a young boy named Valerio, where the hypermasculinized, hyperreal images of Rambo and Schwarzenegger were juxtaposed with photos of Porsches and hot rods.[3] A young man like Joe didn't need to idolize such images, since in a serious way he often embodied them.

Jack Katz discusses gangs as a means to get from *here* to *there*, to transcend limitations and ridicule through incontrovertible dangerousness.[4] When someone who knows how to get from *here* to *there* is provided the means of making a moderate yet respectable income simply by enrolling and monitoring young people in a federal program, the opportunity may seem golden to those of us who have bought into the semiconscious dream of middle-class America, but for those like Joe, in the fantastic, open-ended dreamscape/nightmare of the inner city, such an opportunity may feel more like a *disappointment*. How to integrate the dual performances of bureaucrat and gangbanger was an issue with which Joe was always struggling, in an embodied way if not consciously.

His hiring and continued employment at the CAA nonprofit that ran the jobs program was not without controversy. Kyle Griffin, the director of the program, hired Joe because he saw leadership potential in him but made his job contingent on passing his high school equivalency exam and taking college courses. Lois Gonzalez, the grants director, believed in Joe as a bridge to the community. Anita Gomez, the office secretary at CAA, loathed Joe's presence, rarely missing an opportunity to point out his faults to others. Finally, the board was highly skeptical of the director's decision but ultimately trusted his judgment.

This is a tale of what I know of Joe, as he presented himself to me and as I recorded our time together, both when he was a student at CAA and years later when he became a federal jobs outreach worker. But this tale is not simply about Joe; much more than that, and perhaps more consequentially, it is about what we make of Joe.[5] Although Joe eventually spoiled this opportunity, Kyle, Lois, and Anita were each right in their own respective views. For any performance, as for any assessment of face or identity, the audience is the ultimate judge and interpreter. We are now the arbiters of this performance. Our interpretations reflect what we make of this protean substance we call youth, the concessions we allow them and the opportunities we afford them. Soon enough they are youth no more.

Making the Rounds

I initially interviewed Joe for ninety minutes in March of 1997 at the CAA alternative school. I was struck by the forthright, no-nonsense quality of his speech as he performed a strong image of masculinity.[6] He made many references to being "hard" and to "having balls" in reference to fighting, playing linebacker on a high school football team, and being part of the Florencia Street gang. He told me he was at CAA simply to get his grades up so he would be eligible for a football scholarship offered by a nearby college. He had spent over six months in a youth authority camp for what he described as "carjacking, armed robbery, shit like that," and had recently had a bullet removed that had been lodged in him since 1994. Although Joe belonged to a rival gang of one of the gangs that dominated CAA, he became student body president. It was this sort of initiative that Kyle Griffin recognized and that led to Joe's employment in a job with middle-class status and income.

When I called the CAA nonprofit in November of 1999, I was pleased and surprised when Joe answered, and he helped me find some of my old consultants. As I entered the storefront nonprofit, where colorful fliers adorned the large plate glass windows, I found Joe talking to Fuller, the director of the local Americorps, a man in his fifties. I watched Joe listening as Fuller told him how a number of ten-foot lengths of pipe had been stolen from the grounds of a local continuation school. As Fuller talked of how much the theft would cost, how inconvenient it would be to the school, and how hard such pipes might be to sell, Joe stood in a squared stance, hands to his sides, hardly blinking, not nodding, not sympathizing, just watching with few discernible movements: a powerful presence. At only nineteen, his silence spoke of experience, self-control, and efficacy that placed him on an equal footing with a man old enough to be his grandfather. I have no doubt that such a strong "decent" presence was the result of his accumulated experiences as a gang member.[7]

As we sat down and listened to our interview from almost three years before, Joe repeatedly shook his head and squirmed in his chair. "That's the old Joe. I was really full of shit back then," he said, reflecting on "doing being" Joe; but I was not quite sure what had changed. As I talked with him, meeting his penetrating eyes, sitting across from his powerful frame, responding to his direct, no-nonsense language, he came across to me as brilliant and dangerous. I think he enjoyed giving off that impression; I'm not sure he could help it.

Lois Gonzalez later told me a few stories over lunch to provide her impression of Joe. She mentioned how she had been walking with Joe one day after lunch when her sandal became stuck in a crack in the sidewalk. As she was falling, she reached out to stop herself and grabbed a barbed wire, severing the nerves and numbing a finger as blood spurted out. She and Joe asked a nearby man if they could use his phone to call 911, but he said no. Eventually they managed to call and get help. Joe brought her to the hospital and then returned to confront the man. "That's the way Joe is," she said. "It turns out the man didn't mean anything; he just didn't want the cops coming because he deals drugs."

"They listen to him," she said, "more than they would listen to someone like me, because I haven't been through the same thing, or probably someone like you either." She told me another story about how Joe had been out with his buddies getting drunk when a man who was trying to steal Joe's car was shot inside of it. She thought the guy had been set up by a rival gang—falsely tipped off that Joe's car would be easy to steal–and that when he got inside they popped him. Joe arrived just as the guy was dying, in convulsions. Joe's buddies called the cops, and when the cops came they took a look at Joe and decided to take him in. "But I'm the victim here," Joe said. They couldn't believe that, so Joe had to have his friends who were there come in as witnesses and back up his story. She said Joe still got beat up by the cops at times. "It's how he looks, who he hangs around with."

Through stories like these, Lois clearly showed that she respected Joe, even idolized him somewhat, and at least valued him as an important colleague although he was about half her age. I also found the stories impressive, thinking I would be unlikely to return, as Joe had, to confront the man who had refused them access to his phone. Joe's street sensibilities provided him the possibility of acting in a decent manner. On one hand, he worked beyond the scope of the law to hold a stranger personally accountable; yet such behavior also defended the honor of a friend and coworker who might have been physically injured by a stranger's snub. The tales also point out the ordinary chaos of Joe's life, insinuating that times when he had run afoul of the law might have been due more to circumstances than to anything Joe had done, a common theme in Joe's accounts as well.

One morning in September of 2000, I arrived at the CAA nonprofit and overheard Joe telling George, an African American in charge of a citywide middle school gang prevention program, how a girl who was Joe's friend had said Joe was talking white. "I know I don't talk slang like I used to, but I didn't think I talked white! And she's white, she oughta know. She said the way I talked changed a lot since she knew me."

"Better watch out, you're *crossing over*," George warned in his debonair style.

"Nah, I'll never cross over," Joe said, shaking his head. But his clothing that day, black slacks with black leather dress shoes, a belt, and a long-sleeve, pale blue dress shirt, belied such intentions.

This was a telling interaction, as Joe revealed his reflexive awareness of straddling two worlds, presented here as office humor. The stigma of "acting white" has been pointed out as a hindrance to African American upward mobility but has been less remarked upon as an issue for Latinos such as Joe.[8] Whether this was a real issue for Joe or not, his mentioning it revealed his office savvy, bringing a moment of camaraderie with his African American colleague.

Joe was on his way out; I was not sure why or where, but he motioned for me to come along so I followed him to his '78 Crown Victoria. He had tinted out the back windows, refurbished the upholstery, and raised the rear struts. Joe showed me how he had gotten the bullet hole removed from the driver's door and repaired the bullet mark on the trunk from the incident when the young man was shot in his car. We got in and Joe slowly, purposefully put on a hair net and popped in a CD of Nelly at high volume. We headed out to the freeway, where Joe drove somewhat fast and recklessly, changing lanes quickly and tailgating drivers. With his driving, the loud music, and the windows down, I felt like I was back in high school. I had to shout over the radio, so he turned it down a bit.

As Joe donned the hair net, he also adopted an icy attitude, starkly at odds with his jocular office humor just moments before. This was code-switching at work, not of the sort Elijah Anderson discusses but of the sort Prudence Carter analyzes.[9] Joe's adopted persona here was neither "decent" nor "street" but a hard-won, ever precarious, closely maintained *social capital*.

I told Joe I was sorry I hadn't been able to make it to the party he'd invited me to, and asked how it had gone. He said it was funny I asked, because they had talked about how I would have felt if I had been there.

"Oh yeah, what happened?" I asked.

"This guy came and pointed a gun at everybody."

"Really?"

"I guess he had a right."

"Why do you say that?"

"We were playing football on the street. Well, not us, some younger guys, and we were watching. It was getting pretty rough, bouncing into cars and shit. He was driving by and he just got out, said this was his neighborhood, and cut that shit out. I could understand."

Joe and his friends, some of whom I had interviewed, such as Marco, Steve, and Ernesto, regularly played tackle football in the streets. They described with relish bouncing off cars, going all out, come what may. In his account to me, Joe found it perfectly understandable that a neighbor would use a gun to break up the game, though he laughed that I might not have found it as comprehensible.

"So did that break up the party?"

"Oh no, we still partied."

"I didn't imagine you guys would be playing football. I thought it'd be more like drinking and smoking."

"Oh there was a lot of that too."

"So when did the game break up?"

"Around eight or nine."

"And how long did the party last?"

"I don't know. I must've passed out," he laughed.

We drove to Southern County and into a high-security apartment complex. I asked what we were doing, as up to this point I had no idea where we were headed. Joe said he had to pick up a tutor since the buses weren't running. He honked his horn by touching to adjacent metal a bare wire that stuck out of the steering column. "I gotta get this fixed," he said. While we waited, we walked to a nearby food truck and he bought a carrot juice for himself and a pear juice for me.

As we returned, the tutor, a young African American woman with her braided hair pulled straight back, came out her front door. "Is your mama home?" Joe called out. He looked at me and laughed, saying he had said that to her when he dropped her off one night. She came closer to the car and he repeated his sly bit of sexual harassment, and she smiled at the flirtation.[10] I let her have the front seat and sat in the back by the thumping speakers. He touched the back of her hair, pulled back by a rubber band, and said it looked like she was getting dreadlocks. "Oh shut up," she said.

After we dropped her off at the school I asked how his weekend had been. "Oh I'm tired," he said. "I was up until four or five with my neighbor last night, this black woman."

"Oh yeah?"

"She came by and asked what I was drinkin'. 'Coronas,' I said. She asked if she could drink with me. I said, 'Sure.' We finished off that six-pack. Then we went out for a twelve-pack. Then I went back out for a twenty-four-pack. Then damn, it was on."

"Oh yeah?"

"She asked if I wanted to go to her house; I asked if she wanted to come to my house." He had a guilty grin on his face.

"So did you?"

"Nah," he said. "But it was nice."

Kyle, Joe's boss, as well as Lois had spoken often with Joe about misogynistic talk and behavior, and they made a point of working with young men on this issue, more than job skills or anger management, for example. Despite having two daughters with different women, Joe especially relished the possibilities of relationships.[11]

"What would you usually do on a day like this?" I asked him.

"This would be my chance to cruise, catch up with the homies."

We drove on, past Eldridge High School. "I used to slang here," Joe said. "I had this whole street. This here was a crack house." He motioned to an empty lot. "I used to stand here"—he pointed to a spot across from the high school—"and deal to the kids coming out."

"What were you sellin', marijuana?"

"Marijuana, crack, primos."

"Crack, really? How'd you get started in that?"

"My brother-in-law. He was a dealer. Still is. I went up to him and said, 'Hook me up with an ounce.' He said, 'An ounce!' That's $500 cocaine. I told him I wanted him to show me how you rock it up. What you do is take a glass container and put it on a stove. Then you take equal parts cocaine and baking soda—they have to be measured exactly the same (he pantomimes eying the measures). You mix 'em up, then put 'em in the water till all the water's gone. After that you can keep adding on to it until you got this big rock. You sell that for $1,000, so you just made your $500. I used that to buy my next batch. Shorty and I, we used to deal here."

Joe didn't have any hesitation, and even took pride in telling me this. I had not been aware that Joe, just out of high school himself, though without graduating, had slung crack right outside the local high school. I don't think Kyle, Joe's boss, knew about this, but I wasn't about to tell him either.

As we drove on, lo and behold, he spotted Shorty, jogging under a freeway overpass in gray workout clothes, looking like a boxer with his hood up. Joe waved hello to him and pulled the car over. Shorty shook hands with Joe, then me. Joe asked him why he wasn't working. Shorty said he was taking a few days off but he would go back soon. He said he had gotten fucked up back at a party. "What happened?" Joe asked. Shorty said he had gotten jumped by these four guys, he wasn't sure why. They had fucked up his eye. He showed his left eye, with a large red blotch on the side, as if the tissue was torn, looking bloody but not bleeding. "Damn, well, I gotta go. I catch you later," Joe said. We pulled away and Joe yelled back at him out the window, "Stop fucking around!" Shorty turned around, smiled and waved.

We drove on to Delaware and Ninetieth, and Joe pointed out a young man in long shorts and a T-shirt. "See that fuckup in the shorts? He used to go to CAA. He used to take crack. Now he just washes windows at the gas station. He was pretty bad, now look at him. . . . His life is fucked up." We headed to Marco's place. I thought it was an interesting irony that Joe was proud of dealing crack but dismissive of a crackhead.[12]

Joe, Marco, and Steve, all Latinos from separate, rival gangs, became fast friends at CAA, and that friendship continued over the years after they left school. We stopped the car across the street and Joe called for Marco. He came out of the house with two gray and white pit bull pups. His eyes lit up as he recognized me from three years ago. I noticed he had the tattoos around his eyes that Joe had described. Two boys in Pendletons were standing in front of the apartment buildings, as if on guard, staring straight at us as we arrived. They looked squarely at Joe and nodded in acknowledgment, then watched me with leveled gazes. Marco had an old raggedy dog toy in his hands, and his pit bull pups rolled and tumbled behind him, nipping at his heels.

"Sure, I remember Bob, how you doin', man?" He reached his hand in and we shook as he grinned deviously. He seemed a bit older and harder to me. "How you like my dogs, man? I'm gonna make me some money with them."

"You gonna fight 'em?" Joe asked.

"No, they bitches. I'm gonna breed 'em." They petted the dogs.

Joe asked him, "How you doin'?"

"I gotta move to Ohio."

"Ohio. Why?"

"I gotta get away. I gotta get outta here."

Joe asked about his girlfriend. "I'm not together with her anymore, man," Marco said grimacing.

"Shit, you wouldn't know what to do in Ohio. Did you smoke?"

Marco smiled.

"You goin' in to work today?" Joe asked.

"Yeah, around 2:00."

"Whachu been doin'?"

Marco picked bits of straw out of the dog toy. He said they'd all gotten stoned and had been playing with the dogs. He laughed, squeezing the dog toy, making it squeak. We took off.

"Same old Marco," Joe said. "See, what'd I tell you? Getting stoned and going to work, that's about all he does." Later, when I interviewed Marco a second time I found he had been working with hydrochloric acid, removing the chrome from auto parts with little protection for his hands or face. He'd been experiencing skin problems and dizziness. Getting stoned was not necessarily an unreasonable way of dealing with the boredom, low status, and toxic fumes of such work. Yet Marco had been getting stoned long before. He often referred to the prominent tattoos on his face, neck, and arms as barriers to finding better work. I made an appointment for him with a friend who ran a tattoo removal clinic, and after numerous attempts to coordinate and reschedule, Marco failed to show up.

"Where did he say he wanted to move? Iowa?" I asked.

"Ohio. He's always saying he wants to move somewhere, Arizona, Texas. Today it's Ohio."

"Why?"

"Fuck if I know."

"What would he do up there?"

"I'm sure he doesn't have any idea. He just thinks he needs to get away from his homies around here sometimes."

Joe parked his car around the corner from the nonprofit. I told Joe that a woman at the small, ramshackle house across the street had talked to me, introducing herself as Ebony. "That place is a crack house," Joe said.

"How do you know?" I asked.

"Whenever I see a place where people are coming and going all the time and there's no real reason, I think it must be a crack house. I don't wanna know. I don't wanna deal with them."

As we passed I saw a paper that I hadn't seen before, posted on the door with words written in thick blue marker: "Don't hang out here." I wondered if it was somehow for my benefit, or because of me. Was I making it "hot" or was I slightly paranoid?

I went out with Joe a number of other times and found that these were more or less his daily rounds. He would also visit other nonprofits, continuation and probation schools, apparently to sign up or check on young people in the jobs program for which he was working. Yet he never explicitly talked about the jobs program with anyone he met. He always seemed to be "Joe," marked more by his personal style than his position, a guy checking out his friends in the neighborhood. I wondered what others in the office thought of Joe's work; I would find out soon enough.

Office Politics

Returning to the nonprofit, I went in the back with Kyle to smoke and talk. He was quiet and tense, alluding obscurely to "office politics." Throughout my fieldwork, we would head to this garagelike area behind his office, where his ashtray was strategically nearby on a column of cardboard file boxes. We were surrounded by old bikes, fans, files, and labeled and unlabeled boxes covered in dust. Particles were suspended in bands of light piercing through gaps between the tin roof and the brick sides; there was no other light, and one's eyes took time to adjust. It felt like a cave. As long as a cigarette was burning the conversation continued, and I was grateful that the cigarettes were slow-burning low tar with long filters. I marked how well I was engaging his interest by how many he smoked. On this day's discussion of Joe, he lit up a good four or five.

"If there's one theme to your study it should be perseverance," Kyle told me. "The guys in this neighborhood keep on, despite the drugs, the violence, the grief. Joe's still trying to finish school, for example. The teachers don't like him because he talks back. They're ready for him to go. . . . I know Joe's a smart kid, and I don't just mean street smart, he's also academically smart." However, he was concerned about Joe's commitment. "He still hangs around the same friends. He says he's changed, but he's doing a lot of the same things he used to do."

"I've heard some in the office say that that's why he's so important for you guys to have around. He's like a bridge that sort of helps you have contact with the other side."

"That's some nationalist bullshit. Joe's *very* selective in who he helps. There's still a lot he doesn't know, and there's a lot he can learn from Jerry." Jerry was the other federal jobs coordinator, an African American man old enough to be Joe's father, with a generation of experience on the streets and in nonprofits. Kyle continued, "Jerry's one of the best job coordinators out there. Some folks have said things about Jerry's history, but this man has faced down men at gunpoint. No question, if there's a need, he's there. There's a lot more Joe could be learning from him. I'm concerned about Joe. I've gotten flak for hiring him. The board asked me questions about him. I said, 'Give him time.' When I took him on, I told him I would have him on three conditions. First, he had to get his GED. Second, he had to take community college classes. Third, he had to transfer to a state school. He took his GED in May, and the results should be out in August. I asked him what he got and he said, 'I don't know yet.' He took it twice, and for this last time, he said, 'I think I failed the math section.'"

"Damn," I said.

Kyle told me Joe had a girlfriend who had had a baby when he was four-teen, and now his current girlfriend had had a baby. "He's leaving for Wash-ington because he wants to see his kid, so she knows who her biological father is. The mother wanted to get far away so that the daughter won't know Joe. Now she has a new boyfriend, and the baby sees him as daddy. Joe was pretty upset when he called home, introduced himself as daddy to this four-year-old girl, and she was confused. The girl asked her mommy, 'This guy on the phone says he's daddy, but daddy's right here.' That's why he's going to Washington. Joe's pretty stressed out. I offered him counseling here, but he said he would just like to talk to me."

In the office three weeks later, Jerry asked me if Joe had written anything on the dry-erase board where office workers noted their whereabouts. I read what I found. "What date is that?" Jerry asked. I said it looked like the six-teenth, but Jerry said Joe had done that last week. I asked Jerry where Joe was. "I don't know," he said, pursing his lips and slowly shaking his head to the side, marking his concern, perhaps disdain. Anita, the office secretary, told Jerry not to let Joe get away with that stuff. She told him that he liked to go hang out with his homies and that "you [Jerry] shouldn't have to pick up the slack." Jerry agreed.

I was immersed in working at the CAA alternative school when four months later, in mid-February, one of the security guards asked me, "Did you hear what happened to Joe? He was driving through a housing project and the cops did a routine check, found he had a number of warrants out on him, so they put him in jail."

"Damn," I said, shaking my head. "When's he getting out?"

"Probably tomorrow."

"That's good. Does he still have his job?"

"Not the same job, although they might put him on something else."

Later at the nonprofit, I asked if Joe was back. "Not here," Kyle told me.

"But he's out of jail, right?"

"Right," Kyle said, "but not back here." He seemed to be coding his words, speaking to foil eavesdroppers or at least minimize rumors.

"Do you think he'll be back?" I asked.

"Not in the same facility. We're looking for something more suitable for his talents," Kyle said diplomatically. He told me they were having a meeting with another service organization that afternoon and that he would mention Joe to them to see if they could do something.

Unsatisfied with Kyle's brief responses, I asked Lois what had happened with Joe. She said he had signed up a lot of people and gotten them jobs but was far behind in the paperwork. It turned out that at this point they were supposed to have over a hundred participants, which they had, but only twelve had been put into the computer so they almost lost the contract. They had to have all the names in by Monday. Jerry had had to come in over the weekend and work nights to catch up. She was perhaps the only worker with any sympathy left for Joe, she told me. "Joe was in over his head, and he really didn't have adequate training. We're now looking for a job for him with another program," she said, echoing Kyle. A few weeks later she told me Joe had found work as a roofer. She said Kyle had told him about other opportunities the nonprofit could find for him, and Joe had said he would keep it in mind, and he appreciated the offer, but he was making good money.

Then in early April, as I talked with Kyle in the back, he asked me if I had heard from Joe. I shook my head. Kyle said he had heard Joe was smoking marijuana just about every day and had recently done some shooting. "Joe learned how to tell people just what they wanted to hear."

In mid-May I saw Joe and Steve pull up in a jeep outside the CAA alternative school and ran out to shake their hands. Joe told me, "Have you heard— Marco's in jail?"

"No, I didn't hear that," I said. Joe nodded. "What for?"

"They found him with a gun." He looked at me. "It's not that so much as what he was doing with it."

"What, shooting it in the air?"

Joe nods. "That and other stuff," he said.

"So how long will he be locked up?"

Joe said for about three weeks, he'd heard. Steve nodded. I stood by the jeep that Joe was driving. They wrote their numbers down for me, and I gave my number to them.

"Nice jeep, yours?" I asked Joe.

"No, Steve's," he said. I nodded appreciatively, and Steve nodded too.

"Can you get me a job, man?" Joe practically begged, his eyes squinting.

"Where are you working now?" I asked.

"I'm over at Mono Park, working with kids," he said with disgust.

"You don't like it?"

"Nah," he said, corners of his mouth downturned. I thought of my own difficult yet gratifying work over the last three years as a teacher and felt unsympathetic and distant from Joe.

"Have you thought about going back over to CAA?"

"Yeah," he said. "They offered me something, but I just want to stay away from there for about six months, you know, sort of lay low."

I told him he should talk to the work experience coordinator at the CAA school. "You graduated, right?"

"Yeah," he nodded. Finally, I thought, something to be proud of.

"All right," I said. That's the last I saw of Joe. The most recent news I have is that he's making a good living on the docks.

Joe's Learner's Permit

Joe's experience might have been similar to that of any young man in his late teens, accommodating to his first "real job," except that for Joe past ties and the opportunities for action in his neighborhood provided especially rich possibilities that sometimes coincided with the demands and freedom of his work. In the midst of Joe's serious way of performing his repertoire of identities, it can be easy to forget that he was only nineteen. Childhood for the majority of youth in the West is extending, as the twenties become merely an extension of the teens. But for young people in the inner city, the responsibilities and risks of adulthood often arrive much sooner.[13]

Joe managed to hold on to the action, to work on the edge of his bureaucratic role as much as possible, keeping odd hours, not signing in on the public dry-erase board, and spending much of his work time out socializing with homies and flirting with women. Joe relished the *feel* of such moments, riding down the street in his Crown Victoria, wearing his hair net as Nelly throbbed through his speakers, even as he wore a baby-blue button-down dress shirt, slacks with a thin leather belt, and black dress shoes. Gangbanger bureaucrat? The title seems almost as ridiculous as the cape worn by the Capeman, or the hypermasculine images on a young boy's wall that Cintron analyzes.[14] From a middle-class perspective we might easily dismiss Joe as irresponsible. Or we might lionize Joe, as Lois did, as an honorable hero of his neighborhood who just happened to be in over his head, since the office lacked the resources to train and assist him properly.

I had a different impression from my times driving around with Joe: *it was on.* He took his job seriously, but he was also deadly serious about that street persona. Respect doesn't come cheap. When Joe returned to confront the man who had not called the ambulance for Lois, he didn't do so simply because it was an idea but because that was where he lived, it was his heart, his *corazón.* Perhaps I take the risk of romanticizing Joe, but it is certainly less than the risk Joe took in romanticizing himself. Joe seemed to be squeezing every last drop from the lemon of life as he made his rounds, working the feds while he worked the streets. It may well have been irresponsible, but with the life experiences and opportunities he had, he did all he could to *make the most* of what was offered. Anything less would have been a betrayal. Out of nothing, young people have arisen to create a landscape of daring possibilities, and Joe was less apt to betray those than to betray the opportunity to rise into the middle class.[15]

Joe well knew what the middle-class, bureaucratic life held in store. He saw it in college tutors' dire struggle for grades and in the endless morning coffees, doughnuts, and cigarettes of his co-workers. He witnessed the infighting over grants, where one nonprofit that happened to be a bit more politically connected or able to use the language of the cognoscenti might win out over another that had a better proposal for people more in need. Is this such a wonderful dream to foist upon those we refer to as "underclass"? Is the middle-class suburban dream so much more than what's possible in the inner city, that young people like Joe should be pitied or feared?

In *Sidewalk*, Mitch Duneier speaks of how some of the men eking out a living on the walkways of Greenwich Village adopted the attitude of "Fuck it," a resigned, embittered hopelessness in the face of a discriminatory society. Jay MacLeod describes how "the brothers" in a Newark housing project maintained high aspirations despite diminishing opportunities.[16] Joe's performance might be considered another way of making something out of nothing. With both the resignation of Duneier's sidewalk sitters and the aspirations of MacLeod's hoopsters, both the bragging of Tally's circle and the hypermasculinity that Valerio proudly displayed in his room, Joe had the best of all available worlds, and for a while at least he could do with it as he pleased.

Conclusion

I despise searching for a definition of what those things are.
But I don't need one until you ask.
The problem isn't me
It's you . . .

—Natasha Pike

The morality of ethnographic representation continually haunts ethnographic practice. From the travelers' and missionaries' accounts of *savages* that provided the troubling foundation for anthropology to contemporary studies of the near and the far, there is no escaping the moral, political context of observations. The foremost question for the would-be criminologist is that posed by Howard Becker more than forty years ago: "Whose side are we on?"[1] The question may seem a bit impolite and even Manichean, but it is inevitable and inescapable. Becker did not mince words. In studying any type of "criminal" activity, one sides with either the moral entrepreneurs, those making the rules, building the prisons, and paying the police, or those who are criminalized. According to Becker, research that respects and even appreciates the perspectives of the criminalized is often faulted, not for reasons of scientific methodology or validity, but for moral and political ones. In this closing chapter we focus on problems with an exogenous, correctional perspective on gangs and posit what might be gained by appreciating young people who happen to claim gangs in our society.

Getting It Wrong

The temptations to study gangs from an exogenous perspective are nearly overwhelming. At the time when Howard Becker wrote *Outsiders*, a widespread and vocal counterculture supported and even celebrated the views of the marginalized and downtrodden. Today, a substantial funding apparatus supports research that reinforces the status quo. Such governmental funding priorities trickle down to affect the likelihood of publication and the allocation of rare, extremely competitive academic positions.² As our society becomes increasingly exclusive, researchers must face sacrifices, risking the same marginalization as those they study for understanding the perspectives of the criminalized.³

Yet what is sociology if it is not working to understand the sense members make of their worlds? One of the classic founders of sociology, Max Weber, advocated that the primary aim of sociology was to be a science of *verstehen*, to understand members' perspectives.⁴ David Matza picked up on this admonition when he stated that the "aim is to comprehend and to illuminate the subject's view and interpret the world *as it appears to him*" (italics in original).⁵

The alternative can be embarrassing in hindsight. David Matza, in his foundational monograph *Becoming Deviant*, contrasts correctional and naturalistic perspectives on deviance. As an example of the correctional perspective, he provides an excerpt from a description of a baseball game played on the West Side of New York in the early part of the last century, spoken in the voice of "the community": "Clearly, from the community's point of view, the playing of baseball in the street is rightly a penal offense. It annoys citizens, injures persons and property, and interferes with traffic."⁶ Similarly, Stuart Hall and his colleagues from the famed Birmingham School of cultural studies mock the "bottomless mediocrity" of some social commentators on youth in the 1960s, who described teenagers on programs akin to *American Bandstand* and *Total Request Live* as having "huge faces, bloated with cheap confectionery and smeared with chain-store make-up, the open, sagging mouths and glazed eyes, the hands mindlessly drumming time to the music."⁷

A correctional perspective is all too tempting when one is averse to appreciating the ways youth stylistically remake the world. As sad as this is, it is especially toxic when race and class are added to the mix. Our criminalization of youth, basically for being youth, serves to reinforce centuries of domination and oppression, ensuring that structural inequalities will be passed on to the next generation. W. E. B. Du Bois's words could have been written by a student at CAA, perhaps a perceptive rapper:

Between me and the other world there is ever an unasked question: unasked by some through feelings of delicacy; by others through the difficulty of rightly framing it. All, nevertheless, flutter round it. They approach me in a half-hesitant sort of way, eye me curiously or compassionately, and then, instead of saying directly, How does it feel to be a problem? they say, I know an excellent colored man in my town; . . . or, Do not these Southern outrages make your blood boil. At these I smile, or am interested, or reduce the boiling to a simmer, as the occasion may require. To the real question, How does it feel to be a problem? I answer seldom a word.[8]

Seeing representations of young people in the inner city and then working with the actual people provides some insight into what Du Bois may have been driving at. Du Bois is quite charitable in his portrait, pointing out the good intentions of those in "the other world" even as he sees himself objectified in their eyes as "a problem." Du Bois acknowledges a problem, but the way he reframes it is educational, even today. For Du Bois, the problem lies not in the former slaves or in the former slave owners, but in the systematic structures of segregation, sustained through commonplace expectations: "the color line." Over one hundred years after Du Bois's prediction that "the problem of the twentieth century is the color line," we still find ourselves bedeviled by this most pernicious demarcation,[9] and we are still challenged to rise to Du Bois's level of awareness. Young people in the inner city are not imprisoned by the many discourses that conceptualize them as "a problem." Rather, as this book has shown, their orientations toward "gangs," "decent" and "street," and "violence," rather than entrapping, are resources they draw upon in understanding the actions of others and in molding themselves to be mutually understandable.

In addition to simply getting it wrong, an exogenous, essentializing view of gang members may contribute to the continued criminalization of young people for claiming a street identity. The best response to the demographic question, "How many young people are gang members?" is "All of them and none of them; it all depends." Our academic discourses and policies often reify the importance of gang membership more than young people themselves do. We should criminalize victimizing behaviors, and while the rituals of gangs may provide opportunities for such behaviors, they also provide opportunities for the expression of *communitas*.[10]

Gangs are worth studying, not necessarily because they are criminal or violent, but because they are an important part of how meanings are constituted in many communities. When we overlook that import because of the fear of the "gang" as a four-letter word, a pejorative way of framing our consultants, we risk missing some of the variety of ways in which local meanings are determined. The director of a nonprofit may invoke the presence of gangs in his neighborhood to ensure funding for his grants while at the same time disdaining such commodification. His young federal worker's gang ties may help him find clients for a federal program and provide opportunities for action along the way. And young people, those who know gangs most intimately, often see a gang member as someone who is poor, bored, and hard to love. Nonetheless, the rituals of gangs may provide ways of resolving what might otherwise be intractable situations and, in the insightful words of Ralph Cintron, *create something out of nothing*.[11] Scholars of community should not avoid highlighting local understandings of gangs; rather, we should rehabilitate the term *gang*, which for too long has been associated merely with violence and criminality.

Uncovering

In the many rich and perceptive studies of communities where gangs exist, there is often a strange silence, as if researchers fear to use the term *gang* because it might marginalize their consultants. Perhaps it is time for community researchers to embrace this term and reclaim it from the criminologists. In his book *Covering* (2006), Kenji Yoshino advocates for the recognition of a new category of civil rights abuse: the imposition of the requirement for various individuals to cover a part of their identity in various spheres. While it is illegal to consider that someone *is* a woman or gay as a basis of discrimination, Yoshino finds discrimination in the ways people are expected to hide such identities. Being a woman or gay may not get you fired, but acting the part may.

Community researchers, wary of the stigma of gang membership, are experts at covering. For instance, Ann Ferguson's wonderful book *Bad Boys* tells how teachers warn kids to avoid certain *groups* wearing similar jackets, and Elijah Anderson shows how a young man gets in with the local *group* of young people by fighting one of them. David M. Kennedy, the director of the Center of Crime Prevention and Control at John Jay College, "dislikes the term 'gang,' which he thinks evokes a misleading Hollywood image of highly organized groups bent on mayhem and destruction."[12] Yet however much we may want to avoid or sidestep this loaded four-letter word, if we hope to take members' meanings seriously, we are left with many young people who call their *group* a gang, a group with which others in the neighborhood must come to terms.

The secretiveness of community scholars on gangs is mirrored in local discourses. One afternoon, when I circulated a petition for a skate park among the secretaries of the alternative school, one asked where it would be located, and after I responded the mood turned somber. "Well, my son won't be able to use it," Ms. Smith said. "Neither will mine," Sally said. "But at least it's something for the community," Ms. Smith said. "Might as well sign it, couldn't hurt."

While schools must grapple with issues of inclusiveness and tend to see gang members as a threat to be controlled, Kyle Griffin, the director of a nearby nonprofit, recognizes that they are resources to be exploited. When I asked Griffin about Joe, he made a general comment on the category into which he must have assumed I placed Joe: gang members. Rather than speaking of their pathology or delinquency, he spoke of their commodification—how the allure, the "sexiness" of gangs brings a cachet to nonprofits that he tried to avoid, not always successfully.

> You have the antiviolence experts, and you have the gang experts, where you've basically commodified this dysfunction. . . . We've had a lot of problems with some funders because we don't want to keep those kinds of identifications, or even reveal that kind of stuff if it comes up in the case of discussion, that this person is identified with XYZ [gang]. . . . Well, this is where CAA is, it's where it is. I delivered mail here too *[laughs]* many years ago. I guess it's like this contradiction. You write a proposal, and you put in all this stuff, the number of teen parents, and the number of single households, and *that has nothing to do with the character of folks who live in this community at all.* It is a real thing when you do that, and then you do like, 'Shhh, this is what these folks wanna hear.' Well, you know, they're gonna give you money—what difference will it make if they give you this money? We won't wear that proudly on our chest. That's my contradiction around some of this stuff.[13]

Thus Griffith commodified gangs without wishing to, warping neighborhood perceptions and understandings into the sort of numerical profiles that would preserve the nonprofit and help the community.

One problem in speaking in terms of gangs is that once one mentions a behavior that is assumed to be a *pathology*, one is called upon to identify causes, in keeping with the medical metaphor. The purported "causes" of gangs contain some elements of feasibility, but they always seem to miss the mark, as they are usually on a different level of analysis than the phenomenon to be explained. The most popular "cause" in the gang literature has been deindustrialization, but a global shift in the economy doesn't explain why some areas losing factories have gangs and others don't, or the different forms gangs may take around the world. The areas supposedly with the most "gang members" are far from those most hobbled by jobs going overseas—to the contrary. Diego Vigil's notion of multiple marginalities incorporates both micro and macro perspectives but doesn't recognize the artful nuances by which gang identity may be invoked, and maintains the discourse of pathology.[14]

Studying gangs as a social movement constitutes an important step away from the discourse of gangs as pathology. Such a perspective, long overdue in the gang literature, recognizes structural, marginalizing conditions but shows that gang members are far from mere victims of circumstance. Instead, as David Brotherton, Luis Barrios, and Louis Kontos have shown, the Almighty Latin King and Queen Nation is about educating young people and building community.[15] All gangs contain some elements of a social movement, just as they contain some elements of pathology. The same might be said for corporations, governments, and families. Let us then bring gangs back to the community, and back to the ingenious young people who have created them. Let us not be afraid to speak of how a young person may perform a gang identity or to speak of the ways gangs might be resisted and violence overcome.

Struggles over the ways gang members are depicted are not simply academic squabbles. Rather, in the words of one nonprofit organization, "It's about the youth." Our representations of gangs have real consequences. If we can appreciate how the rituals of gangs are cultural resources that must be understood and can be used strategically by any young person in an ecology with gangs, then we might see how profiling young people as gang members to determine a "population" is deeply misguided. While we should not hesitate to speak of the creative agency of gangs and their members, to refer to a young person simply as a "gang member," as if this might summarize his or her identity, misinterprets and maligns how young people use identity as a resource and reifies a highly situated and contingent construction. To then multiply this misunderstanding through statistical analysis adds injury to insult.

Recognizing Soft Versions of Gang Identity

This book has shown that young people problematize how we might think of gang "members." A young person may claim a gang in which he is not a member in order to create "action" or a sense of prestige. A young person may "kick it" with a gang without being a member, even if his homies have "jumped him in" and claim him as a member. Another may still consider himself in a gang, although he no longer gangbangs. Some—even those who are at times recognized as hard-core—may "rank out," and refuse to claim gang membership if they are in a circumstance in which they do not wish their gang membership to be invoked, such as on a date, while shopping, or perhaps while completing a survey. In short, out of the tool kit of culture, gangs are a wonderful resource for molding identity in the inner city.[16] Community researchers ought to recognize this and appreciate it as much as young people, and not be cowed by commodifying and criminalizing discourses.

Posing gang identity as performance, as a situated, creative, contingent accomplishment by a young person, does not obviate that deeper structural issues may be at play, that gang members constitute groups, or that the performance of gang identity may have deadly serious consequences. What it does do, however, is step away from the notion of gang membership as pathology and recognize that gang identity, like gender, race, or class identity, is fundamentally an achievement.

Perhaps at one time "soft" versions of identity could be called avant-garde or "strange," but this is no longer the case. Perhaps in part because of the work of social scientists, but certainly much more substantially because of the ever expanding currents of globalization, for many young people complexifying identity is nothing new. It is as easy as a walk through a major urban center, where a Little Japan strives for rental space against an adjacent Little El Salvador, and restaurants offer such lively culinary possibilities as Mexican-Korean or Polish-Brazilian. In music, art, and architecture, and everywhere on the Internet, traditions are resources, and identity is malleable, flexible, and contingent. Deconstructionism, hybridization, and bricolage have become unavoidable aspects of our contemporary world.[17]

Researchers who posit the reified existence of class, race, gender, or gangs take the risk that these concepts are as tangible and relevant to the researched as they are to the researchers. Evidence for problematizing such purported identities might come from many sources, not the least of which is the researcher's own lived experience. If one fails to notice such dynamics in everyday life, hard data are readily available from freshman and seniors who took part in an ongoing study of student engagement in the University of California system. According to Marc Flacks, "The survey item respondents most frequently chose to comment on and complain about was one that asked them to identify themselves with particular social groups and/or cliques at their institution."[18] Asked to choose among fourteen categories such as "party-goers," "intellectuals," and "athletes," many students instead claimed to identify most with "people who don't like categories," "people uninterested in associating themselves with a group," and "students who don't assume stupid labels like those listed above." As Flacks notes, "Researchers ought to be methodologically circumspect when pursuing such questions. . . . We need to ask better questions of young respondents."[19]

Such an admonition should be taken especially to heart by gang research-ers. In my exposure to only a few hundred young people in a gang-relevant area, I met young people who had switched from Crips to Bloods, blacks in ostensibly Mexican gangs (and vice versa), and young people who claimed a gang of which they were not a part in order to seek a thrill. I knew young people who were hard-core at one time of the day (for example, "holding down the corner" before or after school) and extremely studious and polite at other times (for instance, in class with a respected teacher). Similarly, Norma Mendoza-Denton met young people who switched from Norte to Sur; who excelled in athletics, jobs, and gangbanging; and who recognized common Norte and Sur allegiances as both became politically active to combat myo-pic immigration laws.[20]

As a means of moving forward, consider what might be gained for gang studies from taking seriously Brubaker and Cooper's insights into how interwoven political consciousness and political responses are with analytic conceptualization:

> This tendency to objectify "identity" deprives us of analytical leverage. It makes it more difficult for us to treat "groupness" and "boundedness" as emergent properties of particular structural or conjunctural settings rather than as always already there in some form. The point needs to be empha-sized today more than ever, for the unreflectively groupist language that prevails in everyday life, journalism, politics, and much social research as well–the habit of speaking without qualification of "Albanians" and "Serbs," for example, as if they were sharply bounded, internally homo-geneous "groups"–not only weakens social analysis but constricts political possibilities in the region.[21]

Let us hope we might worry as much about constricting "political possi-bilities in the region" of our inner cities. As Susan Driver notes, "As a viewer and a researcher I remain uncertain of what is fabricated and what is real, compelling me to wonder why I need to make such distinctions in the first place."[22]

Kites

On an ordinary day of school, Chris was hunched over his math work-sheet, absorbed in drawing figures over the crosses that the teacher's aide had placed next to his incorrect answers. I asked him what he was drawing.

"They are kites," he said simply without looking up, lengthening their tails to fill the margin of his page. Then he started talking.

"I'm gonna go to school, set my mind to the go ahead. 'Cause see, they have me held back to the ninth. I done made it all the way to the eleventh grade, half a year. There ain't been a whole year. I check into this school January eighth. They had me held back to the ninth. I made it to the eleventh like that," he said.

"Mm hm," I said.

"So I'm not, that right there is just a malfunction, you hear what I'm sayin'?"

"Mm hm."

"'Cause I tol' 'em, I said, 'watch this.' I told Mr. Merritt, I say, 'Watch this. I'm gonna get to the eleventh, work faster than air. You don't believe me? 'Cause that's the grade I'm supposed to be in.' He didn't believe me. I was doin' the work like 'wham.' And every day, people be stealin' my work outta the check-in box, puttin' they name on it and I wouldn't get credit but I'd do it over."

However we might think of the inner city, for young people it is a place of dreams.[23] Some dream of escape, some of control, and some of poetry. They are all too human and very much Americans. Like all children, they may be difficult to love at times. Like all humans, they want to create something marvelous, to show what they can do. The city can nurture or repress such dreams. Collectively, we create the ambience of future possibilities.

I give the last word to one of CAA's teachers, expressing his view of possibilities lost.

If you go back down the street here to Fifty-second and Central you'll find a little community park, and in the community park you'll find boulders, and Bob, these boulders gotta be about four feet tall. They must weigh a thousand, fifteen hundred pounds, and they're strategically placed on the grass at this park. And the reason they did that was to stop us from playing football. Now this is a sadness, because we were considered a gang, but every Saturday we would march to that park and we would challenge high schools, car clubs, neighboring blocks, other streets in playing football, and that's how we got our aggression out, which was perfectly legitimate. But they put the rocks there because we wore cleats and we'd dig up the grass every Saturday. So they put rocks there and that prevented us from playing football, so now what do we start doing? [That was] one of the only outlets we had. So these kids have no outlets. The basketball court's still there. But we would throw the football back and forth, and we'd go out there and tackle one another. We'd hit, legitimate football, without referees. The game was very organized, the whole league was organized. We played different people. Ghost wagon club this week. We played another opposing block next week. The Jefferson football team would come the next week, and it was always on our turf, right there on Central and Fifty-second. We did that for about two years, and the maintenance men were really hot, and they told us to get off the grass with our cleats. But what do you want us to do?

We'd go over to Randolph Park. There's an amphitheater over there that's never used. There's dry weeds and leaves and brush and trash. We'd go over early in the morning and clean that baby up. We'd take probably two hundred feet of electrical from the PA back over to this two-story house. There was power in the amphitheater, but since we didn't have a permit we had to get power where we could. We had already sited it out, so we took a plug, with a plug outlet, and screwed it into the light socket, plug it up there. Run that baby over there. We rented equipment, big speakers and turntables and stuff, and then we'd have a showcase, a talent show, right there at the park. When people heard the music, they would gravitate to us. And then whoever wanted to, we'd invite 'em up on the stage. The way we were able to pay for our equipment was we sold hot dogs and cokes, and we made money that way until the police came and told us we couldn't do it. Put us out. But many of the early videos came from that kind of thing.

Appendix: Getting Schooled

Into the Field

I originally visited CAA in the spring of 1995 as part of an evaluation study of a school-to-work program coordinated by my university. I remember the educational coordinator, Candice, a short Caucasian, fluent in Spanish, who, with a bit of a snicker, asked, "Ever been to the ghetto?" I had not. She gave me directions for negotiating the twenty-five miles of freeways and surface streets. "Does it matter what colors I wear?" I asked naively. "No," she said with a chuckle.

The area, still mostly undeveloped years after riots had destroyed many businesses, seemed to consist primarily of windowless churches and liquor stores among the empty lots. Over the years, community organizing reduced the number of liquor stores while storefront, community-based organizations multiplied. I drove down a wide central avenue past a median strip with conifers growing out of green asphalt, giving the street a spacious if surreal quality. Often a couple dogs trotted along this strip, warily making their way into traffic. Along the sides of the street a number of small businesses, such as a VCR repair shop, a nail salon, and an eyeglasses shop were set off from the main strip by another concrete strip in order to provide parking away from traffic.

The school sat a few hundred feet from this main boulevard, down a side street. I parked at the curb, checking the signs to make sure it wasn't street-cleaning day, and walked down the sidewalk to the school, carrying a backpack with my surveys. I passed old Craftsman homes with lawns in front and wide porches. Some were well manicured, with roses and bougainvillea plants engulfing short chain-link fences running around the front of the yards. But others were a nondescript gray or a faded pink, sometimes with the shell of a car or two in the front yard, along with assorted trash blowing onto the sidewalk.

After being buzzed in at two gates attached to twelve-foot high chain-link fences, I distributed the surveys inside an English classroom. I noticed that the students were all African American or Latino, many with tattoos and hairstyles I didn't recognize, extremely baggy T-shirts, and jeans. They looked at me warily without paying much attention to what I said about the survey. Instead, they sought help from Candice, who warmly circulated among them, helping them decipher the questions.

Arriving at CAA felt like landing on the moon. Of over twenty inner-city high schools I visited in the city as part of a school-to-work study, it seemed to have the most dire conditions. Also, since the school was small and the principal accommodating, it seemed more manageable than the sprawling bureaucratic structures set up for teenagers throughout the city. Finally, since every student at CAA was a dropout, by working there I could learn more about why kids leave school.

In January of 1997 I visited Kyle Griffin at the community-based organization (CBO) connected with CAA. I had worked with Kyle at the university's school-to-work program on and off since 1988, and his presence near my field site was a comfort and another motivator for me to choose CAA. As the months passed, I cherished our times in the backroom, smoking Carltons and bullshitting.

Ms. Reynolds, the principal of CAA, was delighted that I would volunteer and conduct research at her school. An African American woman with a strong sense of southern manners and hospitality, she was always dressed fashionably. She told me that the young man she had hoped to match me up with was no longer attending. He had been in the school in the past but had had some altercation, and when he returned from camp she met with him and his parents, who begged and pleaded that he be allowed to return. "Camp?" I asked. "Juvenile?" "Yes," she said, and continued nonchalantly. She said she had written out a detailed contract of what he needed to do.

"He only lasted two days. He's gone now. Said he was too tied down. There were too many restrictions."

I shook my head. "That's too bad."

"But we have someone else for you." She seemed to be grinning. She said his name was Chris and he was in the special education room.

"Now what is it you're looking at?" she asked. This was the first of many requests to explain myself and my research to staff, students, or outsiders. I told her I wanted to look at young men's attempts to be nonviolent even when they might have felt compelled to be violent. She nodded and said that this young man might be very helpful. I told her I would like to interview about twenty young men. She said I could talk to them and take notes but that if they were under eighteen and I was going to tape-record them I would need to make out permission slips to be signed by their parents. I told her I understood. I also assured her that I would guarantee the anonymity and confidentiality of each person, as well as the school.

Ms. Reynolds walked me past five African American young men playing basketball and led me up the ramp to Mr. Merritt's class. Mr. Merritt was an African American who looked to be in his late forties or early fifties, with gray hair and a beard with some strands of black. As I entered his room I saw a chalkboard filling the opposite wall, faced by twelve seats with attached desks, three chairs in each of four rows. At the wall to the right were two computers and a printer separated into study carrels by wooden dividers. Behind the chairs in the far corner was a round table surrounded by four chairs, and behind that was a large locked aluminum cabinet that Mr. Merritt unlocked, placing my backpack inside, and locked again.

Mr. Merritt asked me what school I was from and what I was studying. I told him I was studying how young men avoid violence and what that meant for their masculinity. He told me these young men assumed that violence and masculinity went hand in hand. He offered me some popcorn, and I got up and stepped out of the room and stood on the landing outside Mr. Merritt's class, resting my arms on the wooden rail and looking toward the basketball court. About fifty students were on the grounds. Most of the African American young men were on or around the basketball court before me. Two teams of three players battled each other, apparently not as interested in keeping score as they were in each other's moves and shots. About ten other students were lined up against the fence by the day care center, chatting and watching the action on the court. Now and then someone made a move or a stuff on the court that those by the fence reacted to viscerally, grimacing with cries of "Ohhh" or "Damn!"

Students at CAA typically used the space of the yard during nutrition in a pattern whose fluid boundaries divided the students by race and gender. While the African American young men were open and enthusiastic, aspiring to be public, the Latinos displayed a more private public persona, huddling in tight, intense circles. The African American young women, unlike the young men, showed little interest in basketball. A young woman might occasionally "shoot around" with the guys, as would some Latinos, but once a game began such students would typically find something else to do. Instead, African American young women usually stood in small clusters by the snack machine and the women's restroom. Latinas tended to congregate on the

benches behind the office, talking and leaning against each other support-
ively. Small groups of friends stooped by the metal box in the empty space
by the bathrooms, at a distance far enough from others so they would not be
overheard. This marked a desire for privacy, as anyone coming to meet them
had to traverse a significant gap. This group was typically more mixed ethni-
cally and in terms of gender, often including some of the few openly gay and
lesbian students.

"Why You Still Bangin'?"

Eventually, the students returned to their classes. As I entered Mr. Merritt's room, a dark, handsome young man with a bit of a mustache greeted me
in an officiously friendly and welcoming way, as if mocking his own role as a
sort of ambassador. He held out his hand. "Hi, my name is Richard," he said
quickly. "What's your name?" I told him my name was Bob, and he showed
me to my seat.

Chris entered, a tall, lanky, light Cherokee/African American of about
seventeen, who wore sneakers and saggy beige pants with a black knit belt
hanging down about a foot in the front, and a T-shirt featuring a huge image
of Bugs Bunny. He often seemed as if he might burst out of the room, rising
from his seat to leap over multiple desks with perfect grace and ease. His
speech and energy level matched his athleticism, as he blurted out comments
on an ongoing basis.

Mr. Merritt, whom many of the kids referred to with a jovial nickname
because of his near-constant smile, introduced Chris to me, telling him that
Ms. Reynolds had appointed me as his tutor. He would be working with me
one on one, occasionally outside the classroom. Mr. Merritt was grinning,
but Chris was taken aback, his eyes and mouth open circles. I sat down with
him somewhat apologetically and helped him answer questions out of his
social studies book. Written in accessible pseudo-street language ("Benjamin
Franklin wanted everyone to get along"), the facts concerning the framing
of the Constitution mattered little in Chris's life, and they were not made to
matter in the class. Instead, he and others spent much of their time conjec-
turing about the type and caliber of guns we heard being fired constantly
nearby.

Bored and frustrated, Chris would suddenly speak up loudly, hop out of
his chair, or flirt with the young African American woman sitting in front
of the computers. Nevertheless, he finished copying all the questions in the
chapter, and I spent about ten minutes near the end of the class helping him

find the answers. He and Emily teased each other's lack of productivity, loudly rustling their papers to ironically prove their own industriousness.

The next day Chris was antsy and pulled out his folder to find something else to do besides the fractions worksheet in front of him. He pulled out some papers he said he had worked on in art class—practice tags, with certain words crossed out but not others. I asked to see it and he showed it to me.

"Why you still bangin'?" Emily asked.

"I don't bang."

"You hang around gangbangers."

"Just because I hang around bangers don't mean I bang. They just my homies. Don't you still hang out with your homies?"

"Not if they gangbang," she said proudly. Chris shrugged. Small moments like this were one way gangs were made relevant at CAA. Students like Emily who were moving away from gangs might criticize friends who presented themselves as involved.

Discipline

Occasionally, Chris and other African American young men joked around, and later I thought it might have to do with me, but at the time it didn't faze me. In the beginning of history class they joked about big words. "Oh, that's a big word," one said in response to another, or "I don't get it, that word's too big." While I couldn't be sure about the joke, I thought that perhaps I looked studious to them in my glasses and they were playing off that.

At one point, they repeatedly called each other "nigga." Another student said they shouldn't talk that way around me. "It don't mean nothin'," Chris said. "It's just talk." Later, Mr. Merritt apologized to me on their behalf.[1]

The next day when I returned to the school, I sat at the back table with Tim, Chris, and Kelly and got a crash course in ghetto culture. Kelly, a debonair-looking African American of medium height, with short hair and a tattoo teardrop in the corner of his left eye, wore clean white pants, a white shirt memorializing Tu-Pac, and a gold chain. He had a history workbook out, while Tim, a large, affable African American wearing a T-shirt and jeans, sat by Chris. Tim and Chris each had a reading book out, but schoolwork, including any of my efforts, was not of interest to them on this day.

Kelly and Chris went back and forth about each other's mamas, with Tim watching, smiling, and occasionally jumping in. Their retorts were ingenious, ever so gradually escalating the ugliness of claims to "do" the other's mama or to know of the other's mama being done by someone. They didn't go to the furthest extreme of nastiness but kept it within limits, for instance by insinuating that the other was his bastard son.

Kelly took umbrage, and the talk shifted from mamas to Kelly taking Chris in a fight. Kelly said he'd do it after school in the bathroom. They alternated between threats about the use of guns, of various calibers, shot in various places (often behind the head), and homosexual threats. Chris offered to beat Kelly up right there in the classroom. Why wait? Chris said that he was the kind of guy who didn't need to hide anything from anybody and that "if you wanna go, let's go." Kelly said he wasn't into any of that and he'd rather go after school because he didn't want to humiliate Chris in front of everyone. They continued like this until nutrition, with Mr. Merritt and Ms. West sitting at their desks nonplussed while I watched uselessly sitting beside them.

At nutrition, Mr. Merritt told me I had to watch them; I couldn't let them get out of hand. I told him I couldn't be much of a disciplinarian because I wanted to have good rapport with them. He said he understood. "Discipline, no, you don't need to do that. Just don't let them take advantage of you."

Ms. West brought me to Room 2, to the left of the main office, where a number of the female teachers were sitting and chatting. Ms. West told me that Chris was not happy about having me work with him and had even complained to Ms. Reynolds. I was surprised. "He'll get used to it," she said. "He has to." We entered the room, where I was introduced to about eight different teachers. They sympathized with my efforts to help Chris. I told them it was difficult doing anything with him that morning because he, Kelly, and Yogi were so busy going at each other. They told me to take the upper hand and not to call him Yogi because that was his gang name; "Call him Tim." They also told me Chris probably acted out so much because he couldn't at home—his mama was so stern with him.

The advice they gave me, to "take the upper hand" and to "call him Tim," was advice I never followed. Instead, I did my best not to coerce or discipline students and always followed their lead on what they needed to do or where they needed help. This left me at odds with the teachers, so after one more visit with this group at nutrition I stopped going there and instead hung out with the students on the yard.

Interviews

Ms. Abigail, a young English teacher, asked me what I was studying, and the room became silent. I told her I was interested in how young men avoid violence. She said it sounded interesting and mentioned Ben, saying he was a sweet kid and would be perfect for me to interview. When I returned to class, Ben was by Mr. Merritt's computer, so I asked him if he would like to do an interview. He told me he'd be eighteen in June, so I gave him a permission form.

After interviewing Emily, I returned to class to find Chris alone, as all the other students were attending an assembly on "black and brown pride." After I had worked with him on a math worksheet, he switched on the radio on top of a file cabinet in the far front-left corner of the room, adjusting it to a rap station, playing with the controls, turning it up louder and louder, watching my response, and then turning it down. He returned and started on a percentages packet, copying down on paper what he would later copy into the workbook. "I hate copying," he said. "I know, I hate copying too," I agreed. Chris walked back to the radio, making up his own rap to go with the rap on the radio. Again he turned up the volume, and I cautioned him that I might get into trouble, so he turned it down. "Is that The Beat?" I asked. He shook his head. "106," he said. "K-Roq?" I asked. "No, Power." Oh, of course, I realized, K-Roq plays rock hits and rarely if ever plays rap.

He rapped along with a song. "Is that a rap you wrote out, or did you just make it up?" I asked. "I just made it up," he said. "That's great!" I said. He was extremely talented in improvising his rhymes and rhythms. Four years later, when I returned to CAA, I found that he was on the road with his own group, selling CDs. An R & B song came on. "Oh this is great," he said. "Trent Sweat," I said. "Yeah," he said, nodding his head, although I realized later it was actually Keith Sweat (did he not correct me out of courtesy?).

Throughout my interview with Chris, we rarely made eye contact. When we did, his eyes looked small and sensitive. When I asked about gangbanging he said, "I knew you were going to ask me that," and he placed his hood over his head, hiding himself under a gangster veneer. He became animated when talking about and replaying his past fights, exclaiming "POW!" and slamming the table. When I asked about something that smacked of mainstream views, such as what he did with the gang now or if he regretted the past, he had stock answers that mirrored conventional morality. I noticed that night in my notes that I had felt shaky throughout the interview. Perhaps I realized that Chris was a big, wiry kid who could easily hurt me if he wanted to, or I might have been worried about keeping up with his pace and finding the next question, or perhaps I was just chilly in the cool breeze. I tried to remember to breathe, and I stayed conscious of my shaking knees and tight stomach and tried to be respectful and cool. Chris certainly was both with me.

Shortly after my interview with Chris I interviewed Larry, who introduced me to Shawn, a key informant who introduced me to "hitting up." When Shawn entered class and sat next to Larry, Larry told him, "You ought to let him interview you." In this way, my snowball sample moved quickly through many of the African American young men at the school; I hardly ever needed to ask for an interview.

"We Get a Lot of That"

That afternoon, Richard, who had greeted me so affably, sat by a computer, refusing to participate during history. As class ended, he remained with the computer, even after Merritt told him it was time to go. "That's my girl!" Richard protested. "What you mean, 'That's your girl'? That's the school's computer, and you ain't been doin' nothin' in class all day anyway," Merritt told him. Richard stormed out, fuming, and screamed, "Go ahead! Call my mother. Kick me out! I don't care!" After he left, Merritt turned to me and said, "I happen to already have a meeting with his mother tomorrow. I can't respond to what's happened in their pasts. We tell them, 'We only know you right now. Doesn't make any sense if you're mad about something that happened before we knew you, because that's not what's happening now.' We get a lot of that." I nodded.

Staff members often recognized that their students were "troubled" with "issues" to explain bewildering behavior. Most notably, the principal of the school urged her staff to see students as "children with needs."[2] For instance, during a discussion concerning whether a student should be expelled for fighting, she remarked, "Remember the students we serve. We should expose them to everything we can. But still, they're the most obnoxious kids out there. That's why we have them. They've dropped out of everywhere else."

Such an understanding was also a background for interpreting students' claims about various exploits. For instance, when I told an older security guard, Bill, how one student had told me about managing his uncle's nightclub, Bill replied, "If you got your shit together, what you doin' here?"

Coming into the Circle

The African American young men were much more willing, even eager to be interviewed initially than the Latinos. I attributed this to my comfort hanging out by the basketball court, talking about basketball, and playing in their games. The Latinos, usually in a closed, quiet circle, seemed more impenetrable. My interviews provided my entrée there. Far from being a burden on my consultants, interviews helped me ease into the setting. After my interview with Marco, a Latino in Mr. Merritt's class, he referred me to others, and gradually the sample expanded. After five months I found myself a practical part of their circle, giving kids rides home from school, going to *quinceañeras,* and talking on the phone at night with my consultants, something that never happened with the African Americans I came to know.

My closest relationships developed with the Belizeans, Ben, Shawn, and Tom. I routinely drove around the city with one or another of them, going out for lunch, looking for mechanics, or searching for apartments. I did not think of this in racial terms at the time, but in hindsight, perhaps since we were both minorities at the setting (there were only about a half-dozen Belizeans at the school, and I was the only white), we weren't pulled by many other ties, so we gravitated toward each other.

Admittedly, I felt like an idiot having lived in former Mexican territory all my life without knowing Spanish, so I missed out on some of their banter as they rapidly code-switched. I knew that before I returned for a longer period of participant observation I should know the language or at least do my best to learn it. This was one of my reasons for becoming a teacher for three years in a neighborhood of recent immigrants from Mexico and Central America. Throughout this time I did not take field notes; planning and teaching my own thematic units, attending classes for teachers, plus homework and journaling took most of my waking hours.[3] I moved into an inner-city neighborhood near the school where I was teaching, not far from CAA, which I visited on occasion, and I spent my breaks at a language school in Mexico.

Round Two

I dropped in at the CAA CBO in the fall of 2000, and to my surprise found Joe. For my first three weeks back doing research, I stayed at the CBO working with Joe and volunteering. Joe told me what he knew of my prior consultants and brought me into the neighborhood to talk with Marco and Steve again. Joe showed me where he had slung crack by the local high school, as well as what his job at the CBO entailed. Eventually, he reintroduced me to CAA, and I began my second round of field research.

At my first day back at CAA, in November of 2000, I reviewed my list of twenty-four prior interviewees with Mr. Merritt, who was now vice principal, Ms. Reynolds, the principal, and some of the office workers. They knew that Chris was a rapper and that Joe was at the CBO, but they were out of touch with many others. They said Richard was in prison. I managed to link up with my two Belizean friends, Ben and Shawn, by repeatedly visiting Ben's job at a local retailer and by catching Shawn when he visited CAA to try to pass his high school equivalency exam, at age twenty-four. I also met up with Marco's brother, Frank, when he came by in the morning to drop off his girlfriend who worked at CAA.

Finding these consultants, showing them their interviews, playing the old tapes, and conducting a follow-up interview was a great experience. Marco was excited, rubbing his hands and purring, "Let's listen to the old Marco!" All my Latino follow-up interviewees spoke for about forty-five minutes, while my Belizeans both filled two ninety-minute tapes, pouring out their hearts. Unfortunately, I was unable to find any of my prior African American consultants.

Aside from locating these young people, I began my second stint of observing at CAA. In my first round, my attention had been entirely focused on the students. I saw the teachers as I think many of the students did, as encumbrances to avoid. My interactions with teachers were limited to tutoring when I wasn't hanging out with or interviewing students. We regarded each other with some suspicion, keeping a respectful distance.

After I became a teacher my entrée at CAA was entirely different. When I returned in fall of 2000 I was embraced by the teachers and the students regarded me with suspicion. I did not particularly try to bond with teachers, but that "teacher persona" that I had thought I could put on or take off like a robe had seeped into how I carried myself. Discussing lesson planning, discipline, first-year teaching experiences, or other topics "only teachers know" was my comfort zone; I fit right in. Though I would have preferred to wait with the students for food at nutrition, they insisted that I cut to the front of the line for food like the teachers. During field trips I was considered an extra chaperone for official purposes, and although I did not enforce discipline I was asked to hold the digital camera. I had no problems getting interviews with the teachers, and each of these lasted at least an hour; they felt like conversations with an old pal.

As I was welcomed by teachers, students were more distant; it took three times as long to interview as many students as I had in the first period of immersion. Many students thought I might be there to offer jobs. Skid, a light-skinned African American/Belizean young man with braids and green eyes who liked to play basketball, asked me what I was doing there. I told him I was doing interviews with young men about their lives and asked him if he would like to be interviewed. "Only for money," he said. "If you got a J-O-B, then we can talk, otherwise, no," leaving no room for argument.

Others could not shake the notion that I was an undercover cop, a problem that had never come up before. As before, I decided to stand up before a class and make an announcement about my research to let them know I was available if they would like to do an interview.

"UC," Angel, a stocky Latino, said.

"UC, what's that?" I asked, thinking of University of California.

"Undercover," he said.

"I promise you I'm not undercover," I said. "Often in classes or in your families you may feel no one wants to listen to you. I'm someone who'll listen. I interviewed Everett," I added as I noticed him passing by me to take his seat. "How was it?" "It was cool," he said, nodding. This announcement, made to about twenty students, did not yield a single interviewee, except, ironically, Angel.

Like Jay MacLeod, I tried playing basketball with students, as I had managed to do in my first immersion period.[4] I kept up with them to an extent, although they seemed much faster and more agile than they had three years before. "I feel like I'm in a pinball machine and the ball just keeps flying by," I told onlookers when I came out of the game. My third time in a game, my shot was blocked and I came down funny, then heard and felt a "crunchiness" in my left knee. This marked my entrée with those who had torn their ACL (anterior cruciate ligament) and my exit from basketball. As I went from crutches to a cane, to various types of supports and braces before and after surgery, my knee became a primary way for others to engage with me for the remainder of my six months at the school.

How did students eventually come to trust me? The main way was through just what I had done before—being with students, working with them and talking with them. I started to follow my own schedule, like any other student, going from class to class in the role of "least adult."[5] I liked to see how long I could keep going to a class and hang out with students before the teacher asked why I was there. Once he or she did, I answered that I was a tutor, which always sufficed. I ate with students at nutrition and lunch, even though Mr. Martin insisted I go to the head of the line, and whenever anyone wanted to do an interview I obliged him or her.

Race

The conception that whites, Anglos, or those of European descent have of themselves as "race-less" is not a pretension that can long be sustained in inner-city areas. Whiteness became relevant in a context where race was not escapable for anyone and was therefore accountable by everyone. Numerous assemblies and discussion were devoted to the "black and brown" issue, since the neighborhood was dominated by two gangs who were sometime rivals inside and outside school: Eighteenth Street for Latinos and Central for African Americans.

When Mr. Ross, an African American teacher, broached this topic with a group of about ten mostly Latino young men in a meeting referred to as a "men's group," Marco was quite specific in delineating an imaginary boundary between the two groups. "Let me tell you," he said, rising to claim the floor. "Over here, Latinos," he said, sweeping his arm to the left. "This side, blacks," he said, sweeping to the right. Mr. Ross tried to interrupt, but Marco drowned him out and became more demonstrative. "They do their thing," he said, pushing his palms outward and away, "and we do ours," bringing his palms inward. "They have their music, their dance, and their language, and we have our music, our dance, and our language. That's the way it is, that's the way it's always going to be. There's no racism at all, man. We each do our thing, we don't have *no* problem."

Marco's ideology smacked of "separate but equal," and it didn't sit well with Mr. Ross, who asked, "But how can we change it?" "Ain't never gonna change," Joe said. "You *can't* change it," Marco insisted, shaking his head. Mr. Ross warned that it could lead to problems, but the young men said they had no problems now; they got along fine. Ernesto then pointed me out explicitly, asking, "What about whites?" Bill, a guard at the school, said that when he had been a kid he had gone to an all-white school and there was a lotta love there, and they all got along. Others nodded. Mr. Ross brought the group to a close by picking up a sheet of paper, saying that he had shown Manny and Joe that to figure out the area of a cylinder you have to take it apart. Turning the tube in his hand, he said that cycles can go on endlessly. Then he let the paper open, saying, "You gotta break it apart and see what's going on, and then you can break the cycle." He then handed out free condoms and everyone went home.

While Bill kindly brushed over Ernesto's concern, my whiteness became a more urgent, inescapable topic when another white person came to work at CAA. Ms. Jones, a woman whose dark hair with light brown highlights hung just past her shoulders, was a frequent substitute at CAA in 1997 and played in a rock band at night. On her first day at CAA, after I had been participating and observing in the setting for four months, she asked me what I did there. I told her I tutored and interviewed young men about resisting and avoiding violence. Her eyes widened and she seemed wary. "Well, how do you go about that?" I told her my rough interview protocol, with its questions regarding where they had lived, why they had moved, how they got to school, if they had ever been in fights or broken up fights, and so on. She seemed concerned and asked if I knew this was a gang-controlled school. I shrugged. Later, when what was described as a small "riot" broke out on campus, purportedly due to the antagonisms of students with rival gang affiliations, she told me as she ran by, "I bet you never thought something like this could happen where you're from!" "No," I said, curtly moving away from her. As I noted that evening, "She was bugging me with her assumptions about who I am, and I don't want this experience filtered through her views."

Later, I talked with Bill, a security guard, and he told me about some of Ms. Jones's confusions when she first came to CAA. He said that she had given an African American young man two to three minutes to go to the bathroom, and in response he had said, "Can't a nigga have at least five minutes to do his business?" As Bill told me, "She thought he was getting racial on her, so she took him to the office." Bill explained to her that it wasn't racial against her–they just used that term all the time with each other.

When my race arose as an explicit topic with a consultant it was often accompanied by laughter, an easing of tension, and a sense of connection. At the end of an interview with Larry, when I told him I didn't know what to ask, he told me of his desire to get away. When I misinterpreted what he said, it became an opportunity for him to explicate himself in a way that he wouldn't have had to do with an insider.

"See, what I'm gonna do," Larry told me, "if I become stable, I'mo have me a house out here, and I'mo also have me a house out in the middle of nowhere, so when I get tired of livin' here I can go out there and take my vacation, you know. That way I can come back in tune. Louisiana, it's pretty dry out there."

"Pretty dry in Louisiana? Louisiana's wet! Practically the whole state's underwater."

"No, no, not as in wet, it's like boring."

"Oh, oh," I said, and laughed.

"That's one of the slang words that we use."

I laughed again. "White people, we take everything literally."

"Yeah," he said, laughing too.

"Huh what?"

"I no— I noticed *[laughter]* the way that I was sayin' a coupla slang words *[laughter]*, you was lookin' at me like, *[laughter]* what the hell are you talkin' about?" And we both laughed.

When I returned to CAA in 2000, the topic of race again arose on a number of occasions, but not always in the ways one might expect. Sitting in the special ed class at the time of the 2000 presidential election recount, Mitch said, "It looks like that whitey is gonna win the election," referring to Bush. "Well, they're both white!" Mr. Dolan said. "Well, you know," Mitch said. "So what color is Bob?" Mr. D asked. "He's Oriental," Mitch said, and Mr. D and I busted up laughing. "Watch out, before you know it, he's gonna have you being blue!" Mr. D said. White people were a rare sight in the neighborhood around CAA, and as Mitch suggested, they were often associated with Republican values. Those who did not espouse such values therefore must not be white, whatever their skin color might be.

At another time when we were talking about the neighborhood, it was not my whiteness but my university affiliation that was singled out for attention. When I told Mr. Dolan how I had never felt especially nervous or frightened in the neighborhood, since "nothing ever happened to me around here," he exclaimed, "Are you kidding? No one would ever do anything to you! You're from the university and all, they know there'd be federal agents and CIA all over this place if anyone ever put a scratch on you." I didn't quite know how to respond when he said this, as I was accustomed to thinking of FBI and CIA as antagonists rather than backup.

In an interview, Antoine, an eighteen-year-old, positive-thinking, stylish and friendly African American, further explained what Mr. Dolan may have meant as he discussed his feel for the local ecology.

"They always hanging out, trying to start trouble. If they see you, they be 'Oh, we know him.' That's why you don't see no drive-bys where you go."

"You're saying that about me?"

"Yeah. Specifically. 'Cause I know some guys, they see you walkin' around there, shoot, they'll keep their eyes on you, 'cause you know, no offense, you white and everything. They'll think, 'He probably a policeman or something.' So they'll watch you hard. So don't do anything fast or nothin' like that."

"I don't," I said, and laughed.

"They would try to rush you, you know? Just watch out, or they'll think you a cop or something. They always think negative like that. They think negative, you know?"

A final instance I'll mention occurred after a shooting rampage by white students at a suburban school near San Diego. During nutrition, McClain, a large security guard passed by and mentioned, "By the way, why is it always white people getting into stuff like that?" I didn't have an answer for him. "You don't see that happening around here in the hood," he said. "Crazy stuff like that just isn't on the news." "They're just crazy," I said. "Yeah," McClain said, loudly and dramatically, looking at me with his face turned sideways, a few inches from my own. "What is it with you white people?" Mr. Dolan, Mr. Pope, and I laughed. In this way, I could be a sort of emissary of "whiteness," representing "my people," if only in a self-mocking way. Such are the ways race became an accountable feature in the setting; if it is not invoked, people find many other ways to understand each other.[6]

If at times I represented white people when I was in the inner city, then I often found myself representing the inner city when I was around white people. Such instances were especially common for me during two activities I engaged on a weekly basis: ocean kayaking and Italian lessons. In both settings I never saw persons of color unless I brought them. Once while kayaking, when I spoke about doing fieldwork with Latinos, a woman responded, "They don't know how to live." Indignantly, I told her that studies show bilingual people are actually more intelligent than monolinguals and that Latinos are more healthy and live longer than Anglos because of their strong family support structure and diet. That shut her up. Similarly, in my Italian class, an instructor, trying to find, I suppose, an innocuous conversation topic, asked, "Do you think it's fair that African American students with lower test scores should eliminate positions for a white student at the university?" With the best Italian I could spit forth, I told her of my experiences as a substitute and a regular teacher in the inner city, where I saw ceilings caving in, where books were often unavailable, and where my class was interrupted by announcements throughout the day. What sort of "universe" does a university represent if it is not filled by those who have built the cities and who suffer from the ills the city foists upon them?

The walls and the prisons we have built are reinforced by much thoughtlessness. In the mornings on my way to CAA, I passed a message scrawled in black paint on a brick wall by a major boulevard, stating, "It only takes one person to make a difference: YOU." The difference is hard to find in the outer environment; perhaps the change the graffiti is referring to is internal.

Notes

1. Proweller (2000) provides a powerful portrayal of the resiliency of, and options for, teen mothers "at promise" rather than "at risk," in an alternative school not unlike CAA. Ruth Horowitz (1995) shows how welfare workers infantilize teen mothers and reinforce a message of dependency, and Jock Young (2007) critiques the scapegoating of teen moms for social ills. Frank Furstenberg (2003:25), who has studied teen moms for over four decades, concludes, "In the United States, the singularity of the issue has more to do with how our political culture has responded to the ancillary problems of poverty, sexuality, gender relations, and the like, than with the threat posed by teenagers having babies before they want to or their families want them or before society thinks is good for their welfare and that of their offspring."

2. On cultivating and distancing oneself from the vicious thug image, see Simpson (2005).

3. See Mendoza-Denton (1996, 2008) for a discussion of how young women in Northern California embody and perform gang identity.

4. Last I heard, she was working a double shift, managing a fast food establishment.

5. I was honored that Emily shared her story with me, but also overwhelmed by it. After hearing her tale, I made the decision in the field not to interview women further. I believe my primary reason was my sense of emotional shock in reaction to her story. Tales of violence and victimization from young men were somehow easier to stomach. When I returned to CAA in 2000 I tried again, gathering three interviews with women before I again gave up. Perhaps a reason can be inferred from this excerpt a few minutes into my interview with Maria, my last interview with a young woman.

"Are there any parts of the city you try to avoid?"
"The city's a mess."
"How?"
"A lot of shooting and killing."
"Has that touched your life?"
"They killed my brother two days after I got married."
"Really."
There was a long pause. She cried for the remainder of the interview and after the tape was turned off.
"Sorry," I offered. "Sometimes in these interviews, this kind of stuff comes up."
Silence. I added, "I was talking to a guy earlier, who said his best friend shot him. Why do people do that?"

"I don't know."

"Is that part of why you want to be a teacher or a social worker?" I asked.

"Mm, no."

"This is the first time someone's really started crying. I feel kind of bad." There was a long silence here. "I feel like I upset you."

"Oh no."

"So you made it through adult school, and now you're graduating from here, so you've really accomplished a lot."

"Mm, yeah."

"Where do you get all that determination?" Silence. "Do you wanna work on that biology project?"

"I'm done. I just have to answer some questions."

"Which ones?"

Here the interview ended.

I regret that I didn't interview more women. However horrendous the stories of men could be, and there were times when they were quite horrendous, I could handle them. I couldn't handle these interviews with women. While I have included their experiences in the analyses, my number of cases, at four, is not sufficient to draw any conclusions from their experiences. I leave those to the many researchers more able to grapple with them, such as Anne Campbell (1991), Ruth Horowitz (1995), Medea Chesney-Lind and Katherine Irwin (2007), Norma Mendoza-Denton (2008), and Jody Miller (2008).

6. See Nightingale (1993) for an insightful discussion of the ways inner-city American young people represent mainstream American values.

1. GANG IDENTITY AS PERFORMANCE

The epigraph is from Susan Talburt (2004:35), quoted in Driver (2007:313).

1. The legal scholar Franklin Zimring (2005) insightfully speaks of adolescence as a "learner's permit," requiring just such a system of justice. This system is being whittled away; for cutting-edge ethnographic studies of this process, see Kupchik (2006), Barrett (2007), and Harris (2007).

2. Glassner (2000) and Thompkins (2000) speak of how exaggerated claims about "gangs" contribute to a culture of fear in the United States. Zatz (1987) and McCorkle and Miethe (2002) examine how fears regarding gangs have led to moral panics, showing how the subjective response to gangs has been far out of proportion to any measure of objective threat they pose. The media play a central role in the spread of moral panics, especially in their use of metaphors and hyperbolic language that incite a disproportionate response to a "problem." Conquergood (1994a, 1997) has repeatedly criticized the metaphors that the media use to describe gangs. As he states (1997:373), "It is difficult for most citizens, progressive educators included, to see anything of value in street culture because our perceptions are skewed by prevailing media metaphors that depict gangs as malignant microbes ('plague,' 'cancer,' 'blight,' 'disease,' 'scourge,' 'virus,' 'infestation,' 'epidemic of violence') or vicious animals ('wilding packs,' 'superpredators,' 'roving,' 'prowling' beasts of prey from the 'urban jungle' seized with 'pack frenzy') or violent terrorists (youths who 'menace' and 'terrorize neighborhoods' creating 'explosions of violence' and 'little Beiruts'

in the inner city)." Hallsworth and Young (2008:184–85) note, "The term *gang* does not designate a social problem in any neutral sense; it denotes and, in a tautological way, explains this problem simultaneously. It is a blinding and mesmerizing concept that has a seductive dimension many cannot resist. This is because, in one simple beguiling term, we find embedded a convenient and simple thesis about why things are as they are. The term *gang* signifies not this or that group out there but a *Monstrous Other*, an organized counter force confronting the good society." As George Lakoff (1991:95) famously noted, "Metaphors can kill." Also see Ibarra and Kitsuse (1993) and Spector and Kitsuse (1987) for discussions of the important role of metaphors in constituting social problems.

3. Decker and Curry (1997:514) are especially adamant that gangs be seen in exclusively criminological terms, claiming, "Gangs facilitate the commission of crime. To ignore that is to ignore, or worse, to excuse the violence gang members commit against each other and their communities." For alternatives, see J. Katz and Jackson-Jacobs (2004) and Hallsworth and Young (2008).

4. Jock Young (1999, 2003, 2007) presents an incisive analysis of such dynamics. According to Young, the marginalized are immersed in the allure of the material trappings of the dominant culture while simultaneously denied them, included culturally but excluded socially and economically in a dynamic he refers to as "social bulimia." Young (2003:394) describes how the excluded must live in a social world that is "full of the liberal mantra of liberty, equality, and fraternity yet systematically in the job market, on the streets, in day-to-day contacts with the outside world, practices exclusion."

5. Massey and Denton (1993). Such segregation also leads to a decline of housing values, ensuring that the poor will stay poor. See K. Jackson (1985), Conley (1999), and Oliver and Shapiro (2006).

6. Kozol (1992).

7. See Gans (1995) on the perpetuation of stereotypes in the social sciences and the media. See Ashamalla (1999) for an extended discussion of the publicity surrounding the case of a supposedly innocent white man and his young daughter shot in a inner-city area after taking "the wrong offramp." Overlooked was the irresponsibility of the white man bringing his three-year-old along for what turned out to be a drug deal gone sour.

8. See Vigil (1988, 2003) on gangs arising out of "multiple marginalities"; see Sibley (1995) for how we perpetuate "geographies of exclusion."

9. Venkatesh (1997, 2000).

10. Kotlowitz (1992), Edin and Lein (1997), and especially Brotherton and Barrios (2004). K. Irwin (2004:475) states that "patterns of exclusion cutting across multiple contexts . . . leave youths with few opportunities but to become violent." Nonetheless, many such youths have the wit and resilience (Rutter 1987) to avoid such outcomes.

11. Ungar (2007:89). Y. Ferguson and Mansbach (1999:85) similarly note that "urban street gangs may offer places of refuge and revitalized identity. . . . Members reveal and reinforce their identity through dress and lifestyle. Such polities can slake the thirst for intimacy, tradition, autonomy, and control in the midst of bewildering change and localism."

12. Ruth Horowitz (2001) explores the dual influences of Mead (1934) and the Chicago School on fieldwork in poor, minority communities. One tradition emphasizes how the marginalized face barriers to public discourse and participation in democracy; the other appreciates the agency of the poor in their creation of social worlds. This book is an effort to contribute to both traditions.

13. Appreciation is a guiding motif of this study. See especially Becker (1963) and Matza (1969).

14. For discussions of dehumanizing and humanizing characterizations of inner-city youth, see the work of Conquergood (1994a, 1994b, 1997).

15. Research using the term *identity* has proliferated over the past fifty years, doubling roughly every ten years. Côté (2006) notes that in the first five years of 2000 alone, keyword searches for *identity* produced over twelve thousand hits on PsychInfo and over eighteen thousand hits on Sociological Abstracts. As Brubaker and Cooper (2000:8) state, "Clearly, the term 'identity' is made to do a great deal of work. It is used to highlight non-instrumental modes of action; to focus on self-understanding rather than self-interest; to designate sameness across persons or sameness over time; to capture allegedly core, foundational aspects of selfhood; to deny that such core, foundational aspects exist; to highlight the processual, interactive development of solidarity and collective self-understanding; and to stress the fragmented quality of the contemporary experience of 'self,' a self unstably patched together through shards of discourse and contingently 'activated' in differing contexts." Côté (2006) also explores various uses of the term *identity,* developing a 2 x 2 x 2 table along the axes of objectivism/subjectivism, individual/social, and status quo/critical or contextual.

16. Brubaker and Cooper (2000).

17. Ibid.

18. Gilligan (1982).

19. W. Wilson (1987:58).

20. Calhoun (1994), quoted in Brubaker and Cooper (2000:6). Nonetheless, essentialism is seen by some as politically useful for motivating individuals to act as a collectivity (see Colebrook 2002; Stone 2004).

21. A. Cohen (1990:12).

22. The fact that this study advocates understanding gang identity as fluid, contextual and "soft" in no way should indicate that the young people studied were any less "hard" as gang members than those in any other gang study.

23. A cursory review of textbooks on gangs or the *Journal of Gang Research* reveals an earnest desire to reify an unproblematized conceptualization of gang members, despite internal contradictions (see J. Katz and Jackson-Jacobs, 2004; Hallsworth and Young 2008). For those conducting quantitative research on the topic, a focus on the *when, how,* and *why* of invoking gang membership—what is important to members—constitutes "noise" or "muddying the waters." Much effort has been expended to reduce such noise. For instance, Malcolm Klein and Cheryl Maxson (2006:23–40) present three tables that come to seventeen pages, citing dozens of gang studies, many with samples of over ten thousand respondents, to show that gang prevalence rates are highly dependent on the restrictiveness of the definition of gangs, and hence to demonstrate the dire need for a consensual definition. Despite extensive discussions of definitions that begin practically every gang monograph, gang researchers commonly acknowledge that "in most street gangs, leadership is ephemeral, turnover is often high, and cohesiveness only moderate" (Klein and Maxson, 2006:163–64). Nonetheless, Klein and Maxson (2006:4) report an emerging consensus in defining a street gang as "any durable, street-oriented youth group whose involvement in illegal activity is part of its group identity," a definition that the authors state has been agreed to at various international conferences of gang researchers.

Nonetheless, this does not resolve the issue of what gangs mean for members. Furthermore, while Klein and Maxson emphasize that their definition applies to groups, not to individual identity, such a definition is used by researchers to categorize individuals, associate findings with them that are based on these categorizations, and criminalize them.

24. Curry and Decker (2003:6).

25. Esbensen et al. (2004:95).

26. Paying heed to members' meanings must be a central concern of gang researchers, since, as Ball and Curry (1995:226) note, "Part of the difference between a scientific and a literary approach to criminology lies in the persistent effort to clarify key terms from time to time by the ostensive method, pointing directly to empirical reality, so that definitions do not stray too far from their empirical referents."

27. Meehan's (2000) ethnographic study shows how police dispatchers and police on patrol routinely record calls regarding groups of young people as "gangs" in order to serve political ends.

28. Huff (1996:1).

29. Spergel (1992:126).

30. W. Miller (1980).

31. Huff (1996); Bursik and Grasmick (2006).

32. Bursik and Grasmick (2006:6), citing Thrasher (1927).

33. W. Miller (1980).

34. Horowitz (1990).

35. Matza (1964).

36. Yablonsky (1997).

37. Quote from Decker and Curry (2002:351). The source from fifty years ago is Cloward and Ohlin (1960). Felson (2002:11) notes that an apt name for a typical street gang would be "the Undependables."

38. Decker and Kempf-Leonard (1991), Brotherton (1997), J. Katz (2000), Meehan (2000), and McCorkle and Miethe (2002).

39. J. Katz and Jackson-Jacobs (2004).

40. Howell, Moore, and Egley (2002). Under the Institute for Intergovernmental Research, the National Youth Gang Center maintains a list of gang-related legislation by state. See www.iir.com/nygc/gang-legis/.

41. Esbensen et al. (2004:58).

42. The title of this section is from Linda McNeil's (1988) book of the same name. In it, she shows that as schools focus more on controlling students, they tend to undermine pedagogical concerns. As she states (xviii), "When the school's organization becomes centered on managing and controlling, teachers and students take school less seriously. They fall into a ritual of teaching and learning that tends toward minimal standards and minimum effort. This sets off a vicious cycle. As students disengage from enthusiastic involvement in the learning process, administrators often see the disengagement as a control problem. They then increase their attention to managing students and teachers rather than supporting their instructional purpose." Also see Brotherton (1996).

43. Bursik and Grasmick (2006:6), citing Thrasher (1927).

44. See S.989, the End Racial Profiling Act of 2001, Serial No. J-107-36.

45. Los Angeles Police Department, "Gang Statistics by Month," www.lapdonline.org/search_results/content_basic_view/24435. Ashamalla (1999) discusses how one such

young man, erroneously profiled as a gang member, is currently serving a life sentence for a crime he did not commit. Many of the male and female honors students I taught at UCLA, who described in detail being stopped, frisked, and photographed by police, were surely part of this tally of suspected gang members. Some of the fellow teachers I knew when I worked for the Los Angeles Unified School District claimed gangs; I often wonder if they were included on the list.

46. Becker (1973:157).

47. Meehan (2000:348, 362), also see C. Katz (2003).

48. Zatz (1985:27).

49. Harris (2007). Harris and Allen (2003) also explore the numerous recent laws, especially in California, that have increasingly criminalized young people purported to be in gangs, leading to the increased incarceration of black and Latino young people and their continuing decline in institutions of higher learning.

50. On the U.S. prison system as the world's largest, see Young (1999:146) and Wacquant (2001). On prison privatization, see Donziger (2002). On the decrease in ethnographic studies of prisons, see Wacquant (2002).

51. J. Irwin (2005); Jerome Miller (1997).

52. On the Almighty Latin King and Queen Nation, see Brotherton and Barrios (2004). On the Mexican Mafia, see E. Cummings (1997). If one follows the theories of gang etiology proposed by scholars such as Thrasher (1927), that gangs arise out of zones of transition, or Vigil (1988, 2003), that gangs arise out of conditions of multiple marginalities, then what more transitional, marginalizing space might be found than the prison? On the increasing symbiosis of prison and ghetto, see Wacquant (2001) and Clear (2009). For an autobiographical statement on the dominance of gangs in prison, see Simpson (2005).

53. *Johnson v. California*, 543 U.S. (2005).

54. See Chen (2004).

55. Travis (2005); Travis and Visher (2005).

56. E. Cummings (1997).

57. G. Scott (2004:120–21), citing Travis, Solomon, and Waul (2002:18).

58. Quotes from G. Scott (2004:121, 122, 107).

59. See Wacquant (2001). For an autobiographical account of such a circular process, see Simpson (2005).

60. See J. Katz and Jackson-Jacobs (2004). As Sullivan (2006:15–16) notes, "The perennial fascination with gangs is partly romantic. It can, and sometimes does, cloud our view of what we should be placing front and center, the problem of youth violence."

61. Ferrell (1996); Prus and Grills (2003).

62. Foucault (1978:42).

63. Zinn (1980).

64. As Brubaker and Cooper (2000:18) note, "Semantically, 'identity' implies sameness across time or persons; hence the awkwardness of continuing to speak of 'identity' while repudiating the implication of sameness."

65. Hall (1996:2).

66. Maynard (1988:316). Also see Schegloff (1992a).

67. Goffman (1967a:3).

68. See Garfinkel (1967/1984), West and Zimmerman (1987), and Moerman (1974).

69. Sacks (1984).

70. Sacks (1972). For a discussion of membership categorization analysis (MCA), see Garot and Berard (forthcoming). For a regularly updated bibliography, see "Bibliography on Membership Categorization Analysis," www2.fmg.uva.nl/emca/MCA-bib.htm#R. For examples outside the MCA canon of how ad hoc categorization may provide the basis for a range of inferences, Venkatesh (1997) shows how young people may be turned down for a job when writing down an address that is associated with the category of "dangerous," and J. Katz (1999) discusses the racist and sexist characterizations that drivers use to categorize other drivers.

71. Wieder (1974). Jimerson and Oware (2006) draw upon Wieder's analysis in contrasting orthodox to ethnomethodological understandings of Elijah Anderson's (1999) notion of the code of the street.

72. The work of phenomenologists such as Maurice Merleau-Ponty (1962, 1968) and pragmatists such as William James (1890/1950) is integral for understanding the powerful insights into bodily practices provided by such authors as Jack Katz (1988, 1999) and Lee F. Monaghan (2001, 2002). Steven Lyng (2004:359) builds from Jurgen Habermas's theory of communicative action to "theorize risk taking in criminal endeavors as an activity linked to the embodied social practices of the life-world."

73. Conquergood (1997:367). He further states that street literacy "is a powerful pedagogy that deeply engages the body as a way of knowing" (370).

74. West and Zimmerman (1987:126).

75. Butler (1991:261).

76. Butler (1990:25).

77. Omi and Winant (1986:55).

78. Karen Brodkin (1999).

79. J. Jackson (2001).

80. Fordham (1996); Ogbu (2003). As Brubaker and Cooper (2000:5) note, one does not "have to use 'race' as a category of analysis–which risks taking for granted that 'race' exists–to understand and analyze social and political practices oriented to the presumed existence of putative 'races.'" On race as a "collective fiction," see Wacquant (1997); on the contextual instability of racial identities, see Hall (1981).

81. Nagel (1994:152).

82. Moerman (1974).

83. R. Cohen (1978).

84. Bruner (1973:225). Also see Wieder and Pratt (1989) for the ways in which the ethnonational category "Indian" is performed, judged, and used as a basis for inclusion or exclusion.

85. B. Anderson (1983/2006:6). For a study of how contradictory myths of "Britishness" are lived in British society, see Hebdige (1996).

86. C. Hirschman (1986); Dirks (1992); R. Jackson and Maddox (1993); Appadurai (1996); R. Jackson (1999); B. Anderson (1983/2006).

87. Nobles (2000); Kertzer and Arel (2002).

88. Calavita (2000).

89. Brubaker (1996:14).

90. See Conquergood (1994a).

91. J. Katz (1988:154).

92. See Vigil (2003).

93. Erikson (1968:22).

94. Côté (2006:4).

95. Erikson (1968). Also see Vigil (2003:227).

96. Raby (2007:42).

97. Susan Driver (2007:311) notes this in discussing the work of Catherine Driscoll (2002).

98. Brubaker and Cooper (2000:5).

99. Conquergood (1994a, 1994b, 1997).

100. Conquergood (1994a:200).

101. Mendoza-Denton (2008:149).

102. Both quotes are from Mendoza-Denton (2008:152).

103. D. Anderson (1998:318).

104. Trump (1996:53). Also see Huff and Trump (1996); Burnett (1999); Bucher and Manning (2003); Struyk (2006). For a more thorough description of such policies and their alternatives as they played out at CAA, see Garot (forthcoming).

105. Frank Tannenbaum (1938) wrote of how processes of punishment dramatize evil, providing a stage to celebrate it rather than a disincentive. For a brilliant contemporary analysis of the rewards of punishment in schools, see A. Ferguson (2001).

106. See Werthman (1983) and Dance (2002).

107. On creating something out of nothing, see Cintron (1997); on gangs' possibilities for political action, see Brotherton and Barrios (2004); on gangs' possibilities for legitimate social and economic uplift, see Dawley (1992).

108. On the ways gangs can limit collective efficacy, see Wilkinson (2007). Regarding gangs' promotion of violence, Alexes Harris (personal communication, 2007), in her observations of proceedings in California to waive juveniles' rights to be tried as juveniles, noticed that many shootings, robbings, and other violent incidents were precipitated by the demand to know another's gang affiliation. Relatedly, it is commonly and rightfully acknowledged that violence associated with gang vendettas is a leading factor in youth homicides, especially among poor youth of color (see Pinderhughes 1997, Kennedy 1998, and the Dwight Conquergood 2007 film, *The Heart Broken in Half*). On how gangs can limit individuals' ability to move freely, see, for instance, Kevin Roy's (2004) article on "three-block fathers," which shows how wariness regarding the likelihood of confronting gang members often limits the strategies of fathers in inner-city neighborhoods.

109. This analysis is also based on my three years of experience working as a substitute and as a credentialed, permanent teacher in K–12 inner-city classrooms, as well as years of supervising many university students' field notes in inner-city educational settings. While many other aspects of young people's lives, such as watching TV (Williams and Kornblum 1985) and minimum wage jobs (Newman 1999), surely breed alienation, I focus on school, as this is a setting that legally requires attendance, often constitutes the bulk of a young person's day, and is integral in molding the self. On how schools make and mold the identity of their students (Davidson 1996), see especially Paul Willis (1977), Penelope Eckert (1989), and Barrie Thorne (1993).

110. My role might be seen as that of "least adult" (Hadley 2007). For guidance and a model for appropriate research conduct in a school setting, I looked to Barrie Thorne (1993). I see my place in the school as similar to that adopted by A. Ferguson (2001), "learning from kids."

111. Emerson, Fretz, and Shaw (1995).

112. This information was provided in an unpublished grant proposal by a local community-based organization.

113. The invalidity and unreliability of gang statistics are notorious, as J. Katz (2000) and Malcolm Klein (1995) point out. Meehan (2000) provides an insider's view of how such statistics are constructed. I provide them here just to give a sense of the data available on the area.

114. Such a setting provides a marked contrast to the image of contemporary U.S. high schools in Milner's (2006) study, where the obsession with status is palpable. M. Fine's (1991) thorough examination of the ways inner-city schools produce dropouts, Kelly's (1993) detailed study of the history and contradictions of continuation schools, and Betsy Rymes's (2001) analysis of the political and social milieu of an alternative urban high school provide a backdrop for the dynamics in which alternative schools are situated.

115. In a national survey of school boards by the National School Boards Association (1993), 66 percent of responding boards claimed to have an alternative program or school as a setting for placing violent students who had been expelled from a traditional school setting. Eighty-five percent of urban districts, 66 percent of suburban districts, and 57 percent of rural districts reported having such a program in place. For a policy argument in favor of alternative schools, see Klagholz (1995).

116. On accounts as resources versus accounts as topics, see Heritage (1984).

117. Driver (2007:315).

118. On conducting life-history interviews with gang members, see Vigil (1988).

119. On the emotional power of interviews, see Hoffman (2007).

120. Driver (2007:308).

121. Driver (2007:317).

122. The process of writing field notes is best formulated by Emerson, Fretz, and Shaw (1995). Glaser and Strauss (1967) and more recently Charmaz (2006) have provided definitive statements on grounded theory. Analytic induction, which involves the constant revision of theory in light of negative cases, was first formulated by Cressey (1953) and Lindesmith (1968) and has since been revisited by J. Katz (2001). Becker (1998) provides excellent analytic sensitizing techniques.

2. MORAL DRAMAS AT SCHOOL

Regarding the second epigraph, Deutsch (2008:88) discusses how the term *ghetto* was used frequently as a negative descriptor by young people in her study.

1. Willis (1977).

2. See Ogbu and Simons (1998) for a partial overview and response to critics. Compare Flores-González (2002) and A. Ferguson (2001).

3. Mateu-Gelabert and Lune (2007); Dow (2007). See especially Carl Werthman (1983) for an important precursor to this chapter, showing how gang members' disruptions in class were often a product of discontent with teaching and grading practices.

4. Mehan (1992), using "felicity conditions," a concept from Austin (1962).

5. The term *pedagogy of oppression* is a play off Paulo Freire's (2000) foundational text *Pedagogy of the Oppressed*, which details the theory and practices of liberating the consciousness of students, accomplishing the opposite of what I often saw at CAA.

6. Willis (2000).

7. See Brotherton (2003) and, on the importance of student voice, M. Fine (1991).

8. On gangs as community organizers, see Brotherton and Barrios (2004). On gangs and street literacy, see Brotherton (2003) and Conquergood (1997). Students might be seen as following a sort of "hidden transcript" to resist marginalization, in what James C. Scott (1976, 1985, 1990) refers to as "infrapolitics." For a lucid discussion and depiction of infrapolitical strategies in an urban high school, see Dickar (2008). For a breathtaking analysis of infrapolitical resistance to gentrification in Harlem, see J. Jackson (2001).

9. On resistance arising out of yet reaffirming class position, see Bowles and Gintis (1976) and Willis (1977). On resistance arising from a history of racial oppression, and the concern among students that achievement means "acting white," see Ogbu (2003) and Fordham and Ogbu (1986). For a classic treatment of how resistance and many other classroom dynamics are enacted and interpreted through the lens of gender, see Thorne (1993). For a definitive and rigorous treatment of the relationship of the structure of the classroom to resistance, see McFarland (2001).

10. Mary Metz (1989) examines those aspects that make up "real schools." The phrase "enchanting a disenchanted world" is from Ritzer (2005). For an application of the term to the radical politics of resistance, see Ferrell (2001) and Notes from Nowhere (2003). A number of sources focus on the somewhat redemptive and marginally transformative power of resistance (Hobsbawm 1973; J. Scott 1985; Kelley 1994). Abu-Lughod (1990) provides a provocative discussion of resistance as a diagnostic of power. For a much-needed look at gangs as a form of resistance, see the work of David Brotherton, especially Brotherton (2008).

11. Marx's insights into alienation (1983:127, italics in original) are apposite to this section: "Man *[sic]* makes his life activity itself an object of his will and consciousness. He has a conscious life activity. . . . Only for this reason is he a species-being. Or rather, he is only a self-conscious being, i.e. his own life is an object for him, because he is a species-being. Only for this reason is his activity free activity. Alienated labour reverses the relationship, in that man because he is a self-conscious being makes his life activity, his *being*, only a means for his *existence*." Furthermore, "The object of labour is, therefore, the *objectification of man's species-life*; for he no longer reproduces himself merely intellectually, as in consciousness, but actively and in a real sense, and he sees his own reflection in a world which he has constructed. While, therefore, alienated labour takes away the object of production from man, it also takes away his *species-life*" (128). For an influential discussion of alienation, see Ollman (1971).

12. This is similar to what Dow (2007) reports.

13. Dow (2007) also speaks of students' frustrations with substitutes.

14. Compare G. Rosenfeld (1971).

15. Usually when I worked with him we put the worksheets aside and focused on sounding out words in a basal reader.

16. See Anyon (1997:31) and A. Ferguson (2001).

17. See Duncan (2000) for an argument that inner-city schools serve as feeders into the prison-industrial complex.

18. McFarland (2001, 2004); see also Newmann, Wehlage, and Lamborn (1992). Mehan (1992:10) notes, "Not all forms of nonconforming behavior stem from a critique, implicit or explicit, of school-constructed ideologies and relations of domination." McFar-

land (2004:1262) makes a useful distinction between deviance and resistance, stating that "the deviant acts out of self-interest and does not try to present himself or herself as an agent of social change. In contrast, the saboteur claims to be an agent of an interpretive stand that is oppositional to the current academic framework. . . . It is always a form of nonconformity that questions the legitimacy of the broader academic framework." Still, a young person might manipulate his or her self-presentation so as to appear to be simply deviating instead of resisting, or vice versa.

19. McFarland (2004:4).

20. Dickar (2008:142–43) draws on J. Scott (1985, 1990), noting that such resistance "flies under the radar because it does not directly confront authority and usually avoids serious sanctions."

21. For insight into teachers' much-needed obsession with procedures, see Wong and Wong (2009).

22. See Fallis and Opotow (2003). Dickar (2008), drawing on McLaren (1986), devotes much of her book, especially chs. 3 and 5, to battles between teachers and students over whether the "street-corner state" embodied in the hall or the ideal of the "student state" of the classroom will prevail.

23. See Mateu-Gelabert and Lune (2007) for similar difficulties on a large urban campus.

24. This ostensible role reversal is worth a deeper look. Why would Bill do Joey's bidding? Perhaps Bill likes Joey, perhaps he's repaying Joey a favor, or perhaps Bill, like Joey, was also bored and thus willing to subvert his formal role.

25. McFarland (2004).

26. See Matthews (2003) on counterfeit classrooms.

27. See A. Ferguson (2001).

28. Conquergood (1997); Brotherton (2003).

29. See Tyack (1974) and Deschenes, Cuban, and Tyack (2001).

30. W. Wilson (1996); Bourgois (1996); Anyon (1997).

31. See Glassner (2000) and Thompkins (2000).

32. G. Rosenfeld (1971:110).

33. Venkatesh (1997).

34. See also Anyon (1997:35–36).

35. McDermott (1987).

36. On "doing nothing," see Corrigan (1975).

37. On dealienating education, see Kalekin-Fishman (1989). For alternatives to the practices described here, see Haberman (1995), Ayers and Ford (1996), Mehan et al. (1996), and McLaren (2003).

38. On the hidden curriculum, see P. Jackson (1990) and Apple (1990).

3. THE CONTRADICTIONS OF CONTROLLING STUDENT DRESS

1. On the alienating nature of low-wage service jobs, see Leidner (1993) and Newman (1999); on alienation and TV watching, see Williams and Kornblum (1985); on "doing nothing," see Corrigan (1975).

2. Theories of fashion place ambiguity at the core of fashion's messages. For Simmel (1904:296–99), fashion represents the tension between unity and differentiation, "satisfy-

ing the demand for social adaptation," which is simultaneous with "social demarcation," especially for the upper classes. Fred Davis (1992:18) extends this analysis by exploring how fashion frames subjective tensions of "youth versus age, masculinity versus femininity, androgyny versus singularity, inclusiveness versus exclusiveness, work versus play, domesticity versus worldliness . . . conformity versus rebellion." Davis posits that the ways fashion resolves these tensions become collective resources for representing social identities (see Blumer 1969a).

Such ambiguities of fashion, and with them possibilities of self-expression, are severely curtailed with uniforms. As McVeigh (2000:2) discusses in his analysis of the seeming ubiquity of uniforms in Japanese society, "Uniforms—especially student uniforms—are a disciplinary link between the individual and the political structures and their allied economic interests." He analyzes uniforms "as tangible symbols of the ability of enormous and extensive politico-economic structures to shape bodily practices, and by implication, subjectivity and behavior" (3).

Davis is helpful in showing how fashions' statements, like music, resist the attribution of unambiguous meanings, yet he does not connect these multilayered meanings to bodily practices and subjectivity as McVeigh does in his discussion of the ways fashion is embodied. The work of Joanne Entwistle (2001) is quite informative in this regard, drawing on Goffman (1959, 1971) to show how actors orient to and perform in the social world, and on Merleau-Ponty (1962, 1968) to highlight how "our bodies are what give us our expression" in that world (Merleau-Ponty 1968:5). For Entwistle (2001:44), "Approaching dress from a phenomenological framework means acknowledging the way in which dress works on the body which in turn works on and mediates the experience of self." For a cogent discussion of the importance of style for criminal identity and social control, see Ferrell (1995).

3. The ways students are allowed to dress in schools in the United States are a recurrent topic of public interest as well as a legal issue. In legal journals, a debate rages between those who argue that school dress codes infringe on students' free rights of expression and those who argue that dress codes should be implemented and enforced for safety and security reasons (DeMitchell, Fossey, and Cobb 2000). The landmark case of *Tinker v. Des Moines Independent School District* (1969) established that students had the right, under the First Amendment, to wear a black armband in school to protest the Vietnam War. While the majority opinion (7–2) established that students do not "shed their constitutional rights to freedom of speech or expression at the schoolhouse gate," the two dissenting opinions foreshadowed what was to come. In citing these dissents, DeMitchell, Fossey, and Cobb (2000:41) note that "schools are not open forums" like public parks and thus school boards "should exercise their discretion to establish reasonable dress code regulations that help to maintain an environment conducive to learning."

Federal circuit courts of appeal split over how this discretionary power should be exercised. For instance, in cases involving hair length and style, the Fifth, Sixth, Ninth, Tenth, and Eleventh Circuit Courts "often dismissed the cases, finding no Constitutional rights involved" (Gullatt 1999:40). The First, Fourth, Seventh, and Eighth Circuits, however, have cited the First Amendment on speech and expression, the Ninth Amendment concerning denial of other rights not enumerated in the Constitution, and the Fourteenth Amendment regarding actions affecting citizens by the states, in finding hair length regulations unconstitutional. Nevertheless, "Since Tinker, the Supreme Court has decided two other significant public school speech cases: *Bethel School District No. 403 v. Fraser,* and *Hazelwood School District v. Kuhlmeier,* both of which have resulted in curtailment of student expression" (Weisenberger 2000:52).

Following President Clinton's lead (U.S. Department of Education 1996), public school officials have similarly become more restrictive and conservative in their regulation of student dress (Gullatt 1999). In a survey of 240 randomly selected elementary, middle school, and high school principals, DeMitchell, Fossey, and Cobb (2000) found that 51 percent of principals had adopted a dress code policy and that principals serving older students tended to show more support for dress codes, but not necessarily for a school uniform. Hence, advice for principals implementing dress codes, presented as a means to foster school safety (see, e.g., "12 School Safety Moves" 1999), is common in journals catering to this population (Essex 2001).

4. Foucault (1977, 1978).

5. Choices Alternative Academy (1997).

6. See Dickar (2008:146–49) for a discussion of how infrapolitical struggles over "the hat rule" reveal how "the classroom becomes a different environment for boys and girls," since such rules are "not as abusive to girls."

7. As Alice, a participant in Dickar's (2008:60) study, noted regarding the security guards who scan and search students on their way into school, "It would be better if they were friendly."

8. On "face," see Goffman (1967a).

9. On impressions given and impressions given off, see Goffman (1959).

10. MacLeod (1995); Holloman et al. (1996); E. Anderson (1999). An ongoing lament among criminologists is that policy is often based on such dramatic yet extremely rare instances and that it overlooks mundane, ordinary meanings (Felson 2002:1–19; Zimring 2005).

11. Walker and Schmidt (1996).

12. Out of a substantial literature on "cool," the insights of Hall and Jefferson's (1976/2006) classic collection, detailing how urban wastelands breed cultural resistance, continue to stand out.

13. Merleau-Ponty (1962).

14. On working the ambiguities, see Davis (1992).

15. As Jaime, another Latino consultant, stated, "A time came that girls, they started liking more gangster guys, Mexican girls like, you know, Latinas. It was like, they would just be attracted to, like, gangsters, you know, bald headed, wanna see your big pants creased up. They think those muthafuckas look clean and shit, think they look nice, you know, young girls, I guess. No, most of 'em they still think that they like gangsters." Or as Antoine, an eighteen-year-old African American, stated, "It seems like all girls, they like a little thug in their man." As Venkatesh (1997:105) notes, cases like Frank's exemplify "the streetwise efforts that are needed not only to move about freely but, in the case of youth, to sustain personal identities that are not dominated by street gang affiliations."

16. E. Anderson (1999). Sadly, the last news I have of Frank is that he was serving a sentence for armed robbery.

17. Mendoza-Denton (1996:62). As one of my consultants, Eric, told me, "You can tell some gangsters—I know you've seen gangsters, they walk like, you know, they all bad, you know, like they're limp or something. I walk normally. I don't really walk like, you know,

all hard or nothing. And then you can tell, the way they talk, the gangsters, you can tell how they talk, like 'Fuck this shit,' and this and that, and you know, I don't really talk like that. I don't gangbang or nothing. I'm cool, you know. I'm straight, you know."

18. See E. Anderson (1999) on staging areas.

19. On civil inattention, see Goffman (1959).

20. Vigil (1988).

21. Garfinkel (1967/1984:116–86).

22. On habitus, see Bourdieu (1984).

23. Entwistle (2001).

24. As Goffman (1967a:252), states, "Minor behaviors can be employed as a serious invitation to a run-in or show-down. One type of truncated act should be mentioned specifically. It is the use of the style of standing or walking as an open invitation to action to all others present."

25. Also available to non–gang members—especially suburban white kids, as a way of "doing being" a badass. See J. Katz (1988:80–113).

26. J. Jackson (2001:231).

27. Garfinkel (1967/1984:18–24).

28. Entwistle (2001).

29. See Willis (1977); McNeil (1988); Hyman and Snook (1999).

30. See Freire (2000).

4. CLAIMS

1. Many still consider Thrasher's pioneering work in 1927 on groups of young people in Chicago the best gang study for the ways it captures the multiple forms of gangs, shows how they change over time, contextualizes them in "zones of transition," and addresses such seemingly contemporary topics as the role of girls in gangs. Huff (1996), W. Miller (1980), and Valdez (2003) also present useful depictions of varieties of gangs. Bursik and Grasmick (2006) note the difficulty of arriving at a definition of a gang, and how fraternities fit many of the standard definitions.

2. Harvey Sacks (1995:40) noted that asking, "Where are you from?" is a common way of initiating an interaction with a stranger. Certain questions like "What do you do?" and "Where are you from?" constitute "some very central machinery of social organization"; by soliciting categories as a basis for a wide range of inferences, they enable members to handle "a vast amount of stuff" (41). They are especially prominent in the early parts of conversation, since after learning the category "you feel you know a great deal about the person, and can readily formulate topics of conversation based on the knowledge stored in terms of that category" (41). Furthermore, the way the addressee of such a question responds reveals a great deal about local expectations, for there are potentially limitless ways to respond, but few are recognized as locally competent (see Heritage 1984:135–78).

3. See also Conquergood (1994b:27). In the general discussion of hitting up that follows, masculine pronouns will be used, since most of the consultants were male.

4. On facework, see Goffman (1967a).

5. Bourdieu (1984).

6. Athens (2005) links all violent crime to attempts to establish dominance.

7. J. Katz (1988:168–176).

8. Molotch and Boden (1985:285).

9. In Venkatesh's (1997:105) analysis, a young man who is not a gang member and has no allegiance to any local gang is referred to by the diminutive term *neutron*.

10. J. Katz (1999:151).

11. J. Katz (1999:145).

12. See Garot (2004).

13. The term *horizons of experience* refers to the ways past and future are implicated in the phenomenological present, as discussed by Gurwitsch (1966), Bittner (1967), and Emerson and Paley (1992). McIntyre (2000:64–68) notes how many inner-city kids recurrently "anticipate the worst."

14. Roy (2004).

15. See E. Anderson (1990) for a nuanced account of the challenges African American men face in simply moving about in public. As he states, "The streetwise individual thus becomes interested in a host of signs, emblems, and symbols that others exhibit in everyday life" (105).

16. I asked this out of a personal as much as a research-based interest; I had been with Ben on precisely such a street the week before.

17. This, of course, speaks volumes about the neglect of inner-city neighborhoods by universities, reflected in residents' disenchantment and even hostility toward institutions that are often within walking distance (see E. Anderson 1999:56, 64).

18. Young men were not the only ones to have such experiences of miscommunication; stories that highlighted such experiences as epitomizing life in the region could become a local currency for acquaintances to exchange. For instance, when I told my dental hygienist, Greg, an African American man of about my age, about my fieldwork as he cleaned my teeth, he told me of a similar encounter he'd had with a neighbor he described as a "gangbanger." Greg told me that he was from Oakwood, Ohio, and that "we don't know about this gang stuff out there." When he nonchalantly asked his neighbor where he was from, Greg told me, the neighbor "looked at me for a long time with a questioning look in his eye, and said finally, 'Uh, what do you mean by that, like what state?'" "Yeah, of course," Greg replied. "Oh, okay,' the neighbor said, laughing, and gave a response. On laughter in response to breaches from the natural attitude, see Garfinkel (1967/1984) and Schutz (1962).

19. Asking an especially young child where he is from is likely to be seen as a deviant act, as in the following interview excerpt with Doogan, an eighteen-year-old African American:

"So when's the first time you remember someone telling you where you're from?"

"Kindergarten."

"What did you say then?"

"At that time I knew what he was saying, but I just ignored it because I was not involved. What is that gonna look like, a big eighteen-year-old kid asking a five-year-old or kindergartner where he's from. That doesn't make no sense."

"What happened?"

"I was on the street and he asked me where I'm from. I looked at him like, 'What's wrong with you, man? I'm five years old. I'm a little kid, and I got this big idiot up here.' It's like if I was to tell somebody like now that some stupid idiot did that, they would probably wanna hang him just for him bein' dumb."

20. Emanuel Schegloff (1992b), an expert on the structure of conversation, addresses why trouble often erupts in the "repair after the next turn," where "repair" is the attempt to draw attention to some problem with what was just stated. As Dingwall (2000:895) states, "I say something, you respond to it, and I am then positioned to decide whether your response is adequate and adequately connected to what I said first."

21. Many commentators have noted the disproportionate number of students of color in special education classes (M. Fine 1991:20; Kozol 1992) and the harmful consequences for students placed in such courses (Varenne and McDermott 1998). Many of such students may well be gifted, as I believe Richard is, but are warehoused away from other students for behavioral reasons. Many scholars have struggled with how to bridge the gap between the amazing skills young people demonstrate on the street and the lack of recognition that they receive for these skills in the classroom, where they perform poorly (Lave and Wenger 1991).

22. Suttles (1968).

23. See E. Anderson (1999).

24. Goffman (1967b:249).

25. Schutz (1962).

26. Consider the following public, tear-filled complaint of an African American teenager during a large regional conference on urban issues in a high-profile hotel ballroom: "How can you expect us to stay in school with all the gang violence? If you wanna do something about why so many kids leave school, why don't you look at that?" He fixed the presenters with a hard focused glare and then sat. After a brief pause, a young man with dreadlocks at the front table responded that violence was a real issue but that the gangbangers were part of the community too and also deserved an education.

27. A hot topic in criminology concerns whether individuals who engage in "deviant" acts lose "self-control" (Megargee 1966; Gottfredson and Hirschi 1990). Yet as Jack Katz (1988) showed, the sensation of "loss of control" is precisely the sort of seduction that compels one to carefully plan and engage in a "deviant" act.

28. J. Katz (1988:168–76).

29. See J. Katz (1988) on the ways of the badass.

30. This instance brings to mind Katz's (2001) insight that members' reluctance to provide information on various topics reveals their sensitivity to the ethnographer not as a sociologist but as a fellow member of the setting.

31. Sanders (1994).

32. See the Tupac Shakur song "The Rose That Grew from Concrete."

33. Athens (2005); Labov (1982).

34. For a discussion of embodied knowledge of how emotions work, see J. Katz (1999).

35. On shame-rage spirals, see Retzinger (1987), J. Katz (1988:12–51), and Scheff (1990).

36. Conquergood (1994a).

37. W. Wilson (1987); Massey and Denton (1993); Gans (1995); Venkatesh (1997).

5. AFFILIATIONS

1. E. Anderson (1978). Also see Annegret Staiger (2006:13), who states, "Identity as identification requires an ongoing assessment of who is inside and who is outside, and an ongoing dialogue with those with whom one identifies." She discusses how gang identification is bolstered by "putting in work" (139–41).

2. Horowitz (1990) raises precisely such important questions with regard to gangs.

3. See J. Katz's (1988:139–42) discussion of the "collective arrangement of spontaneous violence."

4. See Thrasher (1927).

5. For discussions of gangs as corporations, see Yablonsky (1997:192) and Taylor (1990). For a gripping tale of running with the Crips in and out of prison, see Simpson (2005).

6. Jody Miller's (2008) book raises profound concerns about the sexual exploitation of young women in the inner city, glossed over in accounts such as Lamont's.

7. See Horowitz (1993) for a glimpse into the substantial literature on this important coming-of-age ritual for young Latinas. In a *quinceañera,* the whole community comes together in a highly formalized celebration that the family spares no expense to stage.

8. There is an extensive literature on tagging. For some exemplary studies, see Castleman (1988), Ferrell (1996, 2001), Conquergood (1997), Phillips (1999), and Snyder (2009).

9. Ferrell (2001) describes how his tagging partner left a short message on his unfinished mural that he would "b back," which was respected by other taggers.

10. On "broken windows" policing, see J. Wilson and Kelling (1982). For some cogent critiques among many, see Duneier (1999) and Ferrell (2001).

11. See J. Katz's (1988) chapter "Sneaky Thrills."

12. On historicizing a fight, see Jackson-Jacobs (2004). On the thrill of mediating edgework experiences through potentially endless loops of video documentation, see Ferrell, Milovanovic, and Lyng (2001).

13. For the results of an amazing graffiti project in Philadelphia, see Golden et al. (2006).

14. Vigil (1988:98–103).

15. See Devitt (1984).

16. See Monti (1994).

17. Monti (1994:31).

18. See Garot (forthcoming) for a discussion of how Central is seen as "owning" CAA, since administrators will transfer students who are harassed by the gang rather than gang members who are harassing.

19. Pollner (1984) describes moments when individuals have differing perceptions of the same event as a "reality disjuncture."

20. For a study of the situated vagaries involved for police departments maintaining statistics on gang members, see Meehan (2000).

21. This excerpt echoes the conversations filled with status-imbued claims in E. Anderson's (1978) analysis.

22. For an exception, see J. Katz's (1988) discussion of the Capeman.

23. J. Katz and Jackson-Jacobs (2004).

24. On hegemonic and subaltern discourses, see Gramsci (1971).

25. Venkatesh (1997, 2000) shows how gang members often assist those in need.

26. See Vigil (1988, 2003).

27. See Garot (forthcoming). Consider how resources might be allocated differently if gang members were framed (Snow et al. 1986) in terms of "homelessness" rather than "crime."

28. On gangs as entrepreneurial efforts, see Sanchez-Jankowski (1991) and Padilla (1992). Deutsch (2008:83) notes, "Almost no studies examine poverty per se as an influence on identity."

29. Malcolm Klein (1995); Vigil (1988); Sanders (1994); J. Katz (1988). On boredom and criminology, see Ferrell (2004).

30. Malcolm Klein (1995:11).

31. Vigil (1988); Williams and Kornblum (1985).

32. Common among my consultants and in the literature on gangs are accounts of initiation rituals involving controlled violence—usually a fight with a prespecified number of persons for a prespecified amount of time—referred to as "jumping in" or, with more feudalistic overtones, "courting in." See Thrasher (1927); Vigil (1994).

33. See Curry and Decker (2003).

34. Deutsch and Hirsch (2002) discuss how youth organizations can serve as "home places" to assist the development of inner-city adolescents' sense of identity and self-esteem.

35. On culture as a tool kit, see Swidler (1986).

36. E. Anderson (1978).

6. VIOLENCE AND NONVIOLENCE

The second epigraph is from "The Doctrine of the Sword" (Gandhi 1999:293).

1. In his definitive treatment of facework, Erving Goffman (1967a:5) defines face as "the positive social value a person effectively claims for himself by the line others assume he has taken during a particular contact."

2. To contextualize this insightful quote, Labov (1982:244) notes that individuals who had engaged in extreme violence "acted as we ourselves might act, if we too had been suddenly deprived of our rightful place in the social world."

3. Jackson-Jacobs (2002) artfully examines such skills, ranging from a subtle bump in a crowded bar to throwing a lit cigarette in another's face. On the other hand, those looking for a fight may turn an innocent "bump" into grounds for insult (see Mullins, Wright, and Jacobs 2004). Herbert Blumer (1969b:8) highlighted precisely such nuances in distinguishing, problematically, between symbolic and nonsymbolic interaction: "Non-symbolic interaction takes place when one responds directly to the action of another without interpreting that action; symbolic interaction involves interpretation of the action. Non-symbolic interaction is most readily apparent in reflex responses, as in the case of a boxer who automatically raises his arm to parry a blow. However, if the boxer were reflectively to identify the forthcoming blow from his opponent as a feint designed to trap him, he would be engaging in symbolic interaction. In this case, he would endeavor to ascertain the meaning of the blow—that is, what the blow signifies as to his opponent's plan." As humans both "live in the moment" (Ostrow 1990) and interpret it, no action can be said

to be inherently symbolic or nonsymbolic. Any behavior, even avoidance, may be grist for the potential fighter's mill.

4. Jones (2008) shows how young women in Philadelphia will not hesitate to fight for respect but do hesitate to use deadly force to the same extent as young men.

5. See Joniak (2005) for a description of how a policy of "tough love" at a homeless drop-in shelter for youth creates an exclusionary environment. Currie (2004) thoughtfully explores the dire, counterproductive consequences of tough love for suburban white youth.

6. A remarkable exception is the work of the fighter-sociologist Curtis Jackson-Jacobs (2002, 2004).

7. Studies of fight narratives, like fights themselves, are fascinating. Morrill et al. (2000) break down 316 ninth graders' written accounts of fights into "action tales," "moral tales," "expressive tales," and "rational tales" in order to examine how teen-agers represent violence, adults, decision making, and conflict resolution in their stories of everyday conflict. Most of the accounts in the present analysis, like those in Morrill's, would be considered "action tales," which begin with a disruption of everyday routines and then move linearly, with few digressions, through a conflict to a resolution. However, I also found many moral, expressive, and rational elements to many tales and had a great deal of difficulty fitting single episodes into single codes. In another provocative study, Labov (1982) analyzes how the structure of narratives of conflict might bring some understanding of the conflict itself. Exploring how these narratives invoke rights and obligations through interactional moves such as challenges, defenses, retreats, counterchallenges, supports, and reinforcements, he explores the logic of violent events. Similarly, Linger (1990) locates commonalities in the scripts of Brazilian man-fights known as *brigas,* both as told in narratives and as enacted, as everyday "schismogenic event[s]" (63). Like the cockfight (Geertz 1973), "an unsettling story the Balinese tell themselves about themselves" (Linger 1990:69), the *briga* "reflects something wrong in the way society is organized" (70) and "explains the emergence of chaos" (72).

Other studies of fights use accounts as resources for understanding actions rather than analyzing such accounts as narrative practices. Felson (1982) uses interviews with ex–mental patients and ex–criminal offenders to show how violence was often linked with impression management (Goffman 1959), for respondents were more likely to express anger after being insulted, and conflicts were more severe when an audience was present. Campbell (1986) discusses the social rules of British girls and women in aggressive encounters, as solicited from questionnaires. Such rules include excluding access to authority figures and limiting possible damage. In a study of 389 English boys' accounts of "their most vicious fight in the last year," Farrington, Berkowitz, and West (1982) distinguish group fights from individual fights, showing that in group fights youth rarely report starting it and almost never report being angry, while in individual fights there is usually a personal provocation, followed by anger. Other studies that use accounts of fights as resources to understand the processes of fights include Davies (1982), Cairns and Cairns (1994), Franke, Huynh-Hohnbaum, and Chung (2002), Athens (2005), and Jones (2008). Finally, a number of studies, such as this one, combine analysis of narratives with direct observation. Boulton (1991) found that the most commonly stated reasons girls and boys gave for fighting were retaliation against teasing or unprovoked assault, disagreements over a game played, dislike of another child, or settlement of a dispute; yet when fights were observed, 43 percent presented no obvious immediate cause to the adult observer, and in situ interviews combined with observations yielded results similar to retrospective accounts. Tomsen (1997) recorded thirty-seven assaults over twelve months of ethnographic observations in bars in Australia, showing how destructive masculinism collided with collective rebellion. Jackson-Jacobs (2004:245) provocatively showed how precisely the narrative possibilities of such encounters "are often the *raison d–être* for risk."

8. E. Anderson (1999:84, 68, 106).

9. Among recent efforts of prominent criminologists to quantify and test Anderson's thesis, see Wilkinson (2001), Kubrin and Weitzer (2003), Brezina et al. (2004), and Stewart and Simons (2006). Such quantitative studies confirm that a code of the street is operative among violent youth, but they have not been as successful in showing just how it is operative or how "decent" young people "code-switch" to street. The notion that "the code" ensures safety has been found wanting by Stewart, Schreck, and Simons (2006). For an application of "the code of the street" to understanding rap music, see Kubrin (2005). Currently, implications of the code of the street are making their way into public policy (see Holder, Robinson, and Rose 2009).

10. Goffman (1967a:20) noted that "violent retaliation" is a "departure from the standard corrective cycle" of facework, which consists of challenge, offering, acceptance, and thanks. While Elijah Anderson depicts such a departure from facework as normative in the inner city, I found it was actually rarer in the inner city than in more upscale areas. For instance, when I walked down the sidewalks strangers often nodded and said "Hello," which never happened when I walked or biked in more upscale areas, where individuals were more likely to honk aggressively and rarely if ever made eye contact.

11. Compare Boulton's (1991) discussion of "play fights."

12. See Fagan and Wilkinson (1998). Horowitz and Schwartz (1974:239) note, "Any provocative or threatening incident can become the basis for a collectively held grievance. But, until it does, we feel that physical conflict between peers should not be classified as gang violence."

13. In addition to the growing literature on the code of the street cited above, many criminologists note that the act of retaliation plays a central role in shaping criminal violence among this population (Mullins, Wright, and Jacobs, 2004). A problem in such studies is that they typically search for and present only confirming cases, overlooking the analytic and explanatory riches that may derive from negative cases (see Cressey 1953; Lindesmith 1968; J. Katz 2001).

14. I also collected nine cases of fighting in response to an attack. Other reasons for fighting included defense of family members (eight cases), a problem in a sport or contest (seven cases), a response to infidelity (five cases), and a response to a robbery (five cases). Categories with fewer than five cases included a response to insults against dress or hair, a fight among friends, a fight within the family, bullying, defense against being wrongly accused, peer pressure, "he say/she say" (see Goodwin 1990), a dirty look, misinterpretation of a signal, defense of one's masculinity, "I was a fighter," "justice," being accused of saying something offensive, and jealousy.

15. Nicholson (1995:29–30).

16. The instances below may also be interpreted according to Harold Garfinkel's notion of the "et cetera clause" (Garfinkel 1967/1984; Heritage 1984). As Garfinkel states (1967/1984:71–73), "The terms of common understandings . . . attain the status of an

agreement for persons only insofar as the stipulated conditions carry along an unspoken but understood et cetera clause." Such a clause is then "used by persons to normalize whatever their actual activities turn out to be" (74). Invoking the "et cetera clause" to understand "the code of the street" means perceiving that actions that appear to "violate" the code may be retrospectively normalized by members in reference to "the code," in two ways. First, "the code" is not self-applying but must be fit to particular situations at particular times. Second, actions that apparently do not follow "the code" are treated as "exceptions" without altering the perceived legitimacy of the code. As is common with Garfinkel's insights, the et cetera clause is not a unique or unusual phenomenon; rather, it is an enduring and commonly unacknowledged resource mundanely used by social actors in general to apply generalized understandings to specific instances, as in interpreting "fights" by means of "the code." On "telling the code of the street," an analysis that draws on Wieder (1974), see Jimerson and Oware (2006).

17. See E. Anderson (1999:88–90 ff.).

18. On the resource of backup as a reason to join a gang, see Sanchez-Jankowski (1991) and Monti (1994).

19. Athens (2005:667).

20. J. Katz (1988:174).

21. Athens (2005:668).

22. Jackson-Jacobs (2002) cites such an "imaginative solution to conflict" as "a way of saving face in terms of the code." As he states, "Saving-face is always imaginatively and prospectively possible."

23. Notions of "decent" and "street" were not common ways of understanding young people in this area. One teacher at CAA came close to making such a distinction when she stated, "You've got 40 percent of these young people out in the world that are not gonna make it. They're gonna end up dead, in the penitentiary, prostituting, on drugs, got a house full of babies, can't take care of 'em, poor, hungry, suicidal, all of the above. And that's pretty sad." Even though this teacher blamed such conditions on structural factors, stating, "Society has now kind of turned their backs on them," such a view of the students was actively discouraged by CAA administrators. As Ms. Reynolds, the school principal, stated, "I don't cherish having anyone on my staff with an attitude about students like that."

24. M. Fine (1991).

25. J. Katz (1999:152)

26. Felson (1982); E. Anderson (1999).

27. Jody Miller (2008:96, 173 ff.) analyzes "the imperative to not hit girls" in depth, showing how hitting girls was framed as unmanly and how the ideology to not hit girls was linked to young men's respect for their mothers (179–80). Nevertheless, "both girls and boys posited several ideologies that justified a violent response when a girl initiated violence" (181).

28. Also see R. Rosenfeld, Jacobs, and Wright (2003).

29. See Athens (2005:668).

30. On "the offering," see Goffman (1967a:20).

31. Compare E. Anderson's (1999:85–91) account of how Tyree "gets cool" with the "bols" and his finding that "the culture of the street doesn't allow backing down" (97).

32. E. Anderson (1999:34).

33. See Whitman and Davis (2007).

34. Merry (1979) analyzes reporting to the police and going to court as weapons of the weak, which are cumbersome and rarely as efficacious as physical retaliation or moving away. R. Rosenfeld, Jacobs, and Wright (2003) plug a wide gap in Anderson's theorizing by exploring the strategic decisions of convicts to become snitches in exchange for benefits, and Wieder (1974) reveals how the dictate "Don't snitch" is better understood as a resource that members use to account for behavior than as a code that predicts and explains it.

35. When Butler (1990) notes that "all gender is drag," we must not lose sight that drag is an extremely difficult performance to successfully pull off! See Garfinkel (1967/1984:116–85).

36. E. Anderson (1999).

37. Benoit et al. (2003:522) also find solid evidence of "street" individuals acting in "decent" ways. Their study of marijuana-using crack sellers born to chronic crack abusers found these individuals to uphold many "decent" values, from working three years in construction, to being anxious to act as a good father, to becoming active in the military. According to the authors, "Labeling certain kinds of behavior as 'street' has the potential to unwittingly reinforce stereotypes associated with young, urban, African-American males," and "positing 'street' and 'decent' codes of conduct may unnecessarily dichotomize the norms that guide young inner-city adults."

38. For a symbolic interactionist approach to the historical development of the use of this term, see Akom (2000).

39. Deutsch (2008:102) found that her sample of inner-city teens did not in fact emulate the "street" in order to be safe and that "images of gangbangers, drug dealers, and school dropouts dominate club members' descriptions of who they do not want to be."

40. E. Anderson (1999:100).

41. See Hartless et al. (1995).

7. AVOIDING RETALIATION

1. "Lumping it" is actually a technical term developed by Felstiner (1974) in the law and society literature.

2. This gap between independent and dependent variables is easily overlooked in criminology, as many consider the primary aim of the discipline to determine which factors lead to crime rather than to determine how an individual in the midst of such factors might decide the best way to respond to a perceived injury. In the United States, a virtual consensus exists in the field that men commit more crime than women, the young more than the old, the urban more than the rural, blacks and Latinos more than whites, and the poor more than the rich (Sampson and Wilson 1995). Accordingly, poor, young, urban men of color are considered "at risk" of engaging in crime, and the act of retaliation plays a central role in shaping criminal violence among this population (Mullins, Wright, and Jacobs 2004). A number of prominent recent studies have specified this risk in elaborate detail, drawing upon Elijah Anderson's notion of the code of the street to show how likely such young men are to commit crime on the basis of a mix of structural and cultural factors (Wilkinson 2001; Kubrin and Weitzer 2003; Brezina et al. 2004; Stewart and Simons 2006). Yet despite the sophistication of such modeling and its intuitive good sense,

researchers are hard-pressed to explain more than 50 percent of the variance. Thus, even when we factor in every currently conceivable variable to predict crime, individuals are more likely not to commit crime in such circumstances than to commit it.

One way to understand how those most at risk of engaging in crime might abstain from it is found in the literature on collective efficacy. Since "there is a consistent, positive relationship between disorder and neighborhood dissatisfaction, citizen withdrawal, and crime and crime levels" (Pattillo 1998:748, citing Skogan 1990), perhaps individuals who pause before retaliating are in neighborhoods with higher collective control of crime. Yet Browning, Feinberg, and Dietz (2004) have shown that stronger social networks may "provide a source of social capital for offenders, potentially diminishing the regulatory effectiveness of collective efficacy." Wilkinson (2007) looks at the willingness to intervene in situations where serious crimes or misdemeanors are happening as assessed by the perpetrators, showing that in cases of vandalism, drug selling, and fighting, the likelihood that someone will intervene to stop it depends on the age, the social ties between interveners and offenders, and the space (public/private, near/far) where the act occurs. Individuals are generally more likely to intervene to stop the behavior of younger children in their neighborhood with whom they share intimate ties. While it is fascinating to gain a lens into the neighborhood through the eyes of offenders, we might also learn from offenders what a neighborhood's collective efficacy *means to them*. As Wilkinson (2007:214) states, "The relationship between network-based social ties, fear and collective efficacy would become clearer if we gather more information from individuals about the situational contingencies that promote or inhibit social control agency. . . . In addition, the voice of non-violent youth in high crime neighborhoods needs to be considered." For excellent articles on the role of neighbors in preventing disputes, see Pattillo (1998) and Carr (2003). For an important contribution of the voices of young people to the discourses concerning them, see the issue of *Journal of Social Issues* devoted to this topic, edited by Daiute and Fine (2003).

    3. E. Anderson (1999:97) holds this view of the "culture of the street," despite Felstiner's (1974) observation that "lumping it" is the most common response to disputes and Merry's (1979:892) finding that "exit" was in fact the modal response in the inner-city neighborhood she studied in Newark.

    4. Stewart and Simons (2006:25), citing Pattillo (1998).

    5. Kubrin and Weitzer (2003:178), citing Black (1976) and Parenti (2000). Kennedy (1988) and J. Katz and Jackson-Jacobs (2004) make similar points.

    6. Felstiner, Abel, and Sarat (1980:630).

    7. For exceptions, see J. Katz (1988), Athens (2005), and Collins (2008). For discussions of the need for more research to address the emotional dynamics of disputes, see De Haan and Loader (2002) and Ferrell (1999:413).

    8. For instance, many of Hochschild's most powerful examples involve flight attendants' management of, or failure to manage, rage arising out of a dispute with a customer. Consider, for example, the following quote from a flight attendant recalling "a personal breaking point": "I guess it was on a flight when a lady spat at me that I decided I'd had enough. I tried. God knows, I tried my damnedest" (Hochschild 1983:128). Similar examples of the necessity for intrapersonal emotion management arising out of interpersonal disputes can be found throughout the emotion management literature, which includes Stenross and Kleinman (1989), Sutton (1991), Dilorio and Nusbaumer (1993), Leidner

(1993), Tolich (1993), Wharton (1993), Wharton and Erickson (1995), Wharton (1999), Copp (1998), Chin (2000), Goodrum and Stafford (2003), Bolton and Boyd (2003), and Garot (2004).

9. Hochschild (1983:90).

10. Sloan (2007) has developed a test of the notion that emotive dissonance and alienation result from abiding by structural constraints on emotional expression, using Turner's (1976) notion of self-concept anchorage, but the results have been inconclusive. Bolton and Boyd (2003) have provided an on-target expansion and critique of Hochschild, adding prescriptive and philanthropic emotion management to Hochschild's model, showing that the latter is far from alienating. Other expansions of emotional management include interpersonal emotion management (Thoits 1996; Francis 1997), emotional sensitivity (Ostrow 1990; Garot 2004), and reciprocal emotion management (Lively 2000).

11. Jennifer Lois (2005) closes the conceptual gap between emotion work and edge-work through her research on the gendered emotion management of rescue workers in establishing confidence levels and suppressing, releasing, and redefining feelings.

12. On the emotional thrill and drawbacks of righteous retaliation, see J. Katz (1988:12–52).

13. On mediation, see Lieberman (2006); on negotiation, see Fisher and Shapiro (2005).

14. Sarat and Felstiner (1995).

15. McClenahen and Lofland (1976).

16. See Thoits (1996) on interpersonal emotional management.

17. J. Katz (1988: 23).

18. J. Katz (1999:18–86).

19. Goffman (1967b); Luckenbill (1977); Felson (1982); Jackson-Jacobs (2004). Athens (2005:668), while not analyzing ambivalence, notes that individuals will deescalate a potentially violent interaction out of "fear that they will destroy their personal relationship with their opponents."

20. A substantial literature on discourse analysis is built on the pioneering work of Foucault (1972).

21. On the dynamics of Manichean distinctions arising out of colonialism and then continuing into decolonialization, see Fanon (1966:29–46).

22. Gadd and Jefferson (2007) draw upon Melanie Klein's (1988a, 1988b) theories of psychosocial development, and especially her analysis of ambivalence, as central to their new psychosocial approach to crime. According to Klein, all individuals wrestle with competing, mutually contradicting desires from the age of infancy. A state of maturity is possible when one is able to reconcile competing desires and settle into an acceptance of ambivalence, learning that one need not destroy that which cannot be controlled. For Gadd and Jefferson, Klein's theories are integral for understanding how criminal behavior may result from an inability to reconcile oneself to ambivalence. Maruna (2001) analyzes the reverse of such processes, showing how ex-convicts struggle to come to terms with past crimes and reintegrate into society by learning to accept perceived harms without resorting to retaliation. Similarly, the tales of the young men presented below might be read as models of how one might overcome emotive dissonance and accept the often ambivalent situations that experience provides. On "the dialectical ambivalence of adversarialism and mutualism," see Barak (2003:281–82).

23. In her classic study of dispute management in an urban neighborhood, Merry (1979) also examines five cases.

24. Such stories have the potential of transforming a sociological interview into a psychological one. I consulted with a psychologist to ensure that I was appropriately managing our interactions and stayed in touch with my consultants often long after the interview to help them cope with difficult feelings that might have been raised.

25. On the importance of honor for Latino gang members, see Horowitz (1983).

26. On rumors, see Suttles (1968:195–202) and G. Fine, Campion-Vincent, and Heath (2005).

27. On deep acting and surface acting, see Hochschild (1983).

28. On earning respect by taking care, see Maruna (2001:117–45).

29. See Merry (1979).

30. J. Katz (1999).

31. Eric's attachment to his truck is similar to the attachment to vehicles described in some of the tales recounted by Amy Best (2006).

32. Brunson and Miller (2006:113) found such experiences common in their sample of African American young men, who often see themselves as "symbolic assailants in the eyes of the police."

33. Transient, lower-income individuals tend to resort to official agencies more often than those with upper incomes to resolve disputes (Kennedy 1988:405). It is typically a weapon of the weak, who are unable or unwilling to pursue more violent and efficacious means of redress. This common practice of resorting to official agencies for assistance contradicts a central thesis of and justification for the code of the street (E. Anderson 1999).

34. On stalking, see Emerson, Ferris, and Gardner (1998), and Dunn (2001). Many families have moved out of the area around CAA to suburban regions, where they often find problems with gangs and violence to be even more pernicious, since they are surrounded by other families who have taken similar steps, neglecting to recognize that their "gang problem" involved their own children. See Emerson (1981) on last resorts.

35. Compare Mullins, Wright, and Jacobs (2004).

36. Note that his reasons are not about academic or social alienation but about frustration with the school's bureaucracy. Faced with an administration that was totally unprepared for him, failed to give him a homeroom class, and kept sending him "back and forth," he simply lost patience and dropped out. Such a phenomenon is all too common in inner-city schools, leading students to speak of those who leave not as "dropouts" but as "push-outs" (M. Fine 1991). As Jacqueline Goldwyn Kingon (2001:30) notes in her first-year teaching journal from a New York City elementary school, "There is a mix-up in the office. Some new parents are trying to find their children's class but their names are not on anyone's list. The children are dressed up, expecting to attend the first day of school[,] but are put on the back burner and told to go home and try again tomorrow. For some, the same thing will happen the next day, and the next."

37. On mixed feelings about prosecuting abusers, see Emerson (1994).

38. Clark (1987) shows how expressions of sympathy reflect an economy of feeling. Ben's sentiments may also be seen as an example of the Stockholm syndrome (Strentz 1980), a term coined by Nels Bejerot for hostages who showed loyalty to their hostage takers during the Norrmalmstorg robbery of Kreditbanken at Norrmalmstorg, Stockholm,

Sweden. The bank robbers held bank employees hostage from August 23 to August 28 in 1973. See A. Hirschman (1970) for an organizational/economic analysis of the dynamics of exit, voice, and loyalty.

39. See M. Fine (1991).

40. See J. Katz (1988, 2000) and J. Katz and Jackson-Jacobs (2004).

41. Duneier (1999:60–62).

42. See Maruna (2001:117–45).

43. Mullins, Wright, and Jacobs (2004).

44. See Emerson and Messinger (1977) for how no incident is self-defining. The way "trouble" is interpreted depends on interactional dynamics between the parties involved and the professional ideology of troubleshooters brought in to manage the matter, among other factors.

45. Pattillo (1998).

46. Carr (2003:1264).

47. Wilkinson (2007).

48. Suttles (1968); Venkatesh (1997); Pattillo (1998); Zatz and Portillos (2000); Brotherton and Barrios (2004).

49. See McGloin (2005).

50. Mullins, Wright, and Jacobs (2004:933).

51. Kubrin and Weitzer (2003:176–77).

8. STREETWORK

1. Goffman (1959).

2. On the other hand, for a discussion of the low wages earned by a drug gang's "foot soldiers," see Levitt and Venkatesh (2000). Bourgois (1997) reports similar findings. Joe, however, was not a foot soldier.

3. Cintron (1997:98–130). The description is reminiscent of the precise detail in Agee and Evans (1941).

4. J. Katz (1988:114–63).

5. Quite intentionally, this chapter is an echo of Elijah Anderson's closing to *The Code of the Street*, in which he discusses his efforts to find employment at the University of Pennsylvania for John Turner, who had been a drug dealer. Anderson also describes the efforts of another young man, Robert, to become legitimate and stand up to the local drug dealers. Both treatments are steeped in middle-class morality, for which Anderson was upbraided in a scathing and controversial critique by Loïc Wacquant (2002) in the pages of a leading sociology journal.

6. See Connell (1995).

7. The decent/street dichotomy, discussed in chapters 6 and 7 and below, is developed most clearly by Elijah Anderson (1999).

8. See Fordham and Ogbu (1986).

9. Carter (2003, 2007).

10. The difference is often far from clear for members. See Jody Miller (2008).

11. For a lively discussion of such themes in Mexican male "working-class speech/body play," and the politics of varied depictions of Latino masculinity, see Limón (1989) and his critics (L. Cummings 1991).

12. See E. Anderson (1978) for an analysis of the nuances of categorizing others.

13. Mortimer and Larson (2002). A. Ferguson (2001) speaks of how African American boys in the fifth grade are seen as little men, their antics interpreted in adult terms and perceived as especially *menacing* through a racialized lens.

14. See J. Katz's analysis of the Capeman (1988:130), as well as Cintron (1997).

15. For an enlightening perspective on the joy that inspires young people and the disappointments that hold them back, see Childress (2000).

16. Duneier (1999); MacLeod (1995).

CONCLUSION

The epigraph is from Natasha Pike's video *Untitled,* as discussed by Susan Driver (2007:321). As Driver notes, "The viewer is confronted by the narrator, who refuses to be pathologized. . . . Am I bothered by this refusal of neat categories?"

1. Becker (1967).

2. Hayward and Young (2004:262–63).

3. Jock Young (1999, 2007) diligently traces the causes, contours, and effects of such increasing exclusiveness in his book *The Exclusive Society* and elaborates on this theme with his follow-up book *The Vertigo of Late Modernity.*

4. In applying *verstehen* to criminology, see Ferrell (1999).

5. Matza (1969:25).

6. Matza (1969:19).

7. Clarke et al. (1975/2006:11).

8. Du Bois (1899/2003:1).

9. See Massey and Denton's (1993) analysis of segregation in the United States; a recent Harvard study finds that segregation in schools is increasing (Frankenberg, Lee, and Orfield 2003).

10. See Conquergood (1994a).

11. Cintron (1997).

12. A. Ferguson (2001); E. Anderson (1999); The quote regarding David Kennedy appears in Furlong (2006:19).

13. For a dramatic and humorous depiction of such contradictions, see the 1984 film *Harold of Orange.*

14. Vigil (2003).

15. Brotherton and Barrios (2003).

16. On understanding "culture" as a tool kit, see Swidler (1986).

17. Young (2007).

18. Flacks (2007:73).

19. Flacks (2007:78–79).

20. Norma Mendoza-Denton (2008).

21. Brubaker and Cooper (2000:27–28).

22. Driver (2007:322).

23. Deutsch's (2008) book opens with such a discussion.

1. A number of teachers at CAA strongly objected to students' referring to themselves by this term, as they considered it degrading and a depressing throwback to the pre–civil rights era. Yet in identifying with a term that has been associated with racist oppression, young people could be perceived as empowering themselves. John Kitsuse (1980:9) proposed "the concept of 'tertiary deviation' to refer to the deviant's confrontation, assessment, and rejection of the negative identity . . . and the transformation of that identity into a positive and viable self-conception." Note that Latinos in this setting also use the term *nigga* to refer to each other with as much frequency, relish, and affiliative overtones as African Americans. For a lucid discussion of historical uses of this term, see Akom (2000).

2. See Garot (forthcoming).

3. See Dickar (2008) for a similar tale of the difficulty of balancing research and teaching in a public school.

4. MacLeod (1995).

5. See Hadley (2007).

6. See Sacks (1995:40–48).

References

Abu-Lughod, Lila. 1990. "The Romance of Resistance: Tracing Transformations of Power through Bedouin Women." *American Ethnologist* 17 (1): 41–55.

Agee, James, and Walker Evans. 1941. *Let Us Now Praise Famous Men*. Boston: Houghton Mifflin.

Akom, A. A. 2000. "The House That Race Built: Some Observations on the Use of the Word Nigga, Popular Culture and Urban Adolescent Behavior." In *Construction Sites: Excavating Race, Class and Gender among Urban Youth,* edited by Lois Weis and Michelle Fine, 140–57. New York: Teachers College Press.

Anderson, Benedict. 1983/2006. *Imagined Communities: Reflections on the Origin and Spread of Nationalism*. London: Verso.

Anderson, David C. 1998. "Curriculum, Culture, and Community: The Challenge of School Violence." In *Youth Violence,* edited by Michael Tonry, 317–64. Chicago: University of Chicago Press.

Anderson, Elijah. 1978. *A Place on the Corner*. Chicago: University of Chicago Press.

———. 1990. *Streetwise: Race, Class, and Change in an Urban Community*. Chicago: University of Chicago Press.

———. 1999. *Code of the Street: Decency, Violence, and the Moral Life of the Inner City*. New York: W. W. Norton.

Anyon, Jean. 1997. *Ghetto Schooling: A Political Economy of Urban Educational Reform*. New York: Teachers College Press.

Appadurai, Arjun. 1996. *Modernity at Large: Cultural Dimensions of Globalization*. Minneapolis: University of Minnesota Press.

Apple, Michael. 1990. *Ideology and Curriculum*. New York: Routledge.

Ashamalla, Rosemarie Ann. 1999. "Lost in the System." PhD diss., University of California, Los Angeles.

Athens, Lonnie. 2005. "Violent Encounters: Violent Engagements, Skirmishes, and Tiffs." *Journal of Contemporary Ethnography* 34:631–78.

Austin, John L. 1962. *How to Do Things with Words*. New York: Oxford University Press.

Ayers, William, and Patricia Ford. 1996. *City Kids, City Teachers: Reports from the Front Row*. New York: New Press.

Ball, Richard A., and G. David Curry. 1995. "The Logic of Definition in Criminology: Purposes and Methods for Defining 'Gangs.'" *Criminology* 33 (2): 225–45.

Barak, Gregg. 2003. *Violence and Nonviolence: Pathways to Understanding*. Thousand Oaks, CA: Sage Publications.

Barrett, Carla. 2007. "A Place Apart: Responding to Youth Charged as Adults in a Specialized New York Criminal Court." PhD diss., City University of New York.

Becker, Howard S. 1963. *Outsiders: Studies in the Sociology of Deviance.* New York: Macmillan.

———. 1967. "Whose Side Are We On?" *Social Problems* 14 (Winter): 239–47.

———. 1973. *Outsiders: Studies in the Sociology of Deviance.* Enl. ed. New York: Macmillan.

———. 1998. *Tricks of the Trade: How to Think about Your Research While You're Doing It.* Chicago: University of Chicago Press.

Benoit, E., D. Randolph, E. Dunlap, and B. Johnson. 2003. "Code Switching and Inverse Imitation among Marijuana-Using Crack Sellers." *British Journal of Criminology* 43:506–25.

Best, Amy. 2006. *Fast Cars, Cool Rides: The Accelerating World of Youth and Their Cars.* New York: NYU Press.

Bing, Léon. 1991. *Do or Die.* New York: Harper Perennial.

Bittner, Egon. 1967. "Police Discretion in Emergency Apprehension of Mentally Ill Persons." *Social Problems* 14 (3): 278–92.

Black, Donald. 1976. *The Behavior of Law.* New York: Academic Press.

Blumer, Herbert. 1969a. "Fashion: From Class Differentiation to Collective Selection." *Sociological Quarterly* 10 (Summer): 275–91.

———. 1969b. *Symbolic Interactionism: Perspective and Method.* Englewood Cliffs, NJ: Prentice Hall.

Bolton, Sharon C., and Carol Boyd. 2003. "Trolley Dolly or Skilled Emotion Manager? Moving on from Hochschild's Managed Heart." *Work, Employment and Society* 17 (2): 289–308.

Boulton, Michael J. 1991. "A Comparison of Structural and Contextual Features of Middle School Children's Aggressive Fighting." *Ethology and Sociobiology* 12:119–45.

Bourdieu, Pierre. 1984. *Distinction: A Social Critique of the Judgement of Taste.* Cambridge, MA: Harvard University Press.

Bourgois, Philippe. 1996. *In Search of Respect: Selling Crack in El Barrio.* Cambridge: Cambridge University Press.

———. 1997. "In Search of Horatio Alger: Culture and Ideology in the Crack Economy." In *Crack in America: Demon Drugs and Social Justice,* edited by Craig Reinarman and Harry Gene, 57–76. Berkeley: University of California Press.

Bowles, Samuel, and Herbert Gintis. 1976. *Schooling in Capitalist America: Educational Reform and the Contradictions of Economic Life.* New York: Basic Books.

Brezina, Timothy, Robert Agnew, Francis T. Cullen, and John Paul Wright. 2004. "The Code of the Street: A Quantitative Assessment of Elijah Anderson's Subculture of Violence Thesis and Its Contribution to Youth Violence Research." *Youth Violence and Juvenile Justice* 2 (4): 303–28.

Brodkin, Karen. 1999. *How Jews Became White Folks and What That Says about Race in America.* New Brunswick: Rutgers University Press.

Brotherton, David C. 1996. "The Contradictions of Suppression: Notes from a Study of Approaches to Gangs in Three Public High Schools." *Urban Review* 28 (2): 95–117.

———. 1997. "Socially Constructing the Nomads. Part One." *Humanity and Society* 21 (2): 110–29.

———. 2003. "Education in the Reform of Street Organizations in New York City." In *Gangs and Society: Alternative Perspectives,* edited by Louis Kontos, David Brotherton, and Luis Barrios, 136–58. New York: Columbia University Press.

———. 2008. "Beyond Social Reproduction: Bringing Resistance Back in Gang Theory." *Theoretical Criminology* 12 (1): 55–77.

Brotherton, David C., and Luis Barrios. 2004. *The Almighty Latin King and Queen Nation: Street Politics and the Transformation of a New York Street Gang.* New York: Columbia University Press.

Browning, Christopher R., Seth L. Feinberg, and Robert D. Dietz. 2004. "The Paradox of Social Organization: Networks, Collective Efficacy, and Violent Crime in Urban Neighborhoods." *Social Forces* 83 (2): 503–34.

Brubaker, Rogers. 1996. *Nationalism Reframed: Nationhood and the National Question in the New Europe.* Cambridge: Cambridge University Press.

Brubaker, Rogers, and Frederick Cooper. 2000. "Beyond 'Identity.'" *Theory and Society* 29 (1): 1–47.

Bruner, E. M. 1973. "The Missing Tins of Chicken: A Symbolic Interactionist Approach to Culture Change." *Ethos* 1:219–38.

Brunson, Rod K., and Jody Miller. 2006. "Young Black Men and Urban Policing in the United States." *British Journal of Criminology* 46:613–40.

Bucher, K. T., and M. L. Manning. 2003. "Challenges and Suggestions for Safe Schools." *Clearing House* 76 (3): 160–64.

Burnett, G. 1999. *Gangs in Schools.* ERIC Digest. http://ericweb.tc.columbia.edu/digests/dig99.html.

Bursik, Robert J., Jr., and Harold G. Grasmick. 2006. "Defining and Researching Gangs." In *The Modern Gang Reader,* edited by Arlen Egley Jr., Cheryl L. Maxson, Jody Miller, and Malcolm W. Klein, 2–13. Los Angeles: Roxbury.

Butler, Judith. 1990. *Gender Trouble: Feminism and the Subversion of Identity.* New York: Routledge.

———. 1991. "Imitation and Gender Insubordination." In *Cultural Theory and Popular Culture: A Reader,* edited by John Story, 255–70. Upper Saddle River, NJ: Pearson Prentice Hall.

Cairns, Robert B., and Beverly D. Cairns. 1994. *Lifelines and Risks: Pathways of Youth in Our Time.* Cambridge: Cambridge University Press.

Calavita, Kitty. 2000. "The Paradoxes of Race, Class, Identity, and 'Passing': Enforcing the Chinese Exclusion Acts, 1882–1910." *Law and Social Inquiry* 25:1–40.

Calhoun, Craig. 1994. "Social Theory and the Politics of Identity." In *Social Theory and the Politics of Identity,* edited by Craig Calhoun, 9–36. Oxford: Blackwell.

Campbell, Anne. 1986. "Self-Report of Fighting by Females: A Preliminary Study." *British Journal of Criminology* 26 (1): 28–46.

———. 1991. *The Girls in the Gang: A Report from New York City.* Oxford: Blackwell.

Carr, Patrick J. 2003. "The New Parochialism: The Implications of the Beltway Case for Arguments Concerning Informal Social Control." *American Journal of Sociology* 108 (6): 1249–91.

Carter, Prudence. 2003. "'Black' Cultural Capital, Status Positioning, and Schooling Conflicts for Low-Income African American Youth." *Social Problems* 50:136–55.

———. 2007. *Keepin' It Real: School Success beyond Black and White.* Oxford: Oxford University Press.

Castleman, Craig. 1988. *Getting Up: Subway Graffiti in New York.* Cambridge: MIT Press.

Charmaz, Kathy. 2006. *Constructing Grounded Theory: A Practical Guide through Qualitative Analysis.* Los Angeles: Sage Publications.

Chen, Cindy I. 2004. "Dealing with Prison Violence, Officials Know the Best! Courts Should Defer to Their Policy to Segregate Prisoners." *Western State University Law Review* 32:127–40.

Chesney-Lind, Medea, and Katherine Irwin. 2007. *Beyond Bad Girls: Gender, Violence and Hype.* New York: Routledge.

Childress, Herb. 2000. *Landscapes of Betrayal, Landscapes of Joy: Curtisville in the Lives of Its Teenagers.* Albany: State University of New York Press.

Chin, Tiffany. 2000. "'Sixth Grade Madness': Parental Emotion Work in the Private High School Application Process." *Journal of Contemporary Ethnography* 29 (2): 124–63.

Choices Alternative Academy [Pseud.]. 1997. "Orientation Handbook."

Cintron, Ralph. 1997. *Angels' Town: Chero Ways, Gang Life, and Rhetorics of the Everyday.* Boston: Beacon Press.

Clark, Candace. 1987. "Sympathy Biography and Sympathy Margin." *American Journal of Sociology* 93 (2): 290–321.

Clarke, John, Stuart Hall, Tony Jefferson, and Brian Roberts. 1975/2006. "Subcultures, Cultures and Class." In *Resistance through Rituals: Youth Subcultures in Post-War Britain,* edited by Stuart Hall and Tony Jefferson, 3–59. London: Routledge.

Clear, Todd. 2009. *Imprisoning Communities: How Mass Incarceration Makes Disadvantaged Neighborhoods Worse.* Oxford: Oxford University Press.

Cloward, Richard A., and Lloyd E. Ohlin. 1960. *Delinquency and Opportunity: A Theory of Delinquent Gangs.* Glencoe, IL: Free Press.

Cohen, Albert K. 1990. "Foreword and Overview." In *Gangs in America,* edited by C. Ronald Huff, 7–21. Newbury Park, CA: Sage Publications.

Cohen, Ronald. 1978. "Ethnicity: Problem and Focus in Anthropology." *Annual Review of Anthropology* 7:379–403.

Colebrook, Claire. 2002. "Certeau and Foucault: Tactics and Strategic Essentialism." *South Atlantic Quarterly* 100 (2): 543–74.

Collins, Randall. 2008. *Violence: A Micro-Sociological Theory.* Princeton: Princeton University Press.

Conley, Dalton. 1999. *Being Black, Living in the Red: Race, Wealth, and Social Policy in America.* Berkeley: University of California Press.

Connell, R. W. 1995. *Masculinities.* Berkeley: University of California Press.

Conquergood, Dwight. 1994a. "For the Nation! How Street Gangs Problematize Patriotism." In *After Postmodernism: Reconstructing Ideology Critique,* edited by Herbert W. Simons and Michael Billig, 200–221. Thousand Oaks, CA: Sage Publications.

———. 1994b. "Homeboys and Hoods: Gang Communication and Cultural Space." In *Group Communication in Context: Studies of Natural Groups,* edited by Lawrence R. Frey, 23–55. Hillsdale, NJ: Lawrence Erlbaum Associates.

———. 1997. "Street Literacy." In *Handbook on Teaching Literacy through the Communicative and Visual Arts,* edited by James Flood, Shirley Brice Heath, and Diane Lapp, 354–75. New York: Simon and Schuster.

Copp, Martha. 1998. "When Emotion Work Is Doomed to Fail: Ideological and Structural Constraints on Emotion Management." *Symbolic Interaction* 21 (3): 299–328.

Corrigan, Paul. 1975. "Doing Nothing." In *Resistance through Rituals: Youth Subcultures in Post-war Britain,* edited by Stuart Hall and Tony Jefferson, 103–5. London: Routledge.

Côté, James. 2006. "Identity Studies: How Close Are We to Developing a Social Science of Identity?—An Appraisal of the Field." *Identity: An International Journal of Theory and Research* 6 (1): 3–25.

Cressey, D. R. 1953. *Other People's Money: A Study in the Social Psychology of Embezzlement.* Glencoe, IL: Free Press.

Cummings, Eric. 1997. "Prison Radicalism and the Return of Civil Death in California: Where Are We Now?" Paper presented at the annual meeting of the Organization of American Historians, April 17–20, San Francisco. www.oah.org/meetings/1997/cummins.htm.

Cummings, Laura. 1991. "'Carne con Limón: Reflections on the Construction of Social Harmlessness." *American Ethnologist* 18 (2): 370–72.

Currie, Eliot. 2004. *The Road to Whatever: Middle-Class Culture and the Crisis of Adolescence.* New York: Metropolitan Books.

Curry, G. David, and Scott H. Decker. 2003. *Confronting Gangs: Crime and the Community.* Los Angeles: Roxbury.

Daiute, Colette, and Michelle Fine. 2003. "Youth Perspectives through History, Culture, and Community: Youth Perspectives on Violence and Injustice." *Journal of Social Issues* 59 (1): 1–14.

Dance, L. Janelle. 2002. *Tough Fronts: The Impact of Street Culture on Schooling.* New York: Routledge.

Davidson, Ann Locke. 1996. *Making and Molding Identity in Schools: Student Narratives on Race, Gender, and Academic Engagement.* Albany: State University of New York Press.

Davies, Bronwyn. 1982. *Life in the Classroom and Playground: The Accounts of Primary School Children.* London: Routledge and Kegan Paul.

Davis, Fred. 1992. *Fashion, Culture and Identity.* Chicago: University of Chicago Press.

Dawley, David. 1992. *A Nation of Lords: The Autobiography of the Vice Lords.* Prospect Heights, IL: Waveland Press.

De Haan, Willem, and Ian Loader. 2002. "On the Emotions of Crime, Punishment and Social Control." *Theoretical Criminology* 6 (3): 243–53.

Decker, Scott H., and G. David Curry. 1997. "What's in a Name? A Gang by Any Other Name Isn't Quite the Same." *Valparaiso Law Review* 312:501–14.

———. 2002. "Gangs, Gang Homicides, and Gang Loyalty: Organized Crimes or Disorganized Criminals?" *Journal of Criminal Justice* 30:343–52.

Decker, Scott, and Kimberly Kempf-Leonard. 1991. "Constructing Gangs: The Social Definition of Youth Activities." *Criminal Justice Policy Review* 5 (4): 271–91.

DeMitchell, Todd A., Richard Fossey, and Casey Cobb. 2000. "Dress Codes in the Public Schools: Principals, Policies, and Precepts." *Journal of Law and Education* 29:31–49.

Deschenes, Sarah, Larry Cuban, and David Tyack. 2001. "Mismatch: Historical Perspectives on Schools and Students Who Don't Fit Them." *Teachers College Record* 103 (4): 525–47.

Deutsch, Nancy L. 2008. *Pride in the Projects: Teens Building Identities in Urban Contexts.* New York: NYU Press.

Deutsch, Nancy L., and Barton J. Hirsch. 2002. "A Place to Call Home: Youth Organizations in the Lives of Inner City Adolescents." In *Understanding Early Adolescent Self and Identity: Applications and Interventions,* edited by Thomas M. Brinthaupt and Richard P. Lipka, 293–320. Albany: State University of New York Press.

Devitt, Michael. 1984. *Realism and Truth*. Princeton: Princeton University Press.

Dickar, Maryann. 2008. *Corridor Cultures: Mapping Student Resistance at an Urban High School*. New York: NYU Press.

Dilorio, Judith A., and Michael R. Nusbaumer. 1993. "Securing Our Sanity: Anger Management among Abortion Escorts." *Journal of Contemporary Ethnography* 21 (4): 411–38.

Dingwall, Robert. 2000. "Language, Law and Power: Ethnomethodology, Conversation Analysis, and the Politics of Law and Society Studies." Review essay. *Law and Social Inquiry* 25 (3): 885–911.

Dirks, Nicholas B. 1992. "Castes of Mind: The Original Caste." *Representations* 37:56–78.

Donziger, Steven D. 2002. "The Prison Industrial Complex." In *Order under Law: Readings in Criminal Justice*, edited by Robert G. Culbertson and Ralph A. Weisheit, 281–300. Prospect Heights, IL: Waveland Press.

Dow, Rosalie Rolón. 2007. "Passing Time: An Exploration of School Engagement among Puerto Rican Girls." *Urban Review* 39 (3): 349–72.

Driscoll, Catherine. 2002. *Girls: Feminine Adolescence in Popular Culture and Cultural Theory*. New York: Columbia University Press.

Driver, Susan. 2007. "Beyond 'Straight' Interpretations: Researching Queer Youth Digital Video." In *Representing Youth: Methodological Issues in Critical Youth Studies*, edited by Amy Best, 304–24. New York: NYU Press.

Du Bois, William E. B. 1899/2003. *The Souls of Black Folk*. New York: Modern Library.

Duncan, Garrett Albert. 2000. "Urban Pedagogies and the Ceiling of Adolescents of Color." *Social Justice* 27 (3): 29–42.

Duneier, Mitchell. 1999. *Sidewalk*. New York: Farrar, Straus and Giroux.

Dunn, Jennifer L. 2001. "Innocence Lost: Accomplishing Victimization in Intimate Stalking Cases." *Symbolic Interaction* 24 (3): 285–313.

Eckert, Penelope. 1989. *Jocks and Burnouts: Social Categories and Identity in the High School*. New York: Teachers College Press.

Edin, Kathryn, and Laura Lein. 1997. *Making Ends Meet: How Single Mothers Survive Welfare and Low-Wage Work*. New York: Russell Sage Foundation.

Emerson, Robert M. 1981. "On Last Resorts." *American Journal of Sociology* 87 (1): 1–22.

———. 1994. "Constructing Serious Violence and Its Victims: Processing a Domestic Violence Restraining Order." *Perspectives on Social Problems: A Research Annual* 6:3–28.

Emerson, Robert M., Kerry O. Ferris, and Carol Brooks Gardner. 1998. "On Being Stalked." *Social Problems* 45:289–314.

Emerson, Robert M., Rachel Fretz, and Linda Shaw. 1995. *Writing Ethnographic Fieldnotes*. Chicago: University of Chicago Press.

Emerson, Robert M., and Sheldon Messinger. 1977. "The Micro-Politics of Trouble." *Social Problems* 25:121–34.

Emerson, Robert M., and Blair Paley. 1992. "Organizational Horizons and Complaint-Filing." In *The Uses of Discretion*, edited by Keith Hawkins, 231–48. Oxford: Clarendon Press.

Entwistle, Joanne. 2001. "The Dressed Body." In *Body Dressing*, edited by Joanne Entwistle and Elizabeth Wilson, 33–58. Oxford: Berg.

Erikson, Erik. 1968. "Psychosocial Identity." In *International Encyclopedia of the Social Sciences*, edited by David L. Sills, 7:61–65. New York: Macmillan.

Esbensen, Finn-Aage, L. Thomas Winfree Jr., Ni He, and Terrance J. Taylor. 2004. "Youth Gangs and Definitional Issues: When Is a Gang a Gang, and Why Does It Matter?" In *American Youth Gangs at the Millennium,* edited by Finn-Aage Esbensen, Stephen G. Tibbetts, and Larry Gaines, 90–108. Long Grove, IL: Waveland Press.

Essex, Nathan L. 2001. "School Uniforms: Guidelines for Principals." *Principal* 80 (3): 38–39.

Fagan, J., and D. L. Wilkinson. 1998. "Guns, Youth Violence, and Social Identity in Inner Cities." *Crime and Justice* 24:105–88.

Fallis, R. Kirk, and Susan Opotow. 2003. "Youth Confronting Public Institutions: Are Students Failing School or Are Schools Failing Students? Class Cutting in High School." *Journal of Social Issues* 59 (1): 103–19.

Fanon, Franz. 1966. *The Wretched of the Earth.* Translated by Constance Farrington. New York: Grove Press.

Farrington, David, Leonard Berkowitz, and Donald J. West. 1982. "Differences between Individual and Group Fights." *British Journal of Social Psychology* 21:323–33.

Felson, Richard B. 1982. "Impression Management and the Escalation of Aggression and Violence." *Social Psychology Quarterly* 45 (4): 245–54.

———. 2002. *Crime and Everyday Life.* Los Angeles: Sage Publications.

Felstiner, William L. F. 1974. "Influences of Social Organization on Dispute Processing." *Law and Society Review* 9 (1): 63–94.

Felstiner, William L. F., Richard L. Abel, and Austin Sarat. 1980. "The Emergence and Transformation of Disputes: Naming, Blaming, Claiming." *Law and Society Review* 15 (3/4): 631–54.

Ferguson, Ann Arnett. 2001. *Bad Boys: Public Schools in the Making of Black Masculinity.* Ann Arbor: University of Michigan Press.

Ferguson, Yale H., and Richard W. Mansbach. 1999. "Global Politics at the Turn of the Millennium: Changing Bases of 'Us' and 'Them.'" *International Studies Review* 1 (2): 77–107.

Ferrell, Jeff. 1995. "Style Matters: Criminal Identity and Social Control." In *Cultural Criminology,* edited by John Ferrell and C. R. Sanders, 169–89. Boston: Northeastern University Press.

———. 1996. *Crimes of Style: Urban Graffiti and the Politics of Criminality.* Boston: Northeastern University Press.

———. 1999. "Cultural Criminology." *Annual Review of Sociology* 25:395–418.

———. 2001. *Tearing Down the Streets: Adventures in Urban Anarchy.* New York: Palgrave.

———. 2004. "Boredom, Crime and Criminology." *Theoretical Criminology* 8 (3): 287–302.

Ferrell, Jeff, Dragan Milovanovic, and Stephen Lyng. 2001. "Edgework, Media Practices and the Elongation of Meaning." *Theoretical Criminology* 5 (2): 177–202.

Fine, Gary Alan, Véronique Campion-Vincent, and Chip Heath. 2005. *Rumor Mills: The Social Impact of Rumor and Legend.* New Brunswick, NJ: Aldine.

Fine, Michelle. 1991. *Framing Dropouts: Notes on the Politics of an Urban High School.* New York: State University of New York Press.

Fisher, Roger, and Daniel Shapiro. 2005. *Beyond Reason: Using Emotions as You Negotiate.* New York: Viking Press.

Flacks, Marc. 2007. "'Label Jars Not People': How (Not) to Study Youth Civic Engagement." In *Representing Youth: Methodological Issues in Critical Youth Studies,* edited by Amy Best, 60–83. New York: NYU Press.

Flores-González, Nilda. 2002. *School Kids/Street Kids: Identity Development in Latino Students*. New York: Teachers College Press.

Fordham, Signithia. 1996. *Blacked Out: Dilemmas of Race, Identity, and Success at Capital High*. Chicago: University of Chicago Press.

Fordham, Signithia, and John Ogbu. 1986. "Black Students' School Success: Coping with the 'Burden of Acting White.'" *Urban Review* 18:176–206.

Foucault, Michel. 1972. *The Archaeology of Knowledge*. London: Tavistock.

———. 1978. *The History of Sexuality: An Introduction*. New York: Random House.

Francis, Lynda E. 1997. "Ideology and Interpersonal Emotion Management: Redefining Identity in Two Support Groups." *Social Psychology Quarterly* 60 (2): 153–71.

Franke, Todd Michael, Anh-Luu T. Huynh-Hohnbaum, and Yunah Chung. 2002. "Adolescent Violence: With Whom They Fight and Where." *Journal of Ethnic and Cultural Diversity in Social Work* 11 (3): 133–58.

Frankenberg, Erica, Chungmei Lee, and Gary Orfield. 2003. *A Multiracial Society and Segregated Schools: Are We Losing the American Dream?* Cambridge, MA: Civil Rights Project, Harvard University.

Freire, Paulo. 2000. *Pedagogy of the Oppressed*. Translated by Myra Bergman Ramos, with an introduction by Donald Macedo. New York: Continuum.

Furlong, Tim. 2006. "David Kennedy's Unconventional Approaches to Crime and Gang Violence Get Results." *John Jay Magazine* 1 (1): 16–19, 29.

Furstenberg, Frank F. 2003. "Teenage Childbearing as a Public Issue and Private Concern." *Annual Review of Sociology* 23:23–39.

Gadd, David, and Tony Jefferson. 2007. *Psychosocial Criminology: An Introduction*. Los Angeles: Sage Publications.

Gandhi, Mohandas K. 1999. "Excerpts from *The Essential Writings of Mahatma Gandhi*." In *Violence and Its Alternatives: An Interdisciplinary Reader*, edited by Manfred B. Steger and Nancy S. Lind, 293–301. New York: St. Martin's Press.

Gans, Herbert J. 1995. *The War against the Poor: The Underclass and Antipoverty Policy*. New York: Basic Books.

Garfinkel, Harold. 1967/1984. *Studies in Ethnomethodology*. Cambridge: Polity Press.

Garot, Robert. 2004. "'You're Not a Stone': Emotional Sensitivity in a Bureaucratic Setting." *Journal of Contemporary Ethnography* 33 (6): 735–66.

———. Forthcoming. "The Gang's School: Challenges of Reintegrative Social Control." *Research in Social Problems and Public Policy* 17.

Garot, Robert, and Tim Berard. Forthcoming. "Ethnomethodology and Membership Categorization Analysis." In *Sage Handbook of Sociolinguistics*, edited by Ruth Wodak, Barbara Johnstone, and Paul Kerswill. Thousand Oaks, CA: Sage Publications.

Geertz, Clifford. 1973. "Deep Play: Notes on the Balinese Cockfight." In *The Interpretation of Cultures: Selected Essays*, 412–53. New York: Basic Books.

Gilligan, Carol. 1982. *In a Different Voice: Psychological Theory and Women's Development*. Cambridge, MA: Harvard University Press.

Glaser, Barney G., and Anselm L. Strauss. 1967. *The Discovery of Grounded Theory: Strategies for Qualitative Research*. Chicago: Aldine.

Glassner, Barry. 2000. *Culture of Fear: Why Americans Are Afraid of the Wrong Things*. New York: Basic Books.

Goffman, Erving. 1959. *The Presentation of Self in Everyday Life*. New York: Anchor.

———. 1967a. *Interaction Ritual: Essays on Face-to-Face Behavior*. New York: Pantheon Books.

———. 1967b. "Where the Action Is." In *Interaction Ritual: Essays on Face-to-Face Behavior*, 149–270. New York: Pantheon Books.

———. 1971. *Relations in Public: Microstudies of the Public Order*. New York: Harper and Row.

Golden, Jane, Robin Rice, Monica Yant Kinney, David Graham, and Jack Ramsdale. 2006. *Philadelphia Murals and the Stories They Tell*. Philadelphia: Temple University Press.

Goodrum, Sarah, and Mark C. Stafford. 2003. "The Management of Emotions in the Criminal Justice System." *Sociological Focus* 36 (3): 179–96.

Goodwin, Marjorie Harness. 1990. *He-Said-She-Said: Talk as Social Organization among Black Children*. Bloomington: Indiana University Press.

Gottfredson, Michael, and Travis Hirschi. 1990. *A General Theory of Crime*. Stanford: Stanford University Press.

Gramsci, Antonio. 1971. *Selections from the Prison Notebooks of Antonio Gramsci*. Edited and translated by Quintin Hoare and Geoffrey Nowell Smith. London: Lawrence and Wishart.

Gullatt, David E. 1999. "Rationales and Strategies for Amending the School Dress Code to Accommodate Student Uniforms." *American Secondary Education* 27:39–47.

Gurwitsch, Aron. 1966. *Studies in Phenomenology and Psychology*. Evanston: Northwestern University Press.

Haberman, Martin. 1995. *Star Teachers of Children in Poverty*. West Lafayette, IN: Kappa Delta Pi.

Hadley, Kathryn Gold. 2007. "Will the Least-Adult Please Stand Up? Life as 'Older Sister Katy' in a Taiwanese Elementary School." In *Representing Youth: Methodological Issues in Critical Youth Studies*, edited by Amy Best, 157–81. New York: NYU Press.

Hall, Stuart. 1981. "Moving Right." *Socialist Review* 55 (1): 113–37.

———. 1996. "Introduction: Who Needs 'Identity'?" In *Questions of Cultural Identity*, edited by Stuart Hall and Paul du Gay, 1–17. Thousand Oaks, CA: Sage Publications.

Hall, Stuart, and Tony Jefferson, eds. 1976/2006. *Resistance through Rituals: Youth Subcultures in Post-war Britain*. Abingdon: Routledge.

Hallsworth, Simon, and Tara Young. 2008. "Gang Talk and Gang Talkers: A Critique." *Crime Media Culture* 4:175–95.

Harris, Alexes. 2007. "Diverting and Abdicating Judicial Discretion: Cultural, Political, and Procedural Dynamics in California Juvenile Justice." *Law and Society Review* 41 (2): 387–428.

Harris, Alexes, and Walter Allen. 2003. "Lest We Forget Thee . . . The Under- and Over-Representation of Black and Latino Youth in California Higher Education and Juvenile Justice Institutions." *Race and Society* 6:99–123.

Hartless, Julie M., Jason Ditton, Gwyneth Nair, and Samuel Phillips. 1995. "More Sinned Against than Sinning: A Study of Young Teenagers' Experience of Crime." *British Journal of Criminology* 35 (1): 114–33.

Hayward, Keith J., and Jock Young. 2004. "Cultural Criminology: Some Notes on the Script." *Theoretical Criminology* 8 (3): 259–73.

Hebdige, Dick. 1996. "Digging for Britain: An Excavation in Seven Parts." In *Black British Cultural Studies: A Reader,* edited by Houston A. Baker Jr., Manthia Diawara, and Ruth H. Lindeborg, 120–62. Chicago: University of Chicago Press.

Heritage, John. 1984. *Garfinkel and Ethnomethodology.* Oxford: Polity Press.

Hirschman, Albert O. 1970. *Exit, Voice, and Loyalty: Responses to Decline in Firms, Organizations and States.* Cambridge, MA: Harvard University Press.

Hirschman, Charles. 1986. "The Making of Race in Colonial Malaya: Political Economy and Racial Ideology." *Sociological Forum* 1:330–61.

Hobsbawm, Eric. 1973. "Peasants and Politics." *Journal of Peasant Studies* 1 (1): 3–22.

Hochschild, Arlie Russell. 1983. *The Managed Heart: Commercialization of Human Feeling.* Berkeley: University of California Press.

Hoffman, Elizabeth. 2007. "Open-Ended Interviews, Power and Emotional Labor." *Journal of Contemporary Ethnography* 36 (3): 318–46.

Holder, Eric H., Laurie O. Robinson, and Kristina Rose. 2009. *The Code of the Street and African-American Adolescent Violence.* Washington, DC: U.S. Department of Justice, Office of Justice Programs.

Holloman, Lillian O., Velma Lapoint, Sylvan I. Alleyne, Ruth J. Palmer, and Kathy Sanders-Phillips. 1996. "Dress-Related Behavioral Problems and Violence in the Public School Setting: Prevention, Intervention, and Policy—A Holistic Approach." *Journal of Negro Education* 65 (3): 267–81.

Horowitz, Ruth. 1983. *Honor and the American Dream: Culture and Identity in a Chicano Community.* New Brunswick: Rutgers University Press.

———. 1990. "Sociological Perspectives on Gangs: Conflicting Definitions and Concepts." In *Gangs in America,* edited by C. Ronald Huff, 37–54. Newbury Park, CA: Sage Publications.

———. 1993. "The Power of Ritual in a Chicano Community: A Young Woman's Status and Expanding Family Ties." *Marriage and Family Review* 19 (3/4): 257–80.

———. 1995. *Teen Mothers: Citizens or Dependents?* Chicago: University of Chicago Press.

———. 2001. "Inequalities, Democracy, and Fieldwork in the Chicago Schools of Yesterday and Today." *Symbolic Interaction* 24 (4): 481–504.

Horowitz, Ruth, and Gary Schwartz. 1974. "Honor, Normative Ambiguity and Gang Violence." *American Sociological Review* 39 (2): 238–51.

Howell, J. C., J. P. Moore, and A. Egley Jr. 2002. "The Changing Boundaries of Youth Gangs." In *Gangs in America III,* edited by C. Ronald Huff, 3–18. Thousand Oaks, CA: Sage.

Huff, C. Ronald. 1996. *Gangs in America.* Thousand Oaks, CA: Sage Publications.

Huff, C. Ronald, and Kenneth S. Trump. 1996. "Youth Violence and Gangs: School Safety Initiatives in Urban and Suburban School Districts." *Education and Urban Society* 28 (4): 492–503.

Hyman, Irwin A., and Pamela A. Snook. 1999. *Dangerous Schools: What We Can Do about the Physical and Emotional Abuse of Our Children.* San Francisco: Jossey-Bass.

Ibarra, Peter, and John I. Kitsuse. 1993. "Vernacular Constituents of Moral Discourse: An Interactionist Proposal for the Study of Social Problems." In *Constructing Social Problems,* edited by Gale Miller and James A. Holstein, 21–54. Hawthorne, NY: Aldine de Gruyter.

Irwin, John. 2005. *The Warehouse Prison: Disposal of the New Dangerous Class.* Los Angeles: Roxbury.

Irwin, Katherine. 2004. "The Violence of Adolescent Life: Experiencing and Managing Everyday Threats." *Youth and Society* 35:452–79.

Jackson, John L. 2003. *Harlemworld: Doing Race and Class in Contemporary Black America.* Chicago: University of Chicago Press.

Jackson, Kenneth T. 1985. *Crabgrass Frontier: The Suburbanization of the United States.* New York: Oxford University Press.

Jackson, Philip. 1990. *Life in Classrooms.* New York: Teachers College Press.

Jackson, Robert H. 1999. *Race, Caste and Status: Indians in Colonial Spanish America.* Albuquerque: University of Mexico Press.

Jackson, Robert H., and Gregory Maddox. 1993. "The Creation of Identity: Colonial Society in Bolivia and Tanzania." *Comparative Studies in Society and History* 35:263–84.

Jackson-Jacobs, Curtis. 2002. "Persisting in Fist-Fights during Adolescence and Early Adulthood: Results from an Ethnographic Study." Paper submitted to the annual meeting of the Pacific Sociological Association, April 18–21, Vancouver, BC.

———. 2004. "Taking a Beating: The Narrative Gratifications of Fighting as an Underdog." In *Cultural Criminology Unleashed,* edited by Jeff Ferrell, Keith Hayward, W. Morrison, and Mike Presdee, 231–44. London: Glasshouse Press.

James, William. 1890/1950. *Principles of Psychology.* New York: Dover.

Jimerson, Jason B., and Matthew K. Oware. 2006. "Telling the Code of the Street: An Ethnomethodological Ethnography." *Journal of Contemporary Ethnography* 35 (1): 24–50.

Jones, Nikki. 2008. "Working 'the Code': On Girls, Gender, and Inner-City Violence." *Australian and New Zealand Journal of Criminology* 41 (1): 63–83.

Joniak, Elizabeth A. 2005. "Exclusionary Practices and the Delegitimization of Client Voice: How Staff Create, Sustain, and Escalate Conflict in a Drop-In Center for Street Kids." *American Behavioral Scientist* 48 (8): 961–88.

Kalekin-Fishman, Devorah. 1989. "De-alienation as an Educational Objective." *Humanity and Society* 13 (3): 309–26.

Katz, Charles. 2003. "Issues in the Production and Dissemination of Police Statistics: An Ethnographic Study of a Large Midwestern Police Gang Unit." *Crime and Delinquency* 49 (3): 485–516.

Katz, Jack. 1988. *Seductions of Crime: Moral and Sensual Attractions in Doing Evil.* New York: Basic Books.

———. 1999. *How Emotions Work.* Chicago: University of Chicago Press.

———. 2000. "The Gang Myth." In *Social Dynamics of Crime and Control: New Theories for a World in Transition,* edited by Susanne Karstedt and Kai-D. Bussman, 171–87. Oxford: Hart.

———. 2001. "Analytic Induction Revisited." In *Contemporary Field Research: Perspectives and Formulations,* edited by Robert M. Emerson, 331–34. Prospect Heights, IL: Waveland Press.

Katz, Jack, and Curtis Jackson-Jacobs. 2004. "The Criminologists' Gang." In *The Blackwell Companion to Criminology,* edited by Colin Sumner, 91–124. Malden, MA: Blackwell.

Kelley, Robin D. G. 1994. *Race Rebels: Culture, Politics, and the Black Working Class.* New York: Free Press.

Kelly, Dierdre M. 1993. *Last Chance High: How Girls and Boys Drop In and Out of Alternative Schools.* New Haven: Yale University Press.

Kennedy, David. 1998. "Crime Prevention as Crime Deterrence." In *What Can the Federal Government Do to Decrease Crime and Revitalize Communities?* Washington, DC: U.S. Department of Justice.

Kennedy, Leslie W. 1988. "Going It Alone: Unreported Crime and Individual Self-Help." *Journal of Criminal Justice* 16 (5): 403–12.

Kertzer, David I., and Dominique Arel. 2002. *Census and Identity: The Politics of Race, Ethnicity and Language in National Censuses.* Cambridge: Cambridge University Press.

Kingon, Jacqueline Goldwyn. 2001. "A View from the Trenches." *New York Times Magazine,* April 8.

Kitsuse, John. 1980. "Coming Out All Over: Deviants and the Politics of Social Problems." *Social Problems* 28 (1): 1–13.

Klagholz, Leo. 1995. "A Safe School Environment for All." *School Safety,* Winter, 4–6.

Klein, Malcolm W. 1995. *The American Street Gang: Its Nature, Prevalence and Control.* Oxford: Oxford University Press.

Klein, Malcolm W., and Cheryl L. Maxson. 2006. *Street Gang Patterns and Policies.* Oxford: Oxford University Press.

Klein, Melanie. 1988a. *Envy and Gratitude and Other Works, 1946–1963.* London: Virago.

———. 1988b. *Love, Guilt and Reparation and Other Works, 1921–1945.* London: Virago.

Kotlowitz, Alex. 1992. *There Are No Children Here: The Story of Two Boys Growing Up in the Other America.* New York: Anchor.

Kozol, Jonathan. 1992. *Savage Inequalities: Children in America's Schools.* New York: Harper Perennial.

Kubrin, Charis E. 2005. "Gangstas, Thugs and Hustlas: Identity and the Code of the Street in Rap Music." *Social Problems* 52 (3): 360–78.

Kubrin, Charis E., and Ronald Weitzer. 2003. "Retaliatory Homicide: Concentrated Disadvantage and Neighborhood Culture." *Social Problems* 50 (2): 157–80.

Kupchik, A. 2006. *Judging Juveniles: Prosecuting Adolescents in Adult and Juvenile Courts.* New York: NYU Press.

Labov, William. 1982. "Speech Actions and Reactions in Personal Narrative." In *Analyzing Discourse: Text and Talk,* edited by Deborah Tannen, 219–47. Washington, DC: Georgetown University Press.

Lakoff, George. 1991. "Metaphor and War: The Metaphor System Used to Justify War in the Gulf." In *Engulfed in War: Just War and the Persian Gulf,* edited by Brian Hallet, 95–111. Honolulu: Mansunaga Institute for Peace.

Lave, Jean, and Etienne Wenger. 1991. *Situated Learning: Legitimate Peripheral Participation.* Cambridge: Cambridge University Press.

Leidner, Robin. 1993. *Fast Food, Fast Talk: Service Work and the Routinization of Everyday Life.* Berkeley: University of California Press.

Levitt, Steven D., and Sudhir Alladi Venkatesh. 2000. "An Economic Analysis of a Drug-Selling Gang's Finances." *Quarterly Journal of Economics* 115 (2): 755–89.

Lieberman, Amy L. 2006. "The 'A' List of Emotions in Mediation from Anxiety to Agreement." *Dispute Resolution Journal* 61 (1): 46–50.

Limón, José E. 1989. "'Carne, Carnales,' and the Carnivalesque: Bakhtinian 'Batos,' Disorder, and Narrative Discourses." *American Ethnologist* 16 (3): 471–86.

Lindesmith, A. R. 1968. *Addiction and Opiates.* Chicago: Aldine.

Linger, Daniel T. 1990. "Essential Outlines of Crime and Madness: Man-Fights in São Luís." *Cultural Anthropology* 5 (1): 62–77.

Lively, Kathryn J. 2000. "Reciprocal Emotion Management: Working Together to Maintain Stratification in Private Law Firms." *Work and Occupations* 27 (1): 32–63.

Lois, Jennifer. 2005. "Gender and Emotion Management in the Stages of Edgework." In *Edgework: The Sociology of Risk Taking,* edited by Stephen Lyng, 117–52. New York: Routledge.

Luckenbill, D. F. 1977. "Criminal Homicide as a Situated Transaction." *Social Problems* 25:176–86.

Lyng, Stephen. 2004. "Crime, Edgework and Corporeal Transaction." *Theoretical Criminology* 8 (3): 359–75.

MacLeod, Jay. 1995. *Ain't No Makin' It: Aspirations and Attainment in a Low-Income Neighborhood.* Boulder, CO: Westview Press.

Maruna, Shadd. 2001. *Making Good: How Ex-convicts Reform and Rebuild Their Lives.* Washington, DC: American Psychological Association.

Marx, Karl. 1983. *The Portable Marx.* Edited and translated by Eugene Kamenka. New York: Penguin Books.

Massey, Douglas S., and Nancy A. Denton. 1993. *American Apartheid: Segregation and the Making of the Underclass.* Cambridge, MA: Harvard University Press.

Mateu-Gelabert, Pedro, and Howard Lune. 2007. "Street Codes in High School: School as an Educational Deterrent." *City and Community* 6 (3): 173–91.

Matthews, Sarah H. 2003. "Counterfeit Classrooms: School Life of Inner-City Children." *Sociological Studies of Children and Youth* 9:209–24.

Matza, David. 1964. *Delinquency and Drift.* New York: John Wiley.

———. 1969. *Becoming Deviant.* Englewood Cliffs, NJ: Prentice Hall.

Maynard, Douglas W. 1988. "Language, Interaction and Social Problems." *Social Problems* 35 (4): 311–34.

McClenahan, Lachlan, and John Lofland. 1976. "Bearing Bad News: Tactics of the Deputy U.S. Marshal." *Sociology of Work and Occupations* 3 (3): 251–72.

McCorkle, Richard C., and Terance D. Miethe. 2002. *Panic: The Social Construction of the Street Gang Problem.* Upper Saddle River, NJ: Prentice Hall.

McDermott, Ray. 1987. "Achieving School Failure: An Anthropological Approach to Literacy and Social Stratification." In *Education and Cultural Process: Anthropological Approaches,* edited by George Dearborn Spindler, 82–118. Prospect Heights, IL: Waveland Press.

McFarland, Daniel A. 2001. "Student Resistance: How the Formal and Informal Organization of Classrooms Facilitate Everyday Forms of Student Defiance." *American Journal of Sociology* 107 (3): 612–78.

———. 2004. "Resistance as a Social Drama: A Study of Change-Oriented Encounters." *American Journal of Sociology* 109 (6): 1249–1318.

McGloin, Jean Marie. 2005. "Policy and Intervention Considerations of a Network Analysis of Street Gangs." *Criminology and Public Policy* 4 (3): 607–36.

McIntyre, Alice. 2000. *Inner-City Kids: Adolescents Confront Life and Violence in an Urban Community.* New York: NYU Press.

McLaren, Peter. 1986. *Schooling as a Ritual Performance: Towards a Political Economy of Educational Symbols and Gestures.* New York: Routledge.

———. 2003. *Life in Schools.* Boston: Allyn and Bacon.

McNeil, Linda M. 1988. *Contradictions of Control: School Structure and School Knowledge.* New York: Routledge.

McVeigh, Brian J. 2000. *Wearing Ideology: State, Schooling and Self-Presentation in Japan.* Oxford: Berg.

Mead, George Herbert. 1934. *Mind, Self and Society.* Edited by C. W. Morris. Chicago: University of Chicago Press.

Meehan, Albert J. 2000. "The Organizational Career of Gang Statistics: The Politics of Policing Gangs." *Sociological Quarterly* 41 (3): 337–70.

Megargee, Edwin. 1966. "Undercontrolled and Overcontrolled Personality Types in Extreme Antisocial Aggression." *Psychological Monographs: General and Applied* 80 (3): 1–29.

Mehan, Hugh. 1992. "Understanding Inequality in Schools: The Contribution of Interpretive Studies." *Sociology of Education* 65 (January): 1–20.

Mehan, Hugh, Irene Villanueva, Lea Hubbard, and Angela Lintz. 1996. *Constructing School Success: The Consequences of Untracking Low-Achieving Students.* Cambridge: Cambridge University Press.

Mendoza-Denton, Norma. 1996. "'Muy Macha': Gender and Ideology in Gang-Girls' Discourse about Makeup." *Ethnos* 61 (1/2): 47–63.

———. 2008. *Homegirls: Language and Cultural Practice among Latina Youth Gangs.* Cambridge: Blackwell.

Merleau-Ponty, Maurice. 1962. *The Phenomenology of Perception.* London: Routledge and Kegan Paul.

———. 1968. *The Visible and the Invisible.* Evanston: Northwestern University Press.

Merry, Sally E. 1979. "Going to Court: Strategies of Dispute Management in an American Urban Neighbourhood." *Law and Society Review* 13:891–925.

Metz, Mary H. 1989. "Real School: A Universal Drama amid Disparate Experience." *Journal of Educational Policy* 4 (5): 75–91.

Miller, Jerome. 1997. *Search and Destroy: African-American Males in the Criminal Justice System.* Cambridge: Cambridge University Press.

Miller, Jody. 2008. *Getting Played: African American Girls, Urban Inequality, and Gendered Violence.* New York: NYU Press.

Miller, Walter B. 1980. "Gangs, Groups, and Serious Youth Crime." In *Critical Issues in Juvenile Delinquency,* edited by David Schichor and Delos H. Kelly, 115–38. Lexington, MA: D. C. Heath.

Milner, Murray. 2006. *Freaks, Geeks, and Cool Kids: American Teenagers, Schools, and the Culture of Consumption.* New York: Routledge.

Moerman, Michael. 1974. "Accomplishing Ethnicity." In *Ethnomethodology: Selected Readings,* edited by Roy Turner, 54–68. Middlesex: Penguin Books.

Molotch, Harvey L., and Deirdre Boden. 1985. "Talk and Social Structure: Discourse, Domination and the Watergate Hearings." *American Sociological Review* 50 (June): 273–88.

Monaghan, Lee F. 2001. *Bodybuilding, Drugs and Risk.* London: Routledge.

———. 2002. "Regulating 'Unruly' Bodies: Work Tasks, Conflict and Violence in Britain's Night-Time Economy." *British Journal of Criminology* 53 (3): 403–29.

Monti, Daniel J. 1994. *Wannabe: Gangs in Suburbs and Schools.* Oxford: Blackwell.

Morrill, Calvin, Christine Yalda, Madelaine Adelman, Michael Musheno, and Cindy Bejarno. 2000. "Telling Tales in School: Youth Culture and Conflict Narratives." *Law and Society Review* 34 (3): 521–65.

Mortimer, Jeylan T., and Reed W. Larson. 2002. *The Changing Adolescent Experience: Societal Trends and the Transition to Adulthood.* New York: Cambridge University Press.

Mullins, Christopher, Richard Wright, and Bruce A. Jacobs. 2004. "Gender, Streetlife and Criminal Retaliation." *Criminology* 42 (4): 911–40.

Nagel, Joane. 1994. "Constructing Ethnicity: Creating and Recreating Ethnic Identity and Culture." *Social Problems* 41 (1): 152–76.

National School Boards Association. 1993. *Violence in the Schools: How America's School Boards Are Safeguarding Our Children.* NSBA Best Practices Series. Alexandria, VA: National School Boards Association.

Newman, Katherine. 1999. *No Shame in My Game: The Working Poor in the Inner City.* New York: Knopf.

Newmann, Fred M., Gary G. Wehlage, and Susie D. Lamborn. 1992. "The Significance and Sources of Student Engagement." In *Student Engagement and Achievement in American Secondary Schools,* edited by Fred M. Newmann, 11–40. New York: Teachers College Press.

Nicholson, David. 1995. "On Violence." In *Speak My Name: Black Men on Masculinity and the American Dream,* edited by Don Belton, 28–34. Boston: Beacon Press.

Nightingale, Carl H. 1993. *On the Edge: A History of Poor Black Children and Their American Dreams.* New York: Basic Books.

Nobles, Melissa. 2000. *Race and the Census in Modern Politics.* Stanford: Stanford University Press.

Notes from Nowhere. 2003. *We Are Everywhere: The Irresistible Rise of Global Anticapitalism.* New York: Verso.

Ogbu, John. 2003. *Black American Students in an Affluent Suburb: A Study of Academic Disengagement.* Mahwah, NJ: Lawrence Erlbaum Associates.

Ogbu, John U., and Herbert D. Simons. 1998. "Voluntary and Involuntary Minorities: A Cultural-Ecological Theory of School Performance with Some Implications for Education." *Anthropology and Education Quarterly* 29 (2): 155–88.

Oliver, Melvin, and Thomas Shapiro. 2006. *Black Wealth / White Wealth: A New Perspective on Racial Inequality.* New York: Routledge.

Ollman, Bertell. 1971. *Alienation: Marx's Conception of Man in Capitalist Society.* Cambridge: Cambridge University Press.

Omi, Michael, and Howard Winant. 1986. *Racial Formation in the United States: From the 1960s to the 1980s.* New York: Routledge.

Ostrow, James M. 1990. *Social Sensitivity: A Study of Habit and Experience.* Albany: State University of New York Press.

Padilla, Felix M. 1992. *The Gang as an American Enterprise.* New Brunswick: Rutgers University Press.

Parenti, Christian. 2000. "Crime as Social Control." *Social Justice* 27:43–49.

Pattillo, Mary E. 1998. "Sweet Mothers and Gangbangers: Managing Crime in a Black Middle-Class Neighborhood." *Social Forces* 76 (3): 747–74.

Phillips, Susan A. 1999. *Wallbangin': Graffiti and Gangs in L.A.* Chicago: University of Chicago Press.

Pinderhughes, Howard. 1997. *Race in the Hood: Conflict and Violence Among Urban Youth.* Minneapolis: University of Minnesota Press.

Pollner, Melvin. 1984. *Mundane Reason: Reality in Everyday and Sociological Discourse.* Cambridge: Cambridge University Press.

Proweller, Amira. 2000. "Re-Writing/-Righting Lives: Voices of Pregnant and Parenting Teenagers in an Alternative School." In *Construction Sites: Excavating Race, Class and Gender among Urban Youth,* edited by Lois Weis and Michelle Fine, 100–120. New York: Teachers College Press.

Prus, Robert, and Scott Grills. 2003. *The Deviant Mystique: Involvements, Realities and Regulation.* Westport, CT: Praeger.

Raby, Rebecca. 2007. "Across a Great Gulf? Conducting Research with Adolescents." In *Representing Youth: Methodological Issues in Critical Youth Studies,* edited by Amy Best, 39–59. New York: NYU Press.

Retzinger, Suzanne M. 1987. "Resentment and Laughter: Video Studies of the Shame-Rage Spiral." In *The Role of Shame in Symptom Formation,* edited by Helen Block Lewis, 151–81. Hillsdale, NJ: Lawrence Erlbaum Associates.

Ritzer, George. 2005. *Enchanting a Disenchanted World: Revolutionizing the Means of Consumption.* Thousand Oaks, CA: Pine Forge Press.

Rosenfeld, Gerry. 1971. *"Shut Those Thick Lips!" A Study of Slum School Failure.* Case Studies in Education and Culture. New York: Holt, Rinehart and Winston.

Rosenfeld, R., B. A. Jacobs, and R. Wright. 2003. "Snitching and the Code of the Street." *British Journal of Criminology* 43:291–309.

Roy, Kevin. 2004. "Three-Block Fathers: Spatial Perceptions and Kin-Work in Low-Income African American Neighborhoods." *Social Problems* 51 (4): 528–48.

Rutter, M. 1987. "Psychosocial Resilience and Protective Mechanisms." *American Journal of Orthopsychiatry* 57:316–31.

Rymes, Betsy. 2001. *Conversational Borderlands: Language and Identity in an Alternative Urban High School.* New York: Teachers College Press.

Sacks, Harvey. 1972. "On the Analyzability of Stories by Children." In *Directions in Sociolinguistics: The Ethnography of Communication,* edited by J. J. Gumperz and D. Hymes, 325–45. New York: Rinehart and Winston.

———. 1984. "On Doing 'Being Ordinary.'" In *Structures of Social Action: Studies in Conversation Analysis,* edited by J. Maxwell Atkinson and John Heritage, 413–29. Cambridge: Cambridge University Press.

———. 1995. *Lectures on Conversation.* Oxford: Blackwell.

Sampson, Robert J., and William Julius Wilson. 1995. "Toward a Theory of Race, Crime, and Urban Inequality." In *Crime and Inequality,* edited by John Hagan and Ruth D. Peterson, 37–54. Stanford: Stanford University Press.

Sanchez-Jankowski, Martín. 1991. *Islands in the Street: Gangs and American Urban Society.* Berkeley: University of California Press.

Sanders, William B. 1994. *Gangbangs and Drive-Bys: Grounded Culture and Juvenile Gang Violence.* New York: Aldine de Gruyter.

Sarat, Austin, and William L. F. Felstiner. 1995. *Divorce Lawyers and Their Clients: Power and Meaning in the Legal Process.* New York: Oxford University Press.

Scheff, Thomas. 1990. *Microsociology: Discourse, Emotion, and Social Structure*. Chicago: University of Chicago Press.

Schegloff, Emanuel A. 1992a. "In Another Context." In *Rethinking Context: Language as an Interactive Phenomenon*, edited by Alessandro Duranti and Charles Goodwin, 191–227. Cambridge: Cambridge University Press.

———. 1992b. "Repair after Next Turn: The Last Structurally Provided Defense of Inter-subjectivity in Conversation." *American Journal of Sociology* 97 (5): 1295–1345.

Schutz, Alfred. 1962. *Collected Papers*. Vol. 1. *The Problem of Social Reality*. Edited by M. Natanson. The Hague: Martinus Nijhoff.

Scott, Greg. 2004. "'It's a Sucker's Outfit': How Urban Gangs Enable and Impede the Reintegration of Ex-convicts." *Ethnography* 5 (March): 107–40.

Scott, James C. 1976. *The Moral Economy of the Peasant: Rebellion and Subsistence in Southeast Asia*. New Haven: Yale University Press.

———. 1985. *Weapons of the Weak: Everyday Forms of Peasant Resistance*. New Haven: Yale University Press.

———. 1990. *Domination and the Arts of Resistance: Hidden Transcripts*. New Haven: Yale University Press.

Sibley, David. 1995. *Geographies of Exclusion: Society and Difference in the West*. New York: Routledge.

Sikes, Gini. 1993. *8 Ball Chicks: A Year in the Violent World of Girl Gangsters*. New York: Anchor Books.

Simmel, Georg. 1904. "Fashion." In *On Individuality and Social Forms*, edited by Donald N. Levine, 294–323. Chicago: University of Chicago Press.

Simpson, Colton. 2005. *Inside the Crips: Life inside L.A.'s Most Notorious Gang*. New York: St. Martin's Press.

Skogan, Wesley. 1990. *Disorder and Decline: Crime and the Spiral of Decay in American Neighborhoods*. New York: Free Press.

Sloan, Melissa M. "The 'Real Self' and Inauthenticity: The Importance of Self-Concept Anchorage for Emotional Experiences in the Workplace." *Social Psychology Quarterly* 70 (3): 305–18.

Snow, David A., E. Burke Rochford Jr., Steven K. Worden, and Robert D. Benford. 1986. "Frame Alignment Processes, Micromobilization, and Movement Participation." *American Sociological Review* 51 (4): 464–81.

Snyder, Gregory J. 2009. *Graffiti Lives: Beyond the Tag in New York's Urban Underground*. New York: NYU Press.

Spector, Malcolm, and John I. Kitsuse. 1987. *Constructing Social Problems*. Hawthorne, NY: Aldine de Gruyter.

Spergel, Irving A. 1992. "Youth Gangs: An Essay Review." *Social Service Review* 66 (March): 121–40.

Staiger, Annegret. 2006. *Learning Difference: Race and Schooling in a Multicultural Metropolis*. Stanford: Stanford University Press.

Stenross, Barbara, and Sherryl Kleinman. 1989. "The Highs and Lows of Emotional Labor: Detectives' Encounters with Criminals and Victims." *Journal of Contemporary Ethnography* 17:435–52.

Stewart, Eric A., Christopher J. Schreck, and Ronald L. Simons. 2006. "'I Ain't Gonna Let No One Disrespect Me': Does the Code of the Street Reduce or Increase Violent Victimization among African-American Adolescents?" *Journal of Research in Crime and Delinquency* 43 (4): 427–58.

Stewart, Eric A., and Ronald L. Simons. 2006. "Structure and Culture in African American Adolescent Violence: A Partial Test of the 'Code of the Street' Thesis." *Justice Quarterly* 23 (1): 1–33.

Stone, Alison. 2004. "Essentialism and Anti-essentialism in Feminist Philosophy." *Journal of Moral Philosophy* 1 (2): 135–53.

Strentz, Thomas. 1980. "The Stockholm Syndrome: Law Enforcement Policy and Ego Defenses of the Hostage." *Annals of the New York Academy of Sciences* 347 (1): 137–50.

Struyk, R. 2006. "Gangs in Our Schools: Identifying Gang Indicators in Our School Population." *Clearing House* 80 (1): 11–13.

Sullivan, Mercer L. 2006. "Are 'Gang' Studies Dangerous? Youth Violence, Context, and the Problem of Reification." In *Studying Youth Gangs*, edited by James F. Short and Lorine Hughes, 15–35. New York: Altamira Press.

Suttles, Gerald D. 1968. *The Social Order of the Slum: Ethnicity and Territory in the Inner City*. Chicago: University of Chicago Press.

Sutton, Robert I. 1991. "Maintaining Norms about Expressed Emotions: The Case of Bill Collectors." *Administrative Science Quarterly* 36:245–68.

Swidler, Ann. 1986. "Culture in Action: Symbols and Strategies." *American Sociological Review* 51 (April): 273–86.

Talburt, Susan. 2004. "Intelligibility and Narrating Youth." In *Youth and Sexualities: Pleasure, Subversion, and Insubordination in and out of Schools,* edited by Mary Louise Rasmussen, Eric Rofes, and Susan Talburt, 17–39. New York: Palgrave.

Tannenbaum, Frank. 1938. *Crime and the Community*. New York: Columbia University Press.

Taylor, Carl S. 1990. *Dangerous Society*. East Lansing: Michigan State University Press.

Thoits, Peggy A. 1996. "Managing the Emotions of Others." *Symbolic Interaction* 19 (2): 85–109.

Thompkins, Douglas E. 2000. "School Violence: Gangs and a Culture of Fear." *Annals of the American Academy of Political and Social Science* 567 (January): 54–71.

Thorne, Barrie. 1993. *Gender Play: Girls and Boys in School*. New Brunswick: Rutgers University Press.

Thrasher, Frederic M. 1927. *The Gang: A Study of 1313 Gangs in Chicago*. Chicago: University of Chicago Press.

Tolich, Martin B. 1993. "Alienating and Liberating Emotions at Work: Supermarket Clerks' Performance of Customer Service." *Journal of Contemporary Ethnography* 22 (3): 361–81.

Tomsen, Stephen. 1997. "A Top Night: Social Protest, Masculinity and the Culture of Drinking Violence." *British Journal of Criminology* 37 (1): 90–102.

Travis, Jeremy. 2005. *But They All Come Back: Facing the Challenges of Prisoner Reentry*. Washington, DC: Urban Institute Press.

Travis, Jeremy, A. L. Solomon, and M. Waul. 2002. *From Prison to Home: The Dimensions and Consequences of Prisoner Reentry*. Washington, DC: Urban Institute, Justice Policy Center.

Travis, Jeremy, and Christy Visher, eds. 2005. *Prisoner Reentry and Crime in America*. Cambridge: Cambridge University Press.

Trump, Kenneth S. 1996. "Gangs and School Safety." In *Schools, Violence and Society,* edited by Allan M. Hoffman, 45–60. Westport, CT: Praeger.

Turner, Victor. 1976. "The Real Self: From Institution to Impulse." *American Journal of Sociology* 81:989–1016.

"12 School-Safety Moves You Can Make." 1999. Editorial. *Curriculum Review* 38 (9): 11.

Tyack, David B. 1974. *The One Best System: A History of Urban Education*. Cambridge, MA: Harvard University Press.

Ungar, Michael. 2007. "Grow 'em Strong: Conceptual Challenges in Researching Childhood Resilience." In *Representing Youth: Methodological Issues in Critical Youth Studies*, edited by Amy L. Best, 84–109. New York: NYU Press.

Valdez, Avelardo. 2003. "Toward a Typology of Contemporary Mexican American Youth Gangs." In *Gangs in Society: Alternative Perspectives*, edited by Louis Kontos, David Brotherton, and Luis Barrios, 12–40. New York: Columbia University Press.

Varenne, Hervé, and Ray McDermott. 1998. *Successful Failure: The School America Builds*. Boulder, CO: Westview Press.

Venkatesh, Sudhir Alladi. 1997. "The Social Organization of Street Gang Activity in an Urban Ghetto." *American Journal of Sociology* 1031:82–111.

———. 2000. *American Project: The Rise and Fall of a Modern Ghetto*. Cambridge, MA: Harvard University Press.

Vigil, James Diego. 1988. *Barrio Gangs: Street Life and Identity in Southern California*. Austin: University of Texas Press.

———. 1994. "Gangs, Social Control, and Ethnicity: Ways to Redirect." In *Identity and Inner-City Youth: Beyond Ethnicity and Gender*, edited by Shirley Brice Heath and Milbrey W. McLaughlin, 94–119. New York: Teachers College Press.

———. 2003. "Urban Violence and Street Gangs." *Annual Review of Anthropology* 32:225–42.

Wacquant, Loïc. 1997. "For an Analytic of Racial Domination." *Political Power and Social Theory* 11:221–34.

———. 2001. "Deadly Symbiosis: When Ghetto and Prison Meet and Mesh." *Punishment and Society* 3 (1): 95–134.

———. 2002. "Scrutinizing the Street: Poverty, Morality, and the Pitfalls of Urban Ethnography." *American Journal of Sociology* 107 (6): 1468–1532.

Walker, Michael L., and Linda M. Schmidt. 1996. "Gang Reduction Efforts by the Task Force on Violent Crime in Cleveland, Ohio." In *Gangs in America*, edited by C. Ronald Huff, 263–69. Thousand Oaks, CA: Sage Publications.

Weisenberger, Clay. 2000. "Constitution or Conformity: When the Shirt Hits the Fan in Public Schools." *Journal of Law and Education* 29:51–61.

Werthman, Carl. 1983. "Delinquents in Schools: A Test for the Legitimacy of Authority." In *Achievement and Inequality in Education*, edited by June Purvis and Margaret Hales, 79–97. London: Routledge.

West, Candace, and Donald H. Zimmerman. 1987. "Doing Gender." *Gender and Society* 1 (2): 125–51.

Wharton, Amy S. 1993. "The Affective Consequences of Service Work: Managing Emotions on the Job." *Work and Occupations* 20 (2): 205–32.

———. 1999. "Feeling It and Faking It: Understanding the Consequences of Emotional Labor." In *Emotional Labor in the Service Economy*, edited by Ronnie J. Steinberg and Deborah M. Figart, 158–76. Thousand Oaks, CA: Sage Publications.

Wharton, Amy S., and Rebecca J. Erickson. 1995. "The Consequences of Caring: Exploring the Links between Women's Job and Family Emotion Work." *Sociological Quarterly* 36 (2): 273–96.

Whitman, Julie L., and Robert C. Davis. 2007. *Snitches Get Stitches: Youth, Gangs, and Witness Intimidation in Massachusetts.* Research Brief. Washington, DC: National Center for Victims of Crime.

Wieder, D. Lawrence. 1974. *Language and Social Reality: The Case of Telling the Convict Code.* The Hague: Mouton.

Wieder, D. Lawrence, and Steven Pratt. 1989. "On Being a Recognizable Indian among Indians." In *Cultural Communication and Intercultural Contact,* edited by Donal Carbaugh. Hillsdale, NJ: Lawrence Erlbaum Associates.

Wilkinson, Deanna. L. 2001. "Violent Events and Social Identity: Specifying the Relationship between Respect and Masculinity in Inner-City Youth Violence." *Sociological Studies of Children and Youth* 8:235–69.

———. 2007. "Local Social Ties and Willingness to Intervene: Textured Views among Violent Urban Youth of Neighborhood Social Control Dynamics and Situations." *Justice Quarterly* 24 (2): 185–220.

Williams, Terry, and William Kornblum. 1985. *Growing Up Poor.* Lanham, MD: Lexington Books.

Willis, Paul. 1977. *Learning to Labor: How Working Class Kids Get Working Class Jobs.* Aldershot: Gower.

———. 2000. *The Ethnographic Imagination.* Cambridge: Polity.

Wilson, James Q., and George L. Kelling. 1982. "Broken Windows: The Police and Neighborhood Safety." *Atlantic Monthly,* March, 29–38.

Wilson, William Julius. 1987. *The Truly Disadvantaged: The Inner City, the Underclass, and Public Policy.* Chicago: University of Chicago Press.

———. 1996. *When Work Disappears: The World of the New Urban Poor.* New York: Vintage Books.

Wittgenstein, Ludwig. 1953. *Philosophical Investigations.* Oxford: Blackwell.

Wong, Harry K., and Rosemary T. Wong. 2009. *The First Days of School: How to Be an Effective Teacher.* Mountain View, CA: Henry K. Wong Publications.

Yablonsky, Lewis. 1997. *Gangsters: Fifty Years of Madness, Drugs, and Death on the Streets of America.* New York: NYU Press.

Yoshino, Kenji. 2006. *Covering: The Hidden Assault on Our Civil Rights.* New York: Random House.

Young, Jock. 1999. *The Exclusive Society: Social Exclusion, Crime, and Difference in Late Modernity.* Thousand Oaks, CA: Sage Publications.

———. 2003. "Merton with Energy, Katz with Structure." *Theoretical Criminology* 7 (3): 388–414.

———. 2007. *The Vertigo of Late Modernity.* Thousand Oaks, CA: Sage Publications.

Zatz, Marjorie. 1985. "Los Cholos: Legal Processing of Chicano Gang Members." *Social Problems* 33 (1): 13–30.

———. 1987. "Chicano Gangs and Crime: The Creation of a Moral Panic." *Contemporary Crisis* 11:129–58.

Zatz, Marjorie, and Edwardo L. Portillos. 2000. "Voices from the Barrio: Chicano/a Gangs, Families, and Communities." *Criminology* 38 (2): 369–402.

Zimring, Franklin E. 2005. *American Juvenile Justice.* New York: Oxford University Press.

Zinn, Howard. 1980. *A People's History of the United States.* New York: Harper and Row.

Index

Consultants, Authors, Subject Index

SUBJECT INDEX

About the Author

ROBERT GAROT is Assistant Professor of Sociology in the John Jay College of Criminal Justice at the City University of New York.